Understanding China

The series will provide you with in-depth information on China's social, cultural and economic aspects. It covers a broad variety of topics, from economics and history to law, philosophy, cultural geography and regional politics, and offers a wealth of materials for researchers, doctoral students, and experienced practitioners.

More information about this series at https://link.springer.com/bookseries/11772

Yanbin Lv · He Tian

Evaluation on Government Transparency Index in China (2009–2016)

SSAP

Springer

Yanbin Lv
Institute of Law
Chinese Academy of Social Sciences
Beijing, China

He Tian
Institute of Law
Chinese Academy of Social Sciences
Beijing, China

Translated by
Jianli Du
Beijing, China

ISSN 2196-3134 ISSN 2196-3142 (electronic)
Understanding China
ISBN 978-981-16-5031-4 ISBN 978-981-16-5032-1 (eBook)
https://doi.org/10.1007/978-981-16-5032-1

Jointly published with Social Sciences Academic Press
The print edition is not for sale in China (Mainland). Customers from China (Mainland) please order the print book from: Social Sciences Academic Press.

Translation from the Chinese language edition: *中国政府透明度 (2009–2016)* by Yanbin Lv, et al., © Social Science Academic Press 2017. Published by Social Science Academic Press. All Rights Reserved.

This Springer imprint is published by the registered company Springer Nature Singapore Pte Ltd.
The registered company address is: 152 Beach Road, #21-01/04 Gateway East, Singapore 189721, Singapore

Contents

Chapter 1
Introduction Openness–A New Governance Method

Openness and transparency is the cornerstone of rule of law. The *Freedom of the Press Act of 1766*, passed by the Swedish Riksdag as *His Majesty's Gracious Ordinance Relating to Freedom of Writing and of the Press* on December 2, 1776, is regarded as the world's first law supporting freedom of information. It abolished the censorship of most publications and granted citizens access to the printing and dissemination of official documents. The *Freedom of Information Act* enacted by the United States in 1966 provided that any person has the right to request access to federal agency records or information in which they have no real stake. From the 1990s, global legislation of information disclosure started to show an accelerating trend as governments attempted to promote openness and transparency. The emergence of freedom of information legislation was a response to citizens' right to know or access to information held by public bodies. In other words, as masters of the state, citizens have the right to know and disseminate official information that involves no state secret. This has been enshrined as a fundamental human right in freedom of information laws in countries such as Australia and South Korea, as well as in some human right-related international conventions such as the *Universal Declaration of Human Rights, the International Covenant on Civil and Political Rights* and the *Convention on the International Right of Correction.*[1] Safeguarding citizens' right to know is undeniably both the logical starting point and the ultimate goal of establishing government information disclosure system, which is of little controversy either in legislation or in theoretical studies. However, it needs to be noted that, functions of

[1] Article 19 of *The Universal Declaration of Human Rights* stipulates that "Everyone has the right to freedom of opinion and expression; this right includes freedom to hold opinions without interference and to seek, receive and impart information and ideas through any media and regardless of frontiers". The full text is provided in the *World Documents of Human Rights*, Sichuan Renmin Press, 1990, p. 960–964. Paragraph 2 of Article 19 of *International Covenant on Civil and Political Rights* stipulates that "Everyone shall have the right to freedom of expression; this right shall include freedom to seek, receive and impart information and ideas of all kinds…", ibid, p. 972–985. The preamble of *Convention on the International Right of Correction* stipulates that "Desiring to implement the right of their peoples to be fully and reliably informed".

Y. Lv and H. Tian, *Evaluation on Government Transparency Index in China (2009–2016)*, Understanding China, https://doi.org/10.1007/978-981-16-5032-1_1

government openness and transparency are expanding as society progresses and no longer just limited to guaranteeing public's access to information.

1.1 Transforming the Operating Mechanism of Government Power Through Openness

The operation mode of government power has evolved from ruling to management, and then to governance. "Ruling" is a by-product of agricultural society. In an agricultural society, farming household is the basic production unit and natural resources such as land play a fundamental role in socioeconomic development. A lack of social mobility forms a relatively closed community where "although the barks of dogs and crocks of cocks could be heard in the neighborhood, people are completely isolated from each other all their lives". People are basically self-sufficient, with only a few deals made to meet the demands of production and life. Imperial power serves as a powerful instrument for ruling and the unidirectional paternalistic approach adopted by the state leaves the public no choice but to obey. Social management is featured by orders, commands and coercion—by issuing orders to the public and forcing them to obey, the state can achieve its purpose of maintaining social orders and stability. Under information asymmetry and knowledge-based monopoly conditions, the public are awed by the government and its power as they lack the capability to make their own judgments.

"Management" is a necessary requirement of industrial society. An industrial society, which is dominated by industrial production and where capital plays an irreplaceable role, is characterized by highly advanced science and technology, overall improved production efficiency and refined division of labor. The law of industrial production also reaches social political life and streamlined modes of production and life require citizens to have a rigid division of labor. To be disciplined, obedient, and subject to management and arrangement are the basic requirements of state to members of society. In an industrial society, although the authority of government is challenged to some extent as social members start to acquire more knowledge, citizens' participation in and influence on national decision making remain rather limited. Common people are just certain "parts" or "screws" that hold society together and maintain its proper functioning. Despite that they could make requests for improving their welfare such as demanding better treatment, improved working conditions, wage and gender equality, ordinary people can hardly participate in state governance, let alone contributing to how government operates and state develops.

"Governance", however, is an essential request of post-industrial society. Also known as information society, post-industrial society is featured by the collection, dissemination and utilization of information and most laborers' work has changed from product manufacturing to information development and use. In the post-industrial society, information supersedes capital as a prime resource and the transmission of information and knowledge serves as an overriding force driving society forward while breaking the knowledge monopoly situation. Hence, citizens' subject position is significantly improved and they desire and are able to participate in and influence national decision-making, leaving no room for the obsolete unidirectional operation mode of government power to survive. Currently, China is still at a stage where agricultural, industrial and post-industrial societies co-exist due to its vast territory and varied stages of development in different areas. Therefore, government governance in China is relatively complicated.

These three modes have different characteristics. The one that emphasizes "ruling" is rooted in the hierarchy of society, making maintain the hierarchical social order its ultimate goal; the one that stresses "management" enhances the administration of society, with the government acting as the management body, while individuals and civil societies as the objects, and the pursuit of efficiency as the final aim. Both of the aforementioned patterns are backed by state coercion, characterized by the clear boundaries between the ruling class (rulers and management bodies) and the ruled (individuals and civil societies), emphasizing the unidirectionality of government power. In contrast, though the pattern accentuating "governance" also considers maintaining social order, pursuing social development efficiency, and safeguarding social equity and justice as important goals, the government operated in this mode additionally needs to better resolve market and government failures. Instead of purely ignoring the stances of individuals and civil societies or emphasizing the unidirectionality of state power, the government shall focus more on the diverse needs and aspirations of individuals and civil societies, and work with them rather than unilaterally issue orders to the public and force them to obey.

Governance comprises of activities and processes that maintain social orders through institutions—using power in different institutions to guide, control, coordinate, and regulate citizens' activities in order to maximize public interests and meet their demand. The biggest difference between governance and former two patterns (ruling and management) is not to deny the role of authority and power in it, nor to abandon maintaining normal social order as its goal, but rather that in concepts and processes. Governance embodies negotiation and cooperation, where neither the government nor state power is the sole authority. Instead of solely depending on the top-down operation of state power, governance relies more on the government interacting, cooperating, and equally consulting with the public and civil societies[2]. "Governance means that 'the meaning of ruling has changed, with a new process, different conditions and new means to rule society coming into being'."[3]

Public access to efficient and convenient means of information dissemination brought by the arrival of post-industrial society accelerates the spread and popularization of knowledge. Hence information is no longer monopolized and controlled by the government as it used to be. This massive flow of information provides the public with constantly increased autonomy. By grasping necessary information, people gain

---

[2] Yu Keping, *Governance and Good Governance: A New Framework for Political Analysis*, Social Science Academic Press, 2009, p. 5–6.

[3] Yu Keping, *Governance and Good Governance: A New Framework for Political Analysis*, Social Science Academic Press, 2009, p. 31.

access to knowledge and tend to make their own judgements on understanding and shaping the world instead of just blindly following others' teachings. The wide availability of the fourth and fifth media has further changed the unidirectional nature of information dissemination and eliminated the information monopoly held by government and traditional mass media, making it easier for people to express opinions and interact with each other, thus driving the closed society to an open one. Government's disregard of a point of view, complaint or demand will not only trigger dissatisfaction of the related administrative counterpart, but may also be promptly exaggerated by the media, incurring doubts, reproaches and even distrust of the whole society. Government decisions made without considering public opinions and suggestions may also lack rationale and popular support, that is, it is difficult for government to effectively implement or gain public support for the major decisions that are made without adequate communication and consultation with and recognition from the public. Even If government enforces such decisions backed by state coercion, it may be challenged, opposed, and even resisted by the public, and confrontation between government and people will be created, threatening government authority and legitimacy. "Information accessibility plays a vital role in the development of the 'New Administrative Law'…In many cases, it is impossible for administrative organs not to disclose information and not to let the public participate in state governance. Information accessibility also provides realistic conditions for the establishment of a transparent government."[4] Despite that many factors have contributed to the transition of government governance from one-way orders and obedience to two-way negotiation and cooperation including the development of democracy and rule of law, the wide accessibility of information has undoubtedly provided both an indispensable material foundation and an objective condition.

As the fundamental role of information in socioeconomic development becomes increasingly obvious, public demands for maximum access to information is growing. Therefore, the government has to proactively disclose information it possesses and keep improving its transparency. In turn, the improvement of government transparency will, to a certain extent, tie the government's hands and raise higher requirements on governance. First of all, the rapid dissemination of information requires the government to provide timely and authoritative responses to the ever-changing social situation—various developments—including communicating accurately, promptly, comprehensively and effectively with the public and offering them information. Any delay or avoidance may lead to severe consequences for governance and the loss of government credibility and the best time to handle the situations. Also, the openness and transparency of information is challenging the traditional mode of government operation. With an wider access to information, citizens become increasingly capable of and willing to participate in government decision-making process instead of just obeying government instructions as they used to be. Hence, the traditional

[4] Jiang Ming'an, *Grasping the Trend of Social Transformation and Strengthening the Study on the New 'Administrative Procedure Law of the People's Republic of China'*, the *Administrative Law Review* VOL. 11, Law Press, 2008, p. 11.

social management mode that is characterized by orders, coercion, and unidirectional obedience can hardly fit the needs of governance. Finally, the openness and transparency of information also puts the government under public supervision. The government has to act with caution and regulate and constrain its own performance, as any misconduct and irregularity may be savaged by the public and endanger its legitimacy.

1.2 Enhancing Government Credibility Through Openness

As the knowledge level of public in modern society has increased substantially, the government needs to make more efforts and pay higher prices to maintain its credibility than it did in an traditional society. Enhancing information openness and fully and effectively utilizing information for governance have become indispensable means for the government to increase its authority and credibility. In order to maintain its credibility, the government has to ensure the openness and transparency of its activities and its smooth communication with the public besides keeping its promises, being resolute in deeds, and avoiding inconsistency in policies. "In the past, a police officer could manage 100 citizens, but now 100 police officers cannot manage one citizen.", a government official signed. This reflects the fact that government authority is being severely challenged. In fact, as democracy and rule of law develop, mysticism and authoritarian politics can no longer bring government credibility, instead, they can only trigger public doubts and resistances, thus hampering governance. However, the transparency of government management and public participation can substantially enhance government credibility. Today, improving the transparency of government activities, disclosing information comprehensively and efficiently, and enhancing communication with the public will certainly play a critical role in boosting government authority and credibility.

At present, the wide availability of new media has raised higher requirements for governance—the government needs to respond quickly to the ever-changing society, provide the public with maximum information, leverage the openness and transparency of government information to curb the spread of rumors and false information, resolve misunderstandings and strengthen its authority.

Responding to public opinions in a timely and accurate manner has become one of the important means for the government to achieve good governance. Responsiveness requires public administrators and administrative agencies to respond promptly and responsibly to public demands, and to actively solicit opinions from, interpret policies for, and answer questions asked by the public regularly. The greater the level of responsiveness is, the higher the level of good governance will be[5]. "For average citizens, the crucial questions are whether their encounters with bureaucrats will elicit

[5] Yu Keping, *Governance and Good Governance: A New Framework for Political Analysis*, Social Science Academic Press, 2009, p. 10.

any response at all and whether the response meets their needs."[6] The government may risk losing control of public opinions, confronting difficulties in governance, or even incurring social crises if it fails to stay abreast of public opinions developments and provide the public with authentic and credible information promptly. The 2008 Weng'an Riot is a typical example of this kind. The reflections of cadres at all levels in Weng'an County illustrate that, at that time, the party committee, the local government, and the public security bureau did not have functional and authoritative information release mechanisms to cope with rumors, lies, and other misinformation circulating in society. The resulted slow release of information, inadequate information disclosed to the public, the weak voice of the government, and especially the government's main struggle to only curb the spread of false news in a period of time eventually led to the fact that ordinary people did not know the truth and were used by those with ulterior motives. Hence, the related government agency that possesses relevant information and is responsible for disclosing it should be held accountable[7]. One of the lessons of the 2008 Weng'an Riot is that after missing the best time to release authoritative information to the public and letting rumors and lies gain the upper hand and circulate, the government will encounter difficulty in getting public recognition and trust of any information it released, which will eventually lead to mass incidents. The 2009 Shishou Incident in Hubei and the 2017 Lu County Incident in Sichuan have many similarities with the 2008 Weng'an Riot.

Also, full openness will certainly foster government credibility. For example, in Jinzhai County of Anhui province—one of the key counties for national poverty alleviation and development—there is a growing public awareness of the distribution of relief funds as the scale of various types of relief funds continues to increase. However, the allocation of funds used to be unreasonable and with the large number of officials and approvals at all levels involved, problems such as corruption, misappropriation, interception, false claim and nepotism were commonly seen. As a result, Relief funds was not well targeted at those who needed them and basic-level cadres tended to break the law, leading to numerous complaint letters and visits from the public. In order to enable the public to fully understand and participate in the supervision and management of relief funds, the government of Jinzhai County has shifted its focus from "the disclosure of results" to "the disclosure of both processes and results", with the "five disclosures" policy—the disclosures of policy publicity, information collection, object review, verification and approval and funds distribution—introduced. For example, when selecting the rural households enjoying the minimum living guarantee in the Baitafan Town, the local government implements a "three-bulletin disclosure" policy besides the disclosure of policy publicity. Under this policy, the list of the names of qualified candidates proposed through the democratic appraisal of Villagers' Congress will be displayed on the town bulletin board for seven days; the modified list deliberated and approved by the town government be

[6] Doris. A. Graber, *The Power of Communication: Managing Information in Public Organizations*, translated by Zhang Xike, Fudan University Press, 2007, p. 247.

[7] Liu Zifu, New Concept of Mass Incidents: Lessons Learned from the '6·28 Riot' in Weng'an, Xinhua Publishing House, 2009, p. 71–75.

displayed on the town bulletin board for seven days; and the final list approved by the county-level competent authority will be publicized on the board for a long time. The full openness of the whole process has dramatically increased the transparency of government work and enhanced public trust in the government that it serves the people.

1.3 Safeguarding Social Justice Through Openness

The notion of justice is divided into substantive justice and procedural justice. The former requires that the distribution of interests shall conform to people's judgments of "good or evil" and "right or wrong" and shall be matched perfectly with the assignees' pay, damage, and status, etc. The latter, however, mainly emphasizes the process of realizing justice and endeavors to control the process, ensuring that the assignees enjoy the same period of time and rules, which are not subject to any private interests, during the distribution. As an idealistic pursuit, substantive justice is influenced by such factors as people's innate characteristics and postnatal environment and achieving absolute substantive justice is a long-term goal pursued by human society. Procedural justice emphasizes the design and control of the distribution process and is the only way to make the results as close to substantive justice as possible. While openness does not necessarily lead to justice, it is an important means to help achieve justice.

Openness means that the rules, processes, factors and results of interests distribution shall all be disclosed to the parties concerned and even to the public. This will not only enable the parties concerned or the public to propose dissents for decision makers or implementers to correct the interests distribution process but also narrow discretionary spaces of decision makers or implementers, thus reducing the likelihood of malpractice. Openness enables all parties to be aware that although there might be a gap between the distribution results and their own expectations, they are all treated, so the distribution can at least be considered as a fair one. Of course, openness can never be equated with justice. It is only a condition and guarantee for achieving justice.

1.4 Regulating the Operation of Government Power Through Openness

The openness of government affairs will undoubtedly bring government bodies and staff under the spotlight, and all their behaviors and consequences except for those that are classified have to be made public for evaluation and supervision. Any wrongdoing of the government may trigger public criticism. Therefore, the government shall further regulate its behaviors and improve its capabilities to avoid feeling trapped and passive or being doubted. In 2011, four years since the implementation of the Regulations *on Government Information Disclosure of the People's Republic of China* (hereinafter referred to as "the Regulations"), some government agencies still did not give enough attention to their work of government information disclosure. For example, as per the Regulations, the Annual report on government information disclosure in the previous year shall be released before the end of March, however, many government agencies failed to release theirs on time or issue accurate information.[8] In 2014, some American television programs were removed from the online media, in response to which some people requested to the State Administration of Press, Publication, Radio, Film and Television (SAPPRFT) for releasing the legal basis of the act[9] and questioned whether there were adequate law enforcement bases and reasons. This illustrates that whether the government's administration of society is well regulated has been under public supervision. By promoting transparency through openness can the government be driven to improve its administrative capacities, regulate the operation of its power, improve its credibility, and achieve social justice and development. It is just because of this that the promotion of openness to strengthen social supervision and to regulate how the government exercises power is emphasized in many institutional arrangements, including the *Guiding Opinions on the Implementation of Power Lists System of Local Government Agencies* published by the General Office of the CPC Central Committee and the General Office of the State Council, which stipulates that the online operation of administrative power shall be vigorously promoted, the level of transparency and openness shall be improved, and effective supervisory mechanism for the operation of power shall be established; and the *Notice on Regulating the Administrative Examination and Approval of the Departments under the State Council and Improving Relevant Work* issued by the State Council, which proposes to standardize administrative discretion and proactively disclose information about administrative approval. Competent departments are required to voluntarily disclose their directory for items under administrative approval and related information unless they involve state secret, commercial secret or personal privacy, and to promptly and accurately disclose information about case handling and results, so as to achieve the "Under Sunshine Approval".

---

[8] *The Annual Reports of Two Different Years Provided on the Website of the Ministry of Human Resources and Social Security are Identical: the Ministry Responds that It was a Technical Error and The Two Reports have been Removed, Southern Urban Daily*, March 31, 2011, p. A15; *The Identical Annual Reports of Three Years have All been Revised: the 2008–2010 Annual Work Reports on Government Information Disclosure of the Statistics Bureau of Dongguan are Re-published Online, Southern Urban Daily,* April 26, 2014, p. AA10.

[9] *Why American TV Series have been Removed from the Internet: College Students have Filed a Request with the State Administration of Press, Publication, Radio, Film and Television for the Disclosure of Relevant Legal Basis*, http://chuansongme.com/n/439794, May 18, 2014.

1.5 Facilitating the Establishment of a Service-Oriented Government Through Openness

Just as the proverb "knowledge is power", in the information ear, "service is power" for governments. Disclosing government information, making information publicly accessible, and lowering barriers to services while improving the quality of services shall be the motto of government agencies at all levels. The *Decision of the Central Committee of the Communist Party of China on Some Major Issues Concerning Comprehensively Deepening Reform* proposes that the essence of establishing a service-oriented government is to implement the purpose of serving the people. Recent years have seen government departments at all levels reforming their administrative approval system by building the Government Affairs Hall, unifying administrative approval authority, and making online and parallel connection approvals so as to improve the quality of government services. Many government departments tend to consider the level of hardware facilities in the Hall, professionalism of staff members and whether there are free printing and copying, and medical kits, etc. as evaluation criteria for service quality. However, some have overlooked a fact—the poor quality of the disclosure of information about government services often causes inconvenience for the public to obtain services and affects the sense of benefit of citizens. For example, the numerous lists of powers and service guides stacked on government websites without being categorized are not convenient for citizens and enterprises to access. Also, the content of the lists of powers is often quite complicated and highly specialized and citizens can usually hardly understand the application procedures and requirements. In addition, as the lists may be disclosed on the platforms of different departments, real-time dynamic management can scarcely be achieved, leading to the widespread problem of inconsistent information disclosed. For instance, the content of the service guides provided in the Government Affairs Hall of many local governments may differ from that on their official websites with information such as addresses, contact numbers, service requirements and procedures being rather divergent. Even worse, the information (should be the same) displayed in different sections of the same government portal is contradicted. The contact numbers provided by many government agencies are invalid—cannot get through, have no answer or accurate information cannot be provided by the person answering the phone. All of these have caused the public unnecessary trouble as they are not informed of the materials and requirements needed. Therefore, despite the relentless efforts made by the government in streamlining administration and delegating power to the lower levels and establishing a service-oriented government, citizens gain no sense of benefit. The issues they are most concerned about are: which department is responsible for the service? What materials to prepare? How much time will be needed? Whether the process can be streamlined? In view of this, the concept of "facilitating the better use of government information and cutting red tape for the public" is largely dependent on information disclosure, which is the foundation of establishing a service-oriented government.

1.6 Maintaining Social Stability Through Openness

Maintaining social stability is an important goal of government governance, and promoting openness is a means to achieve it. Almost all of such incidents as the Guangyuan Navel Orange Incident,[10] the 2009 Hangzhou Mitsubishi Sports Car Accident,[11] the 2012 Shifang Protest, the PX incidents in Xiamen, Dalian, Ningbo and Kunming, the Heshan Radioactive Materials Incident[12] and the Hangzhou Waste Incinerator Incident,[13] were partially caused by the failure of disclosing timely and accurate information. By analyzing the causes and processes of the 2012 Shifang Protest and the PX incidents that frequently occurred in recent years, it is not difficult to find that local governments' intention on introducing such projects is to develop local economy, which is quite good, and various approval processes have been fulfilled while some even established sound decision-making participation mechanisms and risk evaluation mechanisms. However, due to the failure of properly absorbing and reflecting public opinions in the decision-making process, especially the lack of timely disclosure of relevant information have triggered citizens' doubts and dissatisfaction, further leading to all-lose situations—governments, citizens and project investors.

Some administrators used to consider information disclosure as a trigger for social instability. In their view, the more information disclosed, the more the public knows, the harder it is for the government to govern, and an increasingly number of unstable factors would occur. In May 2014, a radioactive source in Nanjing was lost, and the situation was not made public until 90 h later as the relevant department worried that early disclosure would cause social panic.[14] However, the cost of delayed disclosure was that more people were exposed to the radioactive source unknowingly, resulting in damaged physical health. Also, around the year 2000, there were incidents of cutting off the postal routes and taking over newspapers by local governments due to fear of information disclosure in the name of maintaining social stability.[15] These practices are nothing more than the fact that administrators were still immersed in the

[10] In October 2008, the rumor—"navel oranges produced in Guangyuan contain bactrocera minax"—was widespread, and due to the lack of publicity in advance and delayed response to the rumor by relevant departments, a large quantity of navel oranges failed to be sold as people were panic, resulting in huge losses in the industry.

[11] In May 2009, when dealing with a Mitsubishi sport car fatal accident case in Hangzhou, the responsible traffic police officers informed the public and media of the accident in a evasive and careless manner, which triggered scathing public indictments against the traffic police department and questioning its capability of handling the case impartially, and some even doubted whether the suspect on trial was a scapegoat.

[12] *Facing Dissent Voices from Society, the Government Decides to Respect Public Will: Government of Heshan Announces Cancellation of the Nuclear Fuel Project, Southern Urban Daily*, July 14, 2013, p. A06.

[13] *Netizens Call for Government Information Disclosure over the Hangzhou Waste Incineration Plant Incident, China Youth Daily*, May 12, 2014, p. 8.

[14] *Tracking the Missing Radioactive Source Incident, Yangtse Evening Post*, May 13, 2014, p. A4.

[15] Examples include: One secretary of the County Committee of a county in Sichuan ordered to recall and burn *Farmers' Daily* of the day, as one article in the newspaper reveled his excessive use

conventional thinking of authoritarianism, considering themselves as parents while treating citizens as children who did not know anything of the world. However, the reality is that the Chinese people now have an increased level of knowledge and with the support of the Internet, some are even highly specialized in some fields. The days of treating the masses as children and making every decision for them are gone forever. In the eyes of citizens, anything that the government tries to cover may not be something good, as it is unnecessary to hide those that are really good. Long-term information withholding can only lead to administrators' decreased political resources and credibility, risking of causing more instability.

1.7 Replacing Conventional Supervision Pattern Through Openness

Information can be a tool influencing and guiding the masses. By disclosing information, the government informs the public of the problems facing the public, society, and the government, and the intentions and purposes of government activities, thereby influencing public awareness and behaviors, and guiding them to behave in the purpose of government governance as much as possible. Information is also an alternative to hard control measures such as orders and coercion. In the process of government governance, the information disclosed provides the public with the ability and opportunity to participate in public affairs, and can avoid the government's strict orders to force the public or its over-intervention in social and private life, thus helping maintain the authority of governance.

The information disclosed by the government can enable government's benign interactions with citizens and to maintain government authority. Providing information to the public helps enhance public choices and their involvement in public affairs. Information cannot be entirely equated with knowledge, but knowledge has to be transmitted through information. By disclosing the information acquired or produced during administration, the government can help raise public understanding of relevant issues. In turn, with the available information, citizens can better express their opinions and insights, criticisms and concerns about public administration, thus communicating with the government more efficiently. This can not only avoid the

---

of cars and construction houses, *Secretary Burns a Party-affiliated Newspaper*, *Southern Weekend*, October 26, 2000, p.15; in a county in Shandong province, the *Legal Daily* of one day "disappeared" because of an article criticizing the county, *Citizens' Rights shall not be Deprived: Commentary on the Case of the Disappearance of Legal Daily by Legal and News Expert*, *Legal Daily*, October 18, 2000, p. 1; and *After the Disappearance of Legal Daily*, *Southern Weekend*, October 5, 2000, p. 1. In Jiangxi province, relevant authorities, in the name of "mainlining social stability", banned the *Manual on Reducing the Burden on Farmers*, which publicized the central government's policy of reducing the burden on farmers, and held those who were related to the manual accountable, *What should be Banned?*, *Southern Weekend*, October 26, 2000, p. 15; *Can Social Stability be Maintained by Prevent Farmers from being Informed?*, *Southern Weekend*, November 16, 2000, p. 1; and *Preventing Improper Police Response*, *Southern Weekend*, November 23, 2000, p13.

government's use of coercion to enforce policies, triggering public resistance and opposition and affecting the effectiveness of policy implementation, but also improve the reasonableness of decision-making by involving public opinions in the process. It has been evidenced that it is more conducive to the realization of "good governance" if the government follows the "mass line" and solicits public opinions. Also, open and transparent government governance will enable the government to maintain its authority rather than losing its credibility.

Information can be used as a "soft measure" in government governance and expected governance outcomes can be delivered through information disclosure. When the government provides sufficient information to the public and maximize their rights to judge and choose, the masses can use the accessible information to make judgments, adopt attitudes and take measures on their own. Therefore, the disclosure and provision of information is also regarded as an important alternative for the unilateral and rigid orders—coercion control measures used in the past.

As per the *Key Tasks in Promoting the Transparency of Government Affairs in 2017* issued by the General Office of the State Council, the government shall have an in-depth interpretation of the development background, legal basis, objectives and tasks, and scope of policies and the highlights in economic transformation and development, and then provide the interpretation to market and enterprises, facilitating the "stability" of market expectations through the "thoroughness" of policy interpretation; the government shall also disclose information about national fiscal revenue and expenditure on a monthly basis, interpret the changes of the revenue and expenditure and reasons behind, predict the trend of fiscal revenue, and proactively explain to citizens the hot issues in the revenue and expenditure that may trigger public concerns; and the government shall hold the briefing on national economic operation on a monthly or quarterly basis, promptly release data on major issues of social concern, and increase the disclosure of information about the quality, efficiency and structure of government work as well as supply-side structural reform. These requirements also reflect the concept of replacing conventional regulation methods through government information disclosure. Also, against the background of streamlining administration and delegating power to the lower levels, the *Interim Regulation on Enterprise Information Disclosure* proposes information about enterprises held by government agencies shall be disclosed to strengthen self-discipline of enterprises and to foster a market environment operated with integrity; in other official documents such as the *Guiding Opinions of the State Council on Establishing and Improving the System of Joint Incentive for Keeping Faith and Joint Punishment for Losing Faith and Accelerating the Advancement of the Development of Social Honesty* (No. 33 [2016] of the State Council) and the *Notice of the General Office of the State Council on Strengthening Environmental Supervision and Law Enforcement* (No. 56 [2014] of the General Office of the State Council), government information disclosure is also considered as an important means to strengthen supervision and enforcement.

Chapter 2
Overview of China's Government Transparency Index Evaluation

The Regulations was approved on the 165th executive meeting of the State Council held on January 17, 2007 and came into effect on May 1, 2008. It embodies a milestone in China's efforts to build a law-based and open government, showing that China's work on government information disclosure has stepped into the path of the rule of law. However, to what extent has such an important rule, which is closely related to the vital interests of people, the rule-based governance of the government and the transition of government functions, been implemented? How does the disclosure system formulated by drawing on foreign theories and experience work? What are the achievements made and problems facing government agencies at all levels when implementing the Regulations? To what extent has the transparency of government agencies satisfied the public's need to obtain information? And how to further implement the disclosure system? All of these questions need to be answered through investigating and analyzing. Although this can be achieved by analyzing some individual cases that have been released, it lacks systematic coherence. Therefore, after many discussions, the Innovation Project Team on the Rule of Law Index of the Institute of Law of Chinese Academy of Social Sciences (hereinafter referred to as "the Project Team") decided to design an evaluation indicator system to conduct third-party evaluations on the implementation of the government information disclosure system in China.

2.1 Evaluation Objectives

In the government transparency index evaluations, by applying a method of researching and developing the indicator system, marking scores for the evaluation objects and statistically analyzing their implementation of the system, we have measured their implementation of the information disclosure system and illustrated the achievements made and problems encountered during the implementation. However, the focus of the work is neither scores or rankings, instead it is to

Y. Lv and H. Tian, *Evaluation on Government Transparency Index in China (2009–2016)*, Understanding China, https://doi.org/10.1007/978-981-16-5032-1_2

identify the common problems and difficulties the evaluation objects encountered in the implementation and the problems of the system itself through quantitative analyses of the disclosure of information by some administrative agencies, and then to put forward methods to improve the system, facilitate the implementation of the disclosure requirements, and constructively promote the transparency of the government.

2.2 Evaluation Principles

First, evaluations should be law-based. A basic principle of conducting government activities is that all actions shall be based on stipulations of laws, which is the basis for administrative agencies to perform their duties, and the foundation of performing well in government information disclosure. Therefore, the indicator system developed in evaluations adheres to the principle of legal compliance, which means that all the indicators are stipulated in laws, regulations and government documents, etc. and none of them are made up by ourselves, nor improvised, so that the evaluation objects and the public can accept them. The evaluation indicators are all based on laws and regulations such as the Regulations, the documents issued by the General Office of the State Council in recent years concerning government information disclosure, and the documents issued by the departments under the State Council to promote their relative work on promoting the openness of government.

Second, evaluations should be objective. The objective of conducting a third-party evaluation is to evaluate the effectiveness of the implementation of the work on government information disclosure by relevant administrative agencies. Hence, subjective evaluations should be avoided and subjective and arbitrary criteria such as "good" and "bad" should be converted into objective and operable indicators, focusing on whether government agencies disclose related information according to law in a timely manner and whether the information made publicly available is accurate and easily accessible to the public. If an evaluation object has disclosed related information in according to law and the information is easily accessible to the public, then a "good" can be scored. Instead of subjectively commenting "good" or "bad", evaluators are required to choose only from "yes" and "no", minimizing their space of discretion. Also, satisfaction surveys are not used as their results are strongly subjective and problems encountered by government agencies in information disclosure cannot be objectively identified.

Third, evaluations should be conducted with some regularity. Third-party evaluations should be based on the daily work of related departments to be evaluated, and "campaign-style" evaluations should be avoided, as in the latter situation evaluation objects may make preparations in advance to achieve "good" results, which do not necessarily reflect the actual situation and will deviate from the original purpose of the evaluation, leading to decreased credibility of the evaluation results. Therefore, the principle of four "NOs"—no prior notice, no advance arrangement, no mobilization, and no evaluation details informed—should be adhered in third-party evaluations.

Fourth, evaluations should be priority-focused. Due to the various categories of the government information that should be disclosed by administrative agencies, the Regulations and the key tasks in the work of government information disclosure issued by the General Office of the State Council every year also propose requirements for information disclosure work in many key areas, and the responsibilities of different agencies vary. Therefore, the indicators selected are mainly those that are critical for facilitating the construction of a law-based and transparent government, satisfying public demands for information, enhancing government credibility, and supervising the government's administration according to law, etc.

Fifth, evaluations should be result-driven. The purpose of disclosing government information is to enable the public to obtain information in a timely, accurate, comprehensive and convenient manner, and to effectively help them gain government services and identify the boundaries of their rights and obligations. Administrative agencies' work on government information is only the first step in performing well in promoting the openness of government affairs and what is more important is to enable the public to have effective access and use of the information. Therefore, the evaluation of the government's work on information disclosure is based on public perspective, results-oriented and during the process we focus on public needs, analyze the actual disclosure effects performed by each evaluation object, and observe whether government information is disclosed according to law and is easily accessible to citizens from a third-party perspective.

2.3 Evaluation Objects

Since the evaluation started in 2009, the scope of the evaluation objects selected has been expanding year by year.

The 2009 evaluation covered 43 large cities (excluding those in national autonomous areas). According to Article 63, Paragraph 4 of the *Legislation Law* prior to amendment, large cities refer to the cities where the people's governments of provinces or autonomous regions are situated, or where the special economic zones are located, and 18 large cities approved to establish by the State Council. These cities were chosen because they have local legislative power and are closely related to citizens' production and life.

In the 2010 evaluation, 59 departments under the State Council were added. The departments under the State Council are consisted of cabinet-level ministries, special organizations directly under the State Council, organizations directly under the State Council, institutions directly under the State Council, state administrations and bureaus administrated by ministry-level agencies, all of which will be referred hereinafter as "departments under the State Council". The selection of specific departments mainly depended on whether the relevant departments have external administrative power and whether they are closely related to citizens' production and life.

In the 2011 evaluation, 26 provinces and municipalities (hereinafter referred to as "the provincial-level governments") were further added, with five autonomous regions temporarily excluded.

In the 2013 evaluation, major adjustments were made in the selection of evaluation objects. The Project Team changed the number of the departments under the State Council to be evaluated to 55 in response to the institutional reform of the State Council. The State Electricity Regulatory Commission, the Ministry of Supervision, and the National Bureau of Corruption Prevention were no longer evaluated. However, though the Ministry of Health and the National Population and Family Planning Commission were integrated into the National Health and Family Planning Commission, their websites had not been integrated as of December 2013, so the two original websites were evaluated separately. As for local governments, the autonomous regions nationwide were all added. Therefore, the 2013 evaluation covered 31 provinces, autonomous regions, and municipalities (the provincial-level governments) and 49 large cities.

The 2014 evaluation covered 54 departments under the State Council, 31 provincial-level governments, and 49 large cities. Among them, as two websites of the State Administration of Press, Publication, Radio, Film and Television (http://www.gapp.gov.cn/ and http://www.chinsarft.gov.cn/) had not been integrated yet, the number of the websites of departments under the State Council evaluated was actually 55.

The 2016 evaluation covered 49 large cities and 100 counties (county-level cities and districts), while the evaluation of 54 departments under the State Council and 31 provincial-level governments are disclosed in the *Third-Party Evaluation Report of Promoting the Openness of Government Affairs of the People's Republic of China*". Considering that the work of government affairs disclosure needs to be improved progressively down to the grass-roots level to meet public demands, the Project Team started to include the county-level governments in the evaluation from 2016. The governments of 100 counties (county-level cities and districts) (hereinafter referred to as "the county-level governments")were chosen based on the *Notice on the Pilot Program of Strengthening the Disclosure of Government Affairs and Government Services at County Level through Electronic Government Affairs Platforms* jointly issued by the office of National Bureau of Corruption Prevention and the Leading Group for Transparency in Administrative Affairs of the Chinese Government on January 4, 2012. All county-level governments were included in the evaluation except one—Dalang Town of Dongguan City.

2.4 Evaluation Indicators

The 2009 evaluation covered six categories of indicators: operation of government portals (10%), the completeness of directory for government information disclosure (22%), the validity of guidelines on government information disclosure (17%), the accessibility of request channels (17%), accessibility of the Annual report on government information disclosure (14%), and public accessibility of information about housing demolition (20%). Although the Regulations puts forward detailed requirements for the disclosure tasks of government agencies, from voluntary disclosure to request-based disclosure, and from the form of disclosure to its content, the evaluation in 2009 did not cover all components, rather only several key aspects, including directory for government information disclosure, guidelines on government information disclosure, request-based disclosure, and annual reports on the disclosure of government information, etc., as these are closely related to the public's easy accessibility of information and their supervision of government information disclosure. Also, considering that housing demolition has been an important factor affecting the vital interests of the public and the relations between the government and citizens since the late 1990s, the disclosure of housing demolition information was set as an exceptional indicator to verify governments' agencies' implementation of information disclosure through the results obtained in obtaining related information.

In the 2010 evaluation, most of the indicators used to evaluate local governments were the same as those of the previous evaluation, though slight adjustments were made on the categories and some of the indicators. For example, as most local governments had established their own official websites, the category "operation of government portals" in 2009 was deleted and the indicators in the category were integrated into other categories. Also, another exceptional indicator—disclosure of information about food safety—was added as it was also a topic of public concern. Meanwhile, some indicators were optimized though not changed. In addition, with 100 total points assigned, the weight of each category was also adjusted—the completeness of directory for government information disclosure (20%), the validity of guidelines on government information disclosure (15%), the accessibility of request channels (20%), forms and content of the Annual report on government information disclosure (15%), disclosure of information about housing demolition (15%), and disclosure of information about food safety (15%).

When designing the indicators to evaluate the departments under the State Council, the Project Team selected the disclosure of information about budgeting as an exceptional indicator. With 100 points assigned, the five categories of indicators and their weights were: the completeness of directory for government information disclosure (20%), the validity of guidelines on government information disclosure (20%), accessibility of the request channels (20%), forms and content of the Annual report on government information disclosure (20%), and disclosure of information about budgeting (20%).

In the 2011 evaluation, the exceptional indicators for evaluating both the departments under the State Council and large cities were adjusted, with the one of the former being the disclosure of normative documents and the ones for the latter being the disclosure of information about food safety and the disclosure of information about administrative approval. The Project Team has also slightly adjusted the remaining indicators of the aforesaid two groups of evaluation objects to enhance the evaluation of substantial disclosure. The exceptional indicator for evaluating provincial-level governments was the disclosure of information about environmental protection. Furthermore, in terms of the points assigned to each category, those for the categories of substantial disclosure were raised while those for the categories of focus-on-form disclosure were lessened.

With 100 points assigned, the five categories of indicators used to evaluate the departments under the State Council and their weights were: the completeness of directory for government information disclosure (25%), the validity of guidelines on government information disclosure (15%), the accessibility of request channels (25%), the accessibility of the Annual report on government information disclosure (15%) and the disclosure of normative documents (20%).

With 100 points assigned, the five categories of indicators used to evaluate the provincial-level governments and their weights were: the completeness of directory for government information disclosure (25%), the validity of guidelines on government information disclosure (15%), the accessibility of request channels (25%), the accessibility of the Annual report on government information disclosure (15%) and the disclosure of information about environmental protection (20%).

With 100 points assigned, the six categories of indicators used to evaluate large cities and their weights were: the completeness of directory for government information disclosure (20%), the validity of guidelines on government information disclosure (15%), the accessibility of request channels (20%), the accessibility of the Annual report on government information disclosure (15%), the disclosure of information about food safety (15%), and the disclosure of information about administrative approval (15%).

Promoted by the State Council and government agencies at all levels, the work of government information disclosure had been carried out smoothly with complete forms of disclosure provided as of 2012. Against such backdrop and to evaluation the work in a more objective manner, the Project Team made some further adjustments on the indicators used in the 2012 evaluation. The evaluation focused less on the forms of information disclosure with both the number of indicators and their weights being reduced, while those of exceptional indicators were increased and more focus was given to the disclosure of key information. In the 2012 evaluation, the category "the validity of guidelines on government information disclosure" was deleted, while "the disclosure of work information" was added to evaluate the departments under the State Council, "the disclosure of government gazettes", "the disclosure of normative documents" and "the disclosure of information about administrative approval" were added to evaluate provincial-level governments, and "the disclosure of normative documents" and "the disclosure of information about environmental protection" were added to evaluate large cities.

With 100 points assigned, the five categories of indicators used to evaluate the departments under the State Council and their weights were: the completeness of directory for government information disclosure (20%), the disclosure of work information (20%), the disclosure of normative documents (25%), the accessibility of request channels (25%), and the accessibility of the Annual report on government information disclosure (10%).

With 100 points assigned, the seven categories of indicators used to evaluate provincial-level governments and their weights were: the completeness of directory for government information disclosure (15%), the disclosure of government gazettes (5%), the disclosure of normative documents (15%), the disclosure of information about administrative approval (15%), the disclosure of information about environmental protection (15%), the accessibility of request channels (25%) and the accessibility of the Annual report on government information disclosure (10%).

With 100 points assigned, the seven categories of indicators used to evaluate large cities and their weights were: the completeness of directory for government information disclosure (15%), the disclosure of normative documents (15%), the disclosure of information about administrative approval (15%), the disclosure of information about food safety (10%), the disclosure of information about environmental protection (10%), the accessibility of request channels (25%), and the accessibility of the Annual report on government information disclosure (10%).

The indicators used in the 2013 evaluation remained almost unchanged compared with those of the 2012 one, though more weights were assigned to categories related to substantial disclosure.

With 100 points assigned, the five categories of indicators used to evaluate the departments under the State Council and their weights were: the completeness of directory for government information disclosure (15%), the disclosure of work information (25%), the disclosure of normative documents (25%); request-based disclosure (25%), and the accessibility of the Annual report on government information disclosure (10%). With 100 points assigned, the seven categories of indicators used to evaluate provincial-level governments and their weights were: the completeness of directory for government information disclosure (15%), the disclosure of government gazettes (5%), the disclosure of normative documents (15%), the disclosure of information about administrative approval (15%), the disclosure of information about environmental protection (15%), request-based disclosure (25%), and the accessibility of the Annual report on government information disclosure (10%).

With 100 points assigned, the seven categories of indicators used to evaluate large cities and their weights were: the completeness of directory for government information disclosure (10%), the disclosure of normative documents (15%), the disclosure of information about administrative approval (15%), the disclosure of information about food safety (15%), the disclosure of information about environmental protection (15%), request-based disclosure (25%) and the accessibility of the Annual report on government information disclosure (5%).

In the 2014 evaluation, with 100 points assigned, the five categories of indicators used to evaluate the departments under the State Council and their weights were: the completeness of directory for government information disclosure (20%), the disclosure of work information (20%), the disclosure of normative documents (25%), request-based disclosure (25%), and the accessibility of the Annual report on government information disclosure (10%).

With 100 points assigned, the six categories of indicators and their weights for evaluating both provincial-level governments and large cities were the same: the completeness of directory for government information disclosure (15%), the disclosure of normative documents (15%), the disclosure of information about administrative approval (15%), the disclosure of information about environmental protection (15%), request-based disclosure (30%), and the accessibility of the Annual report on government information disclosure (10%).

In consideration of the new developments of and requirements appeared in the key areas of government information disclosure and the implementation of the disclosure system in 2015, the Project Team made major adjustments on the indicators.

The five categories of indicators used to evaluate the departments under the State Council and their weights were: the validity of a special section for government information disclosure (15%), the disclosure of normative documents (25%), the disclosure of financial information (20%), the accessibility of the Annual report on government information disclosure (15%) and request-based disclosure (25%).

The seven categories of indicators used to evaluate provincial-level governments and their weights were: the validity of a special section for government information disclosure (10%), the disclosure of normative documents (15%), the disclosure of financial information (15%), the disclosure of information about administrative approval (15%), the disclosure of information about environmental protection (15%), the accessibility of the Annual report on government information disclosure (10%) and request-based disclosure (20%).

The seven categories of indicators used to evaluate large cities and their weights were: the validity of a special section for government information disclosure (10%), the disclosure of normative documents (15%), the disclosure of financial information (15%), the disclosure of information about administrative approval (15%), the disclosure of information about environmental protection (15%), the accessibility of the Annual report on government information disclosure (10%) and request-based disclosure (20%).

In the 2016 evaluation, the indicators were designed in accordance with the requirements stipulated in the Regulations and the *Key Tasks in Promoting the Transparency of Government Affairs in 2016* issued by the General Office of the State Council.

The eight categories of indicators used to evaluate large cities and their weights were: the accessibility of government information disclosure platforms (10%), the disclosure of normative documents (15%), the disclosure of information about administrative approval (15%), the disclosure of information about administrative punishment (15%), the disclosure of information about environmental protection (15%), the disclosure of information about shanty town redevelopment (10%), the accessibility of the Annual report on government information disclosure (5%) and request-based disclosure (15%).

The eight categories of indicators used to evaluate county-level governments and their weights were: the accessibility of government information disclosure platforms (10%), the disclosure of normative documents (15%), the disclosure of information about administrative approval (15%), the disclosure of information about administrative punishment (15%), the disclosure of information about social assistance (10%), the disclosure of information about education (15%), the accessibility of the Annual report on government information disclosure (5%) and request-based disclosure (15%).

2.5 Evaluation Methods

In each year's evaluation, the Project Team used the aforesaid indicator system respectively to observe and analyze the results of voluntary disclosure and request-based disclosure. The evaluation method applied was "observation and verification"—the Project Team browsed and analyzed the sections and information about the official websites of government agencies being evaluated, and then verified the validity of information links, search systems, contact number, email address, and request submission systems, etc. Also, to ensure the objectiveness, authenticity and effectiveness of the evaluation results, if the verification failed the first time, the Project Team would then verify related items multiple times. For example, if the link was invalid and the webpage could not be opened, the Project Team would verify the findings by going online on a different computer, through a different access or at a different time and it would be considered invalid if all were failed. If calls were busy or with no one answering, multiple calls would be made in another office time and if still unable to connect after two working days, then the number would be considered invalid. As for the submission of information disclosure requests, if online request platforms (including email addresses) were provided, requests would all be sent via these platforms, and for those without an online platform, written requests would be sent in hardcopy through the China Post Express (EMS).

The evaluation of government transparency started in 2009. The 2009 evaluation was conducted from November 9 to December 15, 2009, the 2010 evaluation from October 22 to December 15, 2010, the 2011 evaluation from March 15 to December 31, 2011, the 2012 evaluation from March 5 to December 15, 2012, the 2013 evaluation from March 5, 2013 to January 23, 2014, the 2014 evaluation from March 5 to December 31, 2014, the 2015 evaluation from March 10 to December 31, 2015, and the 2016 evaluation from October 17 to December 31.

Chapter 3
The 2009 Evaluation of China's Government Transparency

3.1 Overview of the Work of Government Information Disclosure in 2009

The evaluation found that the government portal has become an important channel for local governments to disclose information. The 43 cities evaluated in 2009 all had their own municipal government portal, and each had a special government information disclosure platform developed in a prominent position. Some even had their own independent website specialized for disclosing government information or promoting the openness of government affairs. Large amount of information was voluntarily disclosed through government information disclosure platforms on local governments' websites, including information about institutional setup, agency responsibilities, policies and regulations, service basis and procedures, and government administration updates.

Most local government portals provided links to the websites of the upper-level departments and subordinate county-level governments. Also, the vast majority of the government portals concentratedly disclosed the information issued by municipal governments, upper-level departments, subordinate county-level governments, and public institutions. Much of the information could be found on the local government portals.

In addition, great majority of local governments highly valued the implementation of the relevant provisions stipulated in the Regulations. For example, as required by the Regulations, they developed sections for the directory for government information disclosure (93.02% without a same-level government directory), the guidelines on government information disclosure (72.09% with the full-text of the same-level government guidelines), request-based disclosure (88.37% with a valid request-based disclosure section), and the annual report on government information disclosure (74.42% with a special section for the annual report) on their website with relevant content provided.

Y. Lv and H. Tian, *Evaluation on Government Transparency Index in China (2009–2016)*, Understanding China, https://doi.org/10.1007/978-981-16-5032-1_3

Government agencies valued highly the convenience for the public to gain the information disclosed on their websites. The evaluation found that many government agencies categorized the information disclosed on their websites intro different sections by items. Some also categorized the information by departments involved or types of documents. Most information could be viewed online, downloaded. Multiple search functions were also provided on the websites to make it convenient to search information. On many government websites information about key issues such as housing demolition was placed in special sections and in prominent position of the websites. In particular, many local government departments managed to make positive and proactive replies within the statutory or shortest time period to the verification consultations via phone or email, or the requests for information disclosure made by the Project.

Nevertheless, some problems were also identified in the evaluation. First, some problems existed in the operation and maintenance of government portals, mainly manifested by slow network speed. The portals of a few governmental subordinate departments could not be opened even after repeated attempts. Some even carried viruses. Second, some government portals showed poor performance on following the requirements of the Regulations. Some failed to provide the directory for government information disclosure or the links in the directory could not be opened; some failed to provide guidelines on government information disclosure or the content of guidelines was incomprehensive; some failed to provide the annual report or the report provided contained little key content and was just a formality. Third, information was disclosed in an decentralized manner. For example, two platforms—the "government information disclosure" platform and the "disclosure of government affair" platform—were provided on some government portals. Some of the information disclosed on the two platforms was overlapped while some was different. For another example, the Project Team selected the disclosure of information about housing and relocation as an exceptional indicator and searched as well as verified relevant information on government websites. It was found that the information provided on many government portals was quite scattered. Some portals only provided demolition regulations and policies, or only demolition announcements. Also, the information provided on a few government portals was inconsistent with that provided by the government agencies that were in charge of housing demolition. Fourth, information disclosed on the websites was not convenient to obtain. The development of sections and information arrangement on some websites were not reasonable. The convenience of users to obtain information was neglected. Users were forced to spend large amount of time and energy to locate the information they were looking for, making them feel like being trapped in an "information maze". Searching for the same information or section, some could locate it while others could not; or even one could locate it at one time but not another time. Search functions for the disclosure of government information were not provided on some websites. Some functions provided were not reasonably designed, resulting in less than satisfactory search results. When examining a few government portals, it took the Project Team three to four hours to finish the scheduled evaluation task. In some extreme scenarios, it took even longer to ensure that there was no information to verify on a certain website. We had sound reasons to believe that it was even more difficult for the public to obtain information. Fifth, information disclosed on a few government websites was more of a formality than providing content. Some government websites were equipped with different sections to disclose various types of information. However, the links provided in the sections either could not be opened or directed to the content unrelated to the title. Some government websites provided inaccurate information, such as wrong contact number or email address. When verifying the contact numbers provided, the Project Team found that some did not exist; some were busy for a very long time or with no one answering the calls. Even when some calls were answered, the people answered were not responsible for or related with related work.

3.2 Operation of Local Government Websites

The operation of local government websites was the first category of the evaluation indicators. The category consisted of four indicators: validity of government portals, links to lower-level government agencies' portals, development of government information disclosure platforms, and disclosure of regulations on government information disclosure. The evaluation of the validity of government portals mainly focused on whether the local governments evaluated had a government portal, and whether the portal could be opened; that of the links to lower-level government agencies' portal mainly focused on whether links to the websites of higher-level departments and district-level as well as county-level governments were provided on the homepages of local government websites and whether the links were valid; that of the development of government information disclosure platforms focused on whether special sections or platforms for disclosing government information were provided on local government portals; and that of the disclosure of regulations on government information disclosure mainly focused on whether the laws, rules or regulations concerning the disclosure of government information at the corresponding level were provided on the local government portals. If the regulations of same-level governments were not formulated, then the provisions developed by higher-level governments or the Regulations shall be provided.

The local government websites evaluated all had their domain names suffixed with gov.cn, and most of them could be opened. This revealed that after years of vigorous promotion by the state, the construction of an e-government across the country has made great achievement. However, the websites of two local governments could not be opened even after repeated attempts. Their subsequent evaluation could only be conducted by browsing relevant information on their "website for disclosing government affairs".

However, some local governments lagged behind in constructing government websites. Among the 43 local government websites evaluated, 35 provided valid links to lower-level government agencies' websites at the bottom of the homepage, accounting for 81.4%. Among the remaining eight websites, the homepage of two could not be opened, leaving the validity of the links unverified; the links to the lower-level agencies' websites of another two could not be opened; one had a list of the names of part of its lower-level agencies, but no links were provided; the links provided by one website were incomplete; one did not provide any links; and one only provided the links to some district-level and county-level government agencies' websites, and did not provide links to its lower-level department websites.

Each of the 43 websites had a section or platform in a prominent position for the disclosure of government information or government affairs. Some local governments even established a special website for the disclosure. The aforementioned two governments whose websites could not be opened had established such a special website. Apart from other sections on government portals, these sections, platforms, and special websites served as an important channel for providing various types of government information to the public. This, to some extent, revealed that with the gradual implementation of the Regulations, local governments have made government information disclosure a key aspect of government administration.

Each of the 43 websites provided regulations concerning government information disclosure in full text on its special platform for information disclosure and in the section of policies and regulations. The regulations concerning government information disclosure developed in the region were also published on many websites. Other regulations disclosed included those concerning request-based information disclosure, fee collection, internal management of government information disclosure, and internal supervision and appraisal mechanisms concerning information disclosure.

3.3 Directory for Government Information Disclosure

The preparation and publication of the directory for government information disclosure (hereinafter referred to as "the directory") is an important duty for government agencies at all levels as stipulated in the Regulations. In the directory, government information was edited and categorized by preparation department, title, keywords, items involved, content summary, time of information generation. The aim of developing the directory was to regulate government agencies' information management activities, to improve the level of management, and to provide the public with convenient access to obtain the information they needed in the vast ocean of digital information. The directory was an important guarantee for the implementation of government information disclosure, especially that of voluntary disclosure. A well-managed voluntary disclosure could free government agencies from responding to large numbers of requests from individuals. Hence, the cost of government administration would be reduced. The level of developing the category determined the quality of government information disclosure. In this information era, the large-capacity information storage function provided by computers and the Internet, multi-functional database programs, along with efficient information transmission and management methods offered a technical platform to develop a e-directory and provide e-services.

This section evaluated the development of the directory, the availability and convenience of the section for the directory, the validity and convenience of links to the content of the directory, and the convenience and availability of search functions of the directory of the same-level governments, affiliated departments, lower-level government agencies, public enterprises and institutions provided on the official websites of local governments.

According to the evaluation, most local governments developed the directory on their portals with links to relevant government information provided. Hence, the public could directly obtain the voluntarily disclosed information online. Among the 43 local government portals evaluated, 40 had the directory of the same-level governments, 39 had the directory of their affiliated departments, 36 had the directory of lower-level governments, and 22 had the directory of public enterprises and institutions (see Fig. 3.1). Local governments all categorized relevant information in the section for the directory according to certain criteria (such as types of items or departments involved). Three websites provided multiple categories of information by genre, theme, object, and relevant organization, to make it more convenient for the public with different needs to obtain information.

When verifying the links contained in the directory of municipal governments, the Project Team randomly selected ten information links on every local government portal evaluated. Among the 43 local government portals evaluated, the number of the portals with all the ten links opened was 33, accounting for 76.74%; that with 7–9 links opened was 3; that with 4–6 opened was also 3; none of the links on one portal could be opened; and the remaining three portals could not be evaluated as they did not have the directory. When verifying the links contained in the directory of affiliated departments, the Project Team chose local development and reform commission, education bureau, civil affairs bureau, public security bureau and labor and social security bureau as samples. Two information links directed to each department provided on the website of every local government were randomly selected.

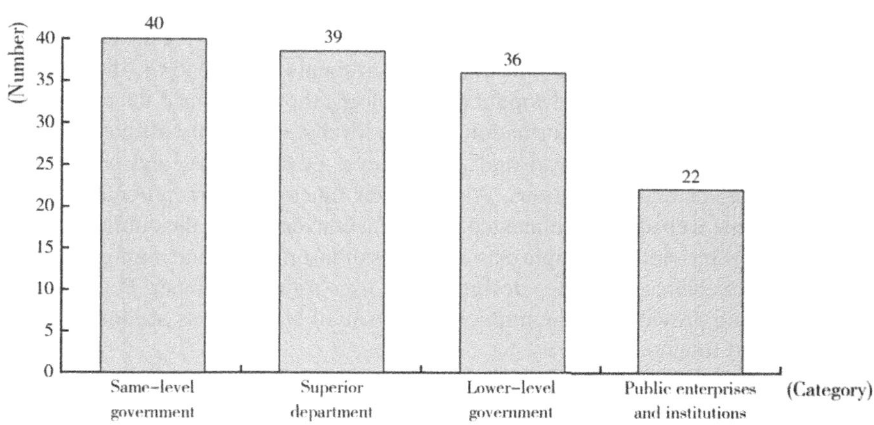

Fig. 3.1 The development of the directory on the websites of local governments

Among the 43 local government portals evaluated, the number of the portals with all the ten links opened was 26, accounting for 60.47%; that with 7–9 links opened was one; that with 4–6 opened was 7; that with 1–3 opened was 2; that with none of the links opened was 3; and the remaining four could not be evaluated as they did not have the directory. When verifying the links contained in the directory of lower-level governments, the Project Team selected three districts or counties listed in the directory. Three information links directed to each county or district provided on the website of every local government were randomly selected. Among the 43 local government portals evaluated, the number of the portals with all the links opened was 27, accounting for 62.79%; that with 7–8 links opened was 2; that with 4–6 links was one; that with 1–3 links was also one; that with none of the links opened was 5; and the remaining seven could not be evaluated as they did not have the directory. When verifying the links contained in the directory of public enterprises and institutions, the Project Team selected three organizations listed in the directory. Two information links directed to each organization provided on the website of every local government were randomly selected. Among the 43 local government portals evaluated, the number of the portals with all the links opened was 13, accounting for 30.23%; that with 3–4 links opened was 3; that with 1–2 links was one; that with none of the links opened or with no links provided was 5; and the remaining 21 could not be evaluated as they did not have the directory.

The evaluation also examined the search functions of the directory on local government portals. The main indicators that were observed and verified were the cross-subdirectory search functions of the directory, and combined search functions as well as their availability. Among the 43 local government portals evaluated, 21 developed a special simple search function (searching under one single condition) for the directory. Also, results can be found with "demolition" as a keyword. Among them, 18 also provided different types of search for the simple search function. Users could search information by using keywords in title, keywords in main body of the document, issuing department, document number, etc. In addition, 13 of the aforesaid 21 websites provided combined search functions. After verification, it was found that the combined search functions provided by all the 12 websites were accessible.

According to the evaluation, most local governments developed the directory on their portals. By employing information technology, they developed the e-directory to integrate various types of information of same-level governments, affiliated departments, subordinate district-level and county-level governments, and subordinate public enterprises and institutions. Also, search functions were provided for the directory. Some websites also managed to make it convenient for the public to search information by providing multiple classifications of information and highlighting key items. Some websites were also designed in a user-friendly manner. For example, the information provided on the municipal website of Ningbo was accompanied by the speech aid function.

However, two major problems were also identified in this respect. First, the directory on some government portals was incomplete, the main manifestations of which were little government information was contained in the directory and some content and sections were still under construction or maintenance. Also, the directory on some websites was not advanced, either without a search function or the function provided failed to work. Second, some problems existed in the information links contained in the directory. To begin with, the links were incomplete. Not all organizations had information links. There were no links directed to some institutions or departments listed on the portals or not all the subordinate departments and district-level as well as county-level governments were listed in the category. Also, some links could not be opened. After clicking the links of many items, "this page cannot be opened" might be displayed, or the information displayed after opening the page had nothing to do with the item itself. Furthermore, some of the information provided by a few websites was not in a commonly used format, thus requiring specific software to read (such as SEP), which brought unnecessary difficulties to public access to information.

3.4 Guidelines on Government Information Disclosure

The preparation of guidelines on government information disclosure (hereinafter referred to as "the guidelines") is another task that the Regulations required government agencies at all levels to accomplish when implementing the government information disclosure system. A guideline serves as an instruction about the government information disclosure system. By reading it, people who are unfamiliar with the system could learn about the rights they are enjoyed, the party that is responsible for providing government information, the agency that is responsible for the disclosure of government information, the ways and means to obtain government information, and channels for seeking relief and assistance when government information cannot be obtained according to laws, etc. The indicators in this category examined by the Project Team were: validity of local government guidelines, validity of information concerning the government agencies responsible for disclosure, a description of voluntary disclosure, a description of the qualifications and procedures of request-based disclosure, and a description of government information disclosure supervision and relief.

The evaluation found that 31 government websites provided the guidelines in fulllines of same-level governments, and no guidelines were found on the remaining websites either by searching on the websites or using popular search engines. Among the 12 websites where no guidelines of same-level governments were found, four disclosed the guidelines of the office of same-level governments instead; one provided a description of the qualifications and procedures of request-based disclosure in the corresponding section; seven failed to provide any content that could serve as a guideline. Although one of the aforesaid seven developed a section for the guidelines, the section was directed to the directory. The vast majority of the 31 websites where guidelines were provided explained items concerning government information disclosure in the guidelines in a unified format. Only one website used the Q and A method to explain the government information disclosure system, which was more vivid and clear.

In accordance with the Regulations, government agencies shall provide relevant information about the agency responsible for disclosing government information in the guidelines to facilitate the public to make consultations and requests. Therefore, the Project Team examined and analyzed the name, address, contact number, fax number, email address and office hours of the agency. Among the 43 government websites evaluated, 31 provided the name of the agency (those that just provided the guidelines of municipal office or a description in the section of requested-based disclosure were also considered as "provided the guidelines"), accounting for 72.09%. Thirty government websites provided the address of the agency, though none of them provided public transport options or location maps. Twenty-three government websites provided office hours of the agency. Also, another two government websites simply referred the time as "working days", which was considered by the Project Team as "failed to provide accurate office hours".

The Project Team verified the contact number and email address of the agency that was responsible for government information disclosure provided on the government websites. The verification found that the contact number and email address provided by some websites were inaccurate. Some calls could not get through and emails could not be sent or some were returned. Some calls were successfully made, however, the person answered either claimed not responsible for the work or refused to reply to any consultations with a terrible attitude. A considerable number of emails that were successfully sent received no replies.

Also, 29 government websites (including those without the guidelines) provided the contact number. Among those provided the guidelines, eight failed to provide the contact number. In the name of an ordinary citizen, the Project Team made phone calls during office hours and asked how to request government information disclosure to verify the contact numbers. For those with no one answering or those calls that were busy, anther one would be made every 30 min or so. If the call could not get through after trying for three times, further calls would be made in the next week. However, if it was still unable to be connected, then no score would be given. According to the verification, the contact numbers provided on two websites were inaccurate—one was out of service, and the other was actually fax number. The number provided on three websites had no one answered. The number provided on one website was always busy. The number provided on 23 websites could be connected, five of which successfully got through during the following week. Among the staff members who answer the 23 contact numbers that were successfully connected, seven either said the agency was not responsible for the disclosure or they themselves were not familiar with the work; one was in a terrible attitude, refusing to answer any questions; 15 replied the consultations made by the Project Team over the phone. Among the 15 calls that successfully got through with answers provided, 12 were connected in the first week, while the remaining three in the second week (See Fig. 3.2). During the verification, the Project Team found that a considerable number of local government staff members who answered the calls were quite cautious about the consultations about government information disclosure, confirming repeatedly the location of the caller. Some even required that the person who requested government information shall have a direct interest in the information and this person shall be the specific

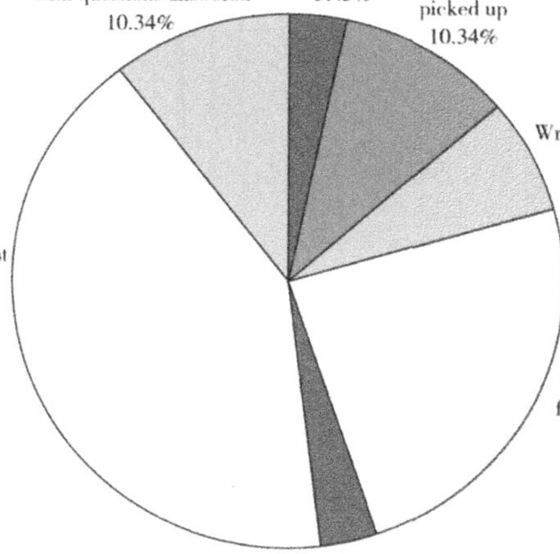

Fig. 3.2 Verification results of the contact number of agency responsible for government information disclosure

party involved in the matter, and stated that local government agencies had discretion in deciding whether the applicant was qualified or not.

Twenty-three government websites provided the email address of the agency responsible for government information disclosure in their guidelines. During the verification, all emails were sent via one email address of the Project Team. The verification found that the email address provided on five websites were inaccurate and emails were returned, while that on 18 websites were accessible. As of the end of the evaluation, only the agency of four local governments replied the consultations via email (see Fig. 3.3). It is worth noting that among the four agencies that replied, the one in Luoyang City responded the fastest—15 min after the email was sent; the one in Changsha City on the next day; the one in Zhengzhou City on the 5th day and the one in Guangzhou on the 14th day after the email was sent. This showed that the staff members of these agencies were professional and were responsible in doing their work. After the evaluation completed and on the afternoon of December 31, 2009, the agency in Qingdao City replied via email. However, considering that it had passed the deadline, no score was given by the Project Team.

All websites that published the guidelines provided a description of the forms of voluntary disclosure, but many of them did not clearly explain the qualifications for request-based disclosure. During the verification, for those without the guidelines, the qualifications listed in the section for requested-based disclosure would be examined. The verification found that 35 websites provided vague qualifications for request-based disclosure. Among them, 25 government websites noted that requests

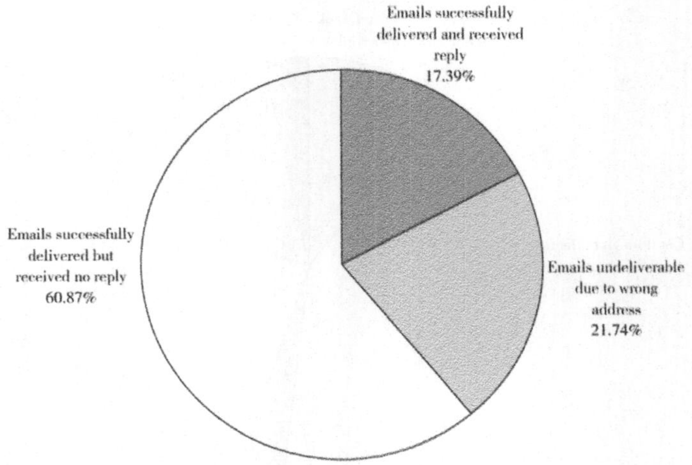

Fig. 3.3 Validity of the email address of agency responsible for government information disclosure

could only be made for the information that was beyond the scope of voluntary disclosure, which confused the relations between voluntary disclosure and request-based disclosure. The remaining did not provide clear qualifications.

Thirty-three websites provided a description of the procedures of request-based disclosure (including the websites that did not have guidelines but provided a description in specific sections). Among them, 20 websites described the procedures both in written words and by using flowcharts; ten only in written words, one only by using flowcharts. The descriptions provided on the remaining two websites did not agree with the real situation. For example, the guidelines on one website suggested that requests could be submitted online, however, the website did not have the function (see Fig. 3.4). The Project Team also noted that, according the guidelines on some local government websites, requests could only be submitted via the Internet, and not in person, by fax, via mail or email.

Among the 31 websites that provided the guidelines in full, 29 described the supervisory mechanism for government information disclosure. Among the aforesaid 29 websites, 21 provided the name of the supervision agency, though 17 of which failed to provide the address and none provided public transport options or location maps. One website did not provide the contact number of the supervision agency; 16 failed to provide the email address; though eight provided an online complaints service platform. Twenty-seven websites explained the ways of government relief on information disclosure in their guidelines.

According to the evaluation, most local government websites provided the guidelines, the content of which basically covered those that required by the Regulations and a description of issues related to information disclosure was also included. However, some problems were identified in this respect. First, in terms of the content

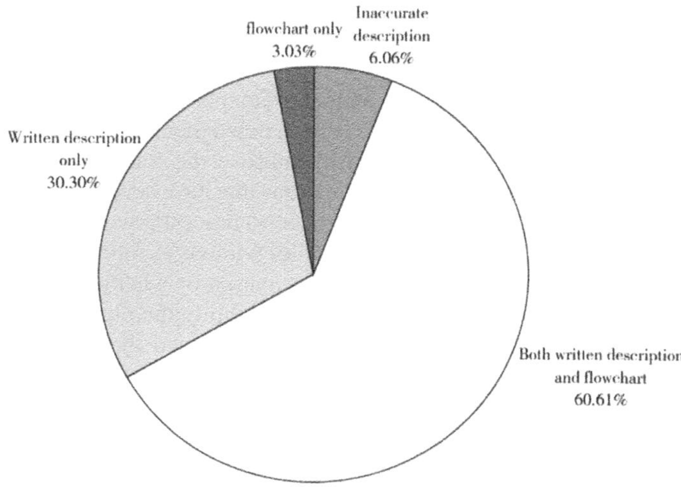

Fig. 3.4 A description of the procedures of request-based disclosure

of the guidelines, some local governments failed to understand thoroughly the government information disclosure system, which was mainly reflected on the description of the qualifications for requesting information disclosure. Second, the requirements on publishing guidelines were not well followed. The evaluation found that not all local governments published the guidelines on their government websites. Some only provided the guidelines of affiliated departments and failed to publish those of same-level governments. Some even confused the guidelines of the same-level governments with those of the office of same-level governments. Third, the information contained in some guidelines did not conform to reality. The two main manifestations of it were invalid contact number and email address and wrong descriptions of disclosure procedures. No answers to calls, busy lines or no replies to the emails could partly because of the limited number of staff member working at the local government agencies. However, as the relevant contact information had been published online, government agencies had the responsibility to ensure that the information could serve as a channel to answer public inquires and to get to know public needs. Finally, some content of the guidelines was not detailed enough. For example, the open hours were vaguely described as "working days" and the public could not know the exact office hours. For another example, in terms of the address of the agency, it was necessary to include public transport options and location maps to help people who were unfamiliar with the routes.

3.5 Request-Based Disclosure

The request-based disclosure system is an important method to safeguard and implement citizens' right to know, to limit and narrow down the discretion of government agencies on information disclosure, and to improve the transparency of government administration. All the countries and regions that have adopted the government information disclosure system allow any citizen to request government agencies to disclose any government information they hold, without examining their purposes of the request, or the potential use of the information or whether they have direct interests in the information. In evaluating the availability the platforms for request-based information disclosure, the Project Team examined the following aspects: whether local government portals provided a section for request-based disclosure, request forms, online request access; whether the online request platforms were user-friendly and effective, and whether the Regulations was appropriately applied to the online platforms. For example, if the collection of information about the applicants was appropriate and if the purposes of the request and the potential use of the information requested were required.

Among the 43 local government portals, 40 provided a special section for requesting government information disclosure. However, the section two websites could not be opened, while the section on the remaining 38 websites could be directed to the online request access page after being clicked. Thirty-two portals provided request forms for the public to request by fax or via the internet. Among them, 27 provided the forms in Microsoft Word (one of the portals required the public to register first and then log on to download the form); three provided the forms in Webpage format; one did not provide unified forms and the applicant needed to download different forms on the websites of different departments and some forms could not be downloaded. Nine portals failed to provide any forms. Although another two portals did have a section to provide downloadable forms, the links to the forms were invalid.

Thirty-four portals provided online request platforms. Among them, one required applicants to submit request forms via emails, while the remaining 33 portals provided access to filling and submitting the forms via the internet. It is worth noting that two of the 33 portals required the public to register and log on before they could make a request.

Among the portals where online request platforms were provided, 31 provided a unified submission platform for all the municipal departments and county-level and district-level governments. For the remaining three local governments, requests could only be submitted on the corresponding portals of different departments. Among the 31 portals with unified platforms, 11 did not require applicants to select the departments from which they request for information, while the remaining 20 did so.

When submitting requests, individual applicants (natural person) were generally required to provide their ID number, place of work, and even gender and age and legal person and other organizations were asked to provide organization code and the gender and age of the person to contact, besides some basic information including name of the applicant, address, contact number, fax number and email address. Among the 34 portals where online request could be made, only four did not require the aforementioned additional information. In addition, according to the guidelines or application forms provided on the nine websites where online request could not be made, the additional information also needed to be included. A few portals even asked applicants to provide a copy of their ID card, or upload the scans of their ID card, organization code and business certificate via the Internet.

Among the 34 portals where online request access was provided, only five did not require applicants to indicate the potential use of the information. Among the remaining 29 portals, the "potential use of information" field on 15 was "required" and on 14 was "optional". In addition, according to the guidelines or application forms provided on the nine websites where online request could not be made, the aforesaid information also needed to be included. This was consistent with the result of the contact number verification completed by the Project Team, that is, many local governments still required the applicant to have direct interests in the information requested.

To verify the availability online request platforms, the members of Project Team, in the name of an ordinary citizen, submitted requests to all the 34 government portals where online request could be made for the disclosure of local demolition compensation standards. Among them, 22 provided receipts of the request (e.g. Acceptance Notice No. or Tracking No.), accounting for 64.71%; eight (23.53%) did not provide any similar message (one website even showed zero request "in process" after the request had been submitted one month before). The submissions to the remaining four (11.76%) were failed—one asked to provide a copy of applicants' ID card; one required to submit via email, but the email was returned; one required to fill in information about a company even the applicant was natural person, and when required information was provided, the submission still failed as the webpage could not be opened; one always indicated that the information entered was incorrect, and the request could not be submitted even after repeated checks and corrections; one needed to verify the virtual ID number of the applicant. In addition, the Project Team also found that in the request form provided by one portal, the allowed maximum number of characters in some fields was less that what was actually needed. Fox example, the number of characters reserved in the email address field was less than the character number of an ordinary email address, so that the email address could not be used in the request.

Among the 34 local government portals where online request could be made, 20 provided the function of tracking requests online; 22 provided the function of checking request results online; and nine provided dynamic information about the requests being processed. However, the corresponding sections on some portals were hidden in other sections, and users needed to search repeatedly to find them. The evaluation also found that a few government portals disclosed the results of all the requests without removing applicants' personal information and details of the requests, which risked damaging the rights and interests of applicants.

As of the end of the evaluation, 12 local government agencies replied within the statutory period. Among them, two responded on the first and the second working day respectively after the submission. The replies of some agencies were made online and applicants needed to check it on the websites. However, the replies of others were given via emails in accordance with related requirements. In terms of the content of the replies, some departments claimed that they were not the agencies responsible for disclosing such information and told the applicants the corresponding agencies to make requests, while some others replied that the information requested had been disclosed voluntarily and applicants were advised to search on their government portals.

The departments that performed the best were the ones in Ningbo, Luoyang and Jinan. The accepting department in Ningbo not only replied on the websites, but also via email, and called the applicant to explain the content of the reply. The accepting department in Luoyang replied in an email that "After communicating with the Municipal Demolition Office, we have confirmed that the compensation standards used in 2009 will remain to be the 2007 one". The accepting department in Luoyang replied in an email that "we do not have any standards on demolition compensation applied in 2009, but we complete related work in accordance with the*Administrative Measures on Urban Housing Demolition in Jinan*". The regulation was attached to the email in full.

According to the verification, many local governments established a platform for request-based disclosure on their government websites. They made an effort to meet citizens' demand for information by virtue of the efficient, convenient and low-cost Internet. Some provided the functions of offering receipts, tracking requests online, checking request results online, and dynamic information about requests. All of these efforts reflected the improvement of their online public service awareness and ability, increased the transparency of handling processes of the requests, and consolidated the self-supervisory mechanism. Many government agencies managed reply within the statutory period. Some not only just fulfilled their responsibility of replying, but also explained the content of their replies in detail via phone calls. When the requested information had been disclosed voluntarily or was no in the scope of their responsibility, some government agencies contacted the relevant departments to disclose the information or even retrieved the information and then sent to the applicant, instead of just refusing the applicant or just provided some instructions on to which department the applicant should make request. These all indicated that local governments and their staff members had relatively high awareness and quality of government service.

Nevertheless, three major problems needed to be concerned about. First, some local governments did not have an online request platform or the platform they created failed to work, and from which people could not obtain information despite the fact that the internet became increasingly developed. Even though it seemed that some governments did have a platform, requests could not be successfully submitted through it, or no receipts provided after the submission and replies were not given within the statutory period. Therefore, the accessibility of the platform should be questioned. Also, the function of tracking requests online provided on some websites did not work. Second, the design and layout of the platform on some websites was less than user-friendly. On some portals, the functions such as tracking requests online were not put in at prominent position nor well arranged on the platform. People needed to search repeatedly to find them, and a slight negligence would make them think that the website did not have the functions. Also, some designs in the process of request were not appropriate, resulting in unnecessary failure of requests. What's more, some websites required applicants to register in real name before they could make requests, which was quite inconvenient for many people who were eager to obtain information but were unfamiliar with the websites. It was also worth noting that some local government agencies violated the provisions of the Regulations by allowing applicants to only submit requests via the internet because this prevented many people who did not have access to internet from making requests, restricting and depriving them of their right to know. Third, some local governments had misunderstandings about the relevant provisions of the Regulations. Local government agencies generally misunderstood the qualification requirements of applicants, so that many required applicants to provide the purposes of their requests and the potential use of the information requested. This was a general misunderstanding of the Article 13 of the Regulations.

3.6 Annual Report on Government Information Disclosure

Releasing the annual report on government information disclosure (hereinafter referred to as "the annual report") within the statutory period is an important duty stipulated by the Regulations, a key supervisory mechanism for the government information disclosure system, and a critical aspect for government agencies to strengthen self-monitoring, fulfill government information disclosure obligation, and subject to public supervision. To this end, the Project Team considered the annual reports of 43 local governments as one category of indicators in the 2009 evaluation. The indicators examined included: availability of the section for the annual report, availability of the annual report, data on voluntary disclosure, data on request-based disclosure, and data on complaints and supervision.

The Project Team mainly examined whether local government websites had a special section for publishing all the annual reports of previous years. The evaluation found that 32 websites developed the section. However, the section on website could not be opened while the section on another two was empty. The remaining 11 websites did not have a special section, though two of them provided their annual reports on the websites anyway. Many websites provided on the 2008 annual report, as it was less than two years since the implementation of the Regulations. Hence, the Project Team only examined the disclosure of the 2008 annual report. The evaluation showed that 34 websites provided the full text of the 2008 annual report. It was worth noting that some of the aforesaid 34 websites did not provide a special section or the section was empty, their annual reports were found by searching on their government portals or by using other search engines.

Among the 34 local government websites that provided the annual report in full, 32 provided the overall data on voluntary disclosure in 2008 and 33 provided the data categorized according to factors such as the forms of voluntary disclosure.

How requests for information disclosure are handled is an important factor for assessing the effectiveness of government agencies in implementing the government information disclosure system. Therefore, the Project Team mainly examined the data on request-based disclosure, including: the number of requests received, the number of requests accepted, the departments received top requests, the items with top requests, and different types of data categorized by ways of requests, decisions on whether the information would be disclosed, and reasons behind the decisions.

Among the 34 websites, only 14 provided the number of requests they received in the previous year. Three of them revealed that they received no request at all. Eleven websites categorized the number of requests received by same-level governments, lower-level governments, and their respective affiliated departments; 16 websites listed the departments received top requests; 20 listed the items with top requests. Nineteen websites provided the categorized data on the requests they received, which was sorted by ways of requests, including in person or via mail, email, fax or the internet. Thirty-three websites (including three that did not receive any request) provided the number of requests accepted in the previous year. It was found that some websites just provided the number of requests accepted without any data on the number of the requests received. Hence, the possibility that some local governments may have confused "received" with "accepted" could not be ruled out. The data on requests provided by 28 websites was categorized by the decisions on whether the information would be disclosed, such as not to be accepted, to be disclosed, not to be disclosed, and to be partly disclosed. The data on requests provided by 17 websites was categorized by the reasons for refusing to disclose, such as involving state secrets, personal privacy or business secrets. Fifteen websites explained the "other reasons" for the refusal. Thirty-two websites listed the number of complaints, administrative reviews and administrative proceedings involving government information disclosure (See Fig. 3.5). Three of them claimed that they did not have any complaints, reviews or proceedings (including three that did not receive any request).

The evaluation found that the vast majority of local governments prepared the annual report in accordance with the requirements of the Regulations. Many also provided a special section for publishing the annual report on their portals or on their government information disclosure platforms. The annual report summarized the agency's work of government information disclosure in the previous year. However, two major problems could not be neglected. First, some local government still failed to prepare and publish their annual reports within the statutory period. Also, some government websites did not develop a special section for publishing the annual reports, causing inconvenience for the public to search. Second, the content of some local governments' annual reports was incomprehensive. The indicators examined by the Project Team were all the core issues of government information disclosure and were all important factors in evaluating the work of local governments on information disclosure. Some were still not included in the annual reports of some local governments. Some local governments confused the difference between "requests

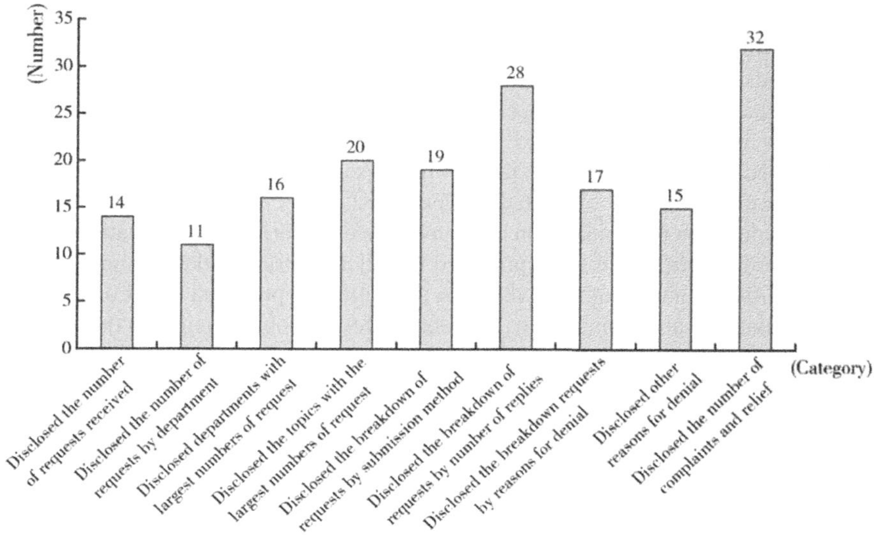

Fig. 3.5 The performance of local governments on publishing data on request-based disclosure

received" and "requests accepted". Some just provided the number of requests accepted, without revealing the rate of acceptance. Some even failed to clearly provide categorized data on either voluntarily disclosed information or request-based information. None of these was conducive to public supervision of local governments' work on government information disclosure.

3.7 Information About Housing Demolition

As China got increasingly urbanized, urban construction and housing demolition activities imposed great influence on people's production and life. Urban housing compensation and relocation were closely related to the vital interests of the public. In the annual report of a considerable number of the 43 local governments, one of the items with top requests in the previous year was information about housing demolition. This revealed that housing demolition has drawn great public attention. Therefore, the Project Team selected the disclosure of information about housing demolition as an exceptional indicator in the 2009 evaluation to examine the openness and transparency of governments' relevant administrative activities.

In this section, the Project Team mainly examined the concentration and disclosure of local governments' information about housing demolition by local governments. As there were competent departments in charge of urban housing demolition, the project team evaluated both local government portals and the websites of the competent departments. It needed to be noted that, this evaluation only involved the examination and analysis of the housing demolition information disclosed on local government portals, hence the results might reflect only some aspects of local governments' implementation of rules and regulations of housing demolition.

The focus of assessing the concentration of information was whether the housing demolition information disclosed by local government websites was relatively concentrated and convenient for the public to search and obtain. Among the 43 local government portals evaluated, 27 provided a special section for publishing housing demolition information on the homepage or government information disclosure platform. Eight out of them provided both demolition regulations and policies and demolition announcements, while the remaining 19 provided either only demolition regulations and policies or only demolition announcements in the section. The competent departments of 23 local governments provided a special section for publishing housing demolition information on the homepage or in other sections. Among them, ten competent departments provided both demolition regulations and policies and demolition announcements, while the remaining 13 only provided either demolition regulations and policies or only demolition announcements.

In terms of the directive standards for demolition compensation and work procedures of housing demolition, 23 local governments provided the standards on their government portals or on the websites of their competent departments. Thirteen local governments provided a description of demolition procedures on their government portals or the websites of their competent departments. Among them, five provided the information both in words and in flowcharts, while eight only provided textual description.

In term of demolition announcements, among the 43 government portals evaluated, 11 provided demolition announcements on their government portals and the websites of competent departments, or published the links on the government portals of municipal governments which could be directed to the webpage of competent departments where the announcements were published. Another 14 local governments only provided demolition announcements on the websites of the competent departments. After searching on the homepage of municipal government portals and websites of any departments that may be a competent authority, the Project team did not find any demolition announcement of the remaining 18 local governments.

The related websites of 13 local governments provided the qualifications of demolition companies and demolition appraisal companies; nine provided information about the location of demolition resettlement housing; and three provided information about the price of resettlement housing.

The evaluation found that many local governments attached great importance to the disclosure of information about housing demolition on their portals and on the websites of the competent departments. Many local governments set up a special section for the disclosure on the websites of two different levels of governments. Some even established a special website to disclose relevant information in a concentrated way. However, some improvements still needed to be made in this area. First, the disclosure of information about housing demolition was less than satisfactory. Some local government websites did not provide any information about housing demolition and related information was hardly to be obtained even by using the search functions provided on the websites. Although some others provided the information, what they disclosed were mainly some related regulations, policies and announcements, and little information about demolition companies, demolition appraisal companies, resettlement housing and others was published. Second, the lack of information concentration made it difficult for the public to search. Although some local government websites provided a special section for publishing information about housing demolition, what published in the section were only regulations, policies and announcements. Some only provided the information on municipal government portals while some others only on the websites of the competent departments. Hence, to obtain comprehensive information, the public needed to search repeatedly on several websites. Third, the information provided lacked consistency. This was mainly reflected in the fact that the number or content of demolition regulations, policies or announcements disclosed on different websites was not completely consistent. The information provided by some local governments was either on the portals of municipal governments or on the websites of competent departments, instead of being published on a uniform platform. This exposed the problem of insufficient information sharing among various government agencies in the construction of e-government, which led to repeated information disclosure.

3.8 Recommendations

The evaluation found that the overall performance of some local governments or some aspects of the performance of some others was less than satisfactory. This illustrated that some local governments still needed to make dramatic improvements in implementing the Regulations and facilitating the work of government information disclosure. The problems may be incurred by the immature existing laws, regulations and related systems, the lack of importance attached by some local governments or the need for improvements in work attitude and working mechanisms. To further improve government transparency, local governments need to make the following improvements.

First, constantly improve related laws and regulations. The Regulations is only a transitional provision for building the government information disclosure system in China. Its legal hierarchy determines its inability to fully resolve issues such as whether information should be disclosed or how to disclose it. Also, in the Regulations, provisions on the definition of information that cannot be disclosed, the relations between voluntary disclosure and request-based disclosure, and the qualifications and procedures of request-based disclosure are not well developed. This creates a gap between the Regulations and the global trend of disclosing information as well as China's need to facilitate the information disclosure system. It is also the root cause of misunderstandings and even misapplications of relevant systems by government agencies at all levels. Therefore, the constant improvement of information disclosure system based on the experience acquired during the implementation of the work is an effort that China has to make.

Second, Foster an open and transparent culture. The successful implementation of the government information disclosure system depends both on the appropriate understanding of the system by the related staff members of government agencies, and on public awareness of the rights they enjoy and their willingness to participate in relevant activities. For one thing, the awareness of related staff members on government information disclosure should be firstly promoted. They should be provided with appropriate training to fully understand the meaning and significance of the system, and to understand that information disclosure is a necessary method and guarantee for improving government ability to manage public affairs and serve the public, instead of viewing it as a burden. For another, public awareness of disclosing information should be fostered. Only when the public actively participate in the disclosure process and continuously submit requests for information disclosure, can government agencies change from closed administration to an increasingly open one.

Third, allocate sufficient manpower and financial resources to conduct information disclosure activities. The cause for some problems occurred in the evaluation, such as unanswered calls or busy lines, and non-replied or slowly replied emails, besides inappropriate work attitude, may be the limited number of related staff members in the government agencies. Therefore, it is necessary for local governments to allocated personnel and financial resources in related work as needed, improving information management work to ensure they can cope with the increasing number of public requests and consultations and to guarantee that related work can be smoothly carried out.

Fourth, local governments should conduct self-inspection on a regular basis. The quality of government information disclosure and website operation should be improved for the convenience of the public. It is recommended that local governments conduct regular inspection and evaluation on their implementation of the Regulations, the work results and work attitude of the departments responsible for government information disclosure and of their staff, the operation of related websites, the rationality of the development and arrangement of the special section for information disclosure and other sections, the validity of search functions, the operation of such online service platforms as request-based platforms, etc. By doing so, problems could be promptly identified and corrected to constantly improve the functions and accessibility of government websites, ensuring that the public could gain the information they need within the least amount of time and at the lowest economic cost.

Fifth, further improve the work of voluntary disclosure. Voluntary disclosure is an activity of government agencies to provide information to the public in accordance with their functions and responsibilities. By disclosing information through government gazettes, government websites, news media, etc., government agencies can prevent the public from requesting every piece of information they need. This is conducive to lower the cost of government agencies to cope with requests and also offer the public easier access to information. Government agencies should conduct routine observations to identify the information that relates to citizens' vital interests, receives high social attention, or is highly demanded by the public. Government agencies then should disclose such information instead of waiting for the public to request. Efforts such as establishing a special section or platform on government portals to voluntarily disclose information should also be made.

Sixth, further integrate the work of government information disclosure. At present, the work of constructing e-government in many regions is still conducted by local government agencies, affiliated departments and district-level and county-level departments establishing their respective websites. Although many local government portals provided the links directed to the aforesaid websites at a prominent position, the lack of concentration and consistency in information could occur. It is recommended that relevant government agencies figure out how to integrate information, and integrate the platforms and sections for "the openness of government affairs" and those for "the disclosure of government information", so that the public can obtain all the information they need on one single website. It is also suggested that local governments pay attention to the continuity of website operations in the process of institutional reform and function adjustment, avoiding repeated establishment and operations of government portals. As for request-based disclosure, it is also necessary to integrate all the platforms or sections into one platform to cope with all the requests, providing one-stop services.

Chapter 4
The 2010 Evaluation of China's Government Transparency

4.1 Overview of the Work of Government Information Disclosure in 2010

The 2010 evaluation found the following aspects of the work of departments under the State Council and local governments in implementing the Regulations and improving the transparency of government administration worthy of recognition.

First, government websites have become an important channel for disclosing government information.

Similar to results of the 2009 evaluation, this evaluation found that both local governments and departments under the State Council disclosed a large amount of information through their websites, playing an essential role in satisfying public demands for information.

Second, the implementation of the government information disclosure system continued to be facilitated.

In accordance with the Regulations and relevant regulations of the State Council, most government websites developed the directory for government information disclosure, published the guidelines on government information disclosure, created an online request platform for request-based disclosure, and disclosed the annual reports on government information disclosure in a timely manner. Local governments' performance on implementing the system in 2010 was better than that in 2009.

Third, great attention was paid to facilitating public access to information and to promoting public interactions.

Many government websites developed sections for public interaction and the directory to enable the public to obtain information quickly to facilitate public interactions through e-government platforms.

Fourth, the disclosure awareness and professionalism of the staff responsible for the work of government information disclosure were worthy of recognition.

In terms of the consultations and requests made by the Project Team via telephone or email, the staff in charge of corresponding work in some departments under the

Y. Lv and H. Tian, *Evaluation on Government Transparency Index in China (2009–2016)*, Understanding China, https://doi.org/10.1007/978-981-16-5032-1_4

State Council and local governments replied in a responsible, proactive and timely manner, and provided detailed explanations politely.

Nevertheless, the following problems were identified in the evaluation.

First, some government websites did not operate well.

The websites of some departments under the State Council and local governments were slow, unstable, and intermittently inaccessible. Some government websites were extremely slow and webpage could not be opened even after repeated trying. Some websites were unstable, and their webpage sometimes could be opened, sometimes could not. And even a few websites could be opened on weekdays but not at weekends. In particular, the website of the Ministry of Housing and Urban–Rural Development—a department under the State council—was under construction for up to two months, during which time this evaluation was conducted, and no information could be searched there. The evaluation found that the operation of the websites was not positively correlated to the large amount of financial resources and manpower invested. This was obviously far from achieving the aim of building a 24/7 government by promoting e-services.

Second, some platforms were repeatedly constructed.

For some local governments, such as the municipal governments of Datong, Guangzhou, and Changchun, the problem of two official websites running at the same time still existed. The repeated websites both had a "gov." domain and information on the websites was updated. The problem also existed in the affiliated departments of some local governments. This problem not only brought about inconvenience for the public to obtain information, but also caused a waste of government resources.

Third, the performance of a few governments on implementing the Regulations was less than satisfactory.

The Regulations, the *Notice of the General Office of the State Council on Doing a Good Job in the Preparatory Work for the Implementation of the Regulations of the People's Republic of China on the Disclosure of Government Information* (No.54 [2007] of the General Office of the State Council), and the *Opinions on Some Issues Concerning the Regulations of the People's Republic of China on the Disclosure of Government Information* (No.36 [2008] of the General Office of the State Council) issued on April 29, 2008 have proposed clear requirements on developing the directory of government information disclosure, publishing the guidelines on government information disclosure, and disclosing the annual report on government information disclosure. The aforesaid documents also emphasized that government websites shall be fully leveraged as an important platform for information disclosure. However, as of the end of this evaluation, some government agencies still did not developed and released the directory for government information disclosure (hereinafter referred to as "the directory"), the guidelines on government information disclosure (hereinafter referred to as "the guidelines"), and the annual report on government information disclosure (hereinafter referred to as "the annual report") in a timely manner. Also, the directory and guidelines provided by a few local governments were just those of their affiliated departments and district-level and county-level governments, not of same-level governments. In accordance with the Regulations, same-level government agencies were also a subject of information disclosure and they shall also develop the directory and guidelines. Their obligations shall not be waived just because their affiliated departments, district-level and county-level governments, and public enterprises and institutions fulfilled theirs. When the Project Team made consultations via phone (using the number provided in the guidelines), staff of a few government agencies refused to answer any question, falsely claiming that they were unfamiliar with related work or were not responsible for the work. In addition, some government agencies, both local and central, did not provide any directory for information links, making it difficult for the public to obtain voluntarily disclosed information directly and effectively. Some local governments and departments under the State Council did not provide any online request platform, and requests could only be submitted via email or in person, which increased the difficulty for the public to obtain information.

Fourth, the information disclosure platforms on some government websites were just a mere formality, as some functions were useless.

Most government websites provided a section for "the openness of government affairs" or "the disclosure of government information" on the homepage. However, some of the sections were not at a prominent position, and some were even hidden in other sections, which was inconvenient for the public to search. The information provided on many government websites was mostly news about officials, and little information related to the vital interests of the people or to the government administration was published. Some government websites established a functional official website and developed categorized sections for information disclosure. However, the problems facing them were either the information links in some sections could not be opened, or the links were directed to nothing, or even the search functions or online request platforms provided on the websites were useless. Although some websites had dynamic information about request-based disclosure, the information had not been updated for almost a year. In addition, the arrangement of information on some websites was in a mess, as either information was not put in corresponding sections or some information could only be found by using search engines and was hidden in other sections. When verifying government agencies' performance on request-based disclosure, the Project Team found that the online submission systems designed by some government agencies were not user-friendly: the fields in some request forms were not wide enough, some did not clearly stated the special requirements for the format of contact numbers, or did not indicate clearly which field was incorrectly filled. This could easily prevent applicants from submitting requests successfully.

Fifth, the information published on some government websites was not updated in a timely manner.

The information provided on some government websites was outdated. The information published several months or even one or two years ago was still listed in the lasted information section. The websites were almost left unattended. The problem was quite obvious for the websites of local competent departments in charge of housing demolition and food safety regulatory departments. The information on some local food safety information websites had not been updated since 2007 or 2008.

Sixth, unnecessary requirements on some government websites incurred extra difficulty and cost for the public to obtain information.

In the 2009 evaluation, the Project Team had already found that a few local governments required potential applicants to register with their real name and sign in before they could make requests. In the 2010 evaluation, the Project Team found that such practice was still popular on the websites of both local governments and departments under the State Council. The purpose of providing online request platform was to provide convenience to the public to make requests. However, some government agencies asked to verify the authenticity of the ID number provided by applicants; some required applicants to upload a copy of ID card in a specific format; some required applicants to print the request form out, sign it, scan it and then attach it to the request in jpg. format; some even required to upload documents to prove purposes of the request, and some required applicants to sign a statement guaranteeing that the information would not be abused. To satisfy these requirements, applicants needed to have equipment including printers, scanners and digital cameras, and they had to master corresponding information processing techniques, the cost and difficulty of which was no less than or even much higher than that of face-to-face request. This went against the original intention of the Regulations.

Seventh, some local governments failed to perform consistently throughout the two years.

Compared with the results of the 2009 evaluation, the performance of local governments on information disclosure in 2010 fell into four categories. The first was that some local governments generally performed quite well throughout the two years. The second was that despite the fact that they did not achieve a positive result in 2009, some local governments performed much better in 2010 or at least made obvious progress in some aspects. The third was that some local governments failed to make any improvement in either government website construction or government information disclosure for two consecutive years. Although the Project Team spent several times more time and energy to search information on these websites, no information needed was found. The fourth was that some government agencies took a step backward either on the overall performance or in some aspects. The main manifestation of this was the unstably operated websites. Some sections or the websites of some departments (e.g. departments in charge of housing demolition or food safety regulation) was poorly operated. Some sections or websites were less user-friendly than they were in 2009 after being redesigned. The sections on a few websites was being redesigned during the time when the evaluation was conducted.

4.2 Directory for Government Information Disclosure

The *Notice of the General Office of the State Council on Doing a Good Job in the Preparatory Work for the Implementation of the Regulations of the People's Republic of China on the Disclosure of Government Information* (No.54 [2007] of the General Office of the State Council) clearly stipulated that "all the information that shall be disclosed shall be included in the directory as required". Based on this, the Project Team added a new indicator—completeness of information contained

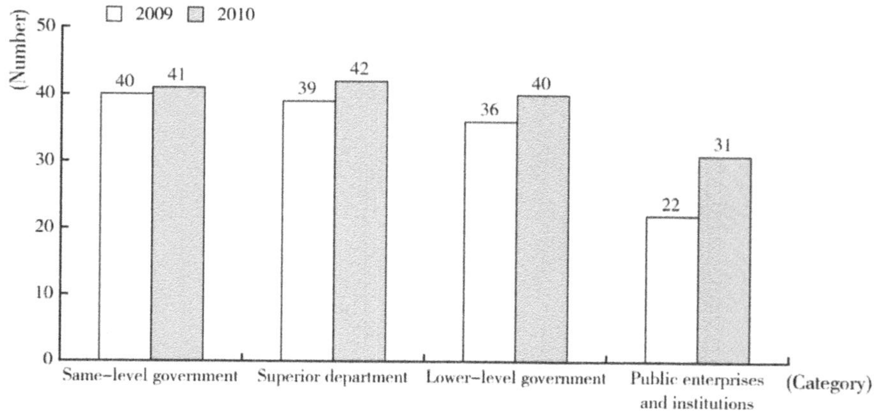

Fig. 4.1 A comparison of the number of government websites with the directory between 2009 and 2010

in the directory—in the two categories of indicators in the 2010 evaluation. The information selected by the Project Team to evaluate the completeness was some important information published on the homepage of websites, such as government papers and official documents.

Among the local governments, the number of those that provided the directory for information disclosure of municipal governments, the directory of affiliated departments, the directory for lower-level governments, and the directory of public enterprises and institutions on their government portals was 41 (95.3%), 42 (97.7%), 40 (93%) and 31 (72.1%) respectively. All figures were higher than those in the 2009 evaluation (see Fig. 4.1). Among the departments under the State Council, 55 provided the directory, accounting for 93.2%.

When evaluating the validity of the directory published on local government websites, the project team randomly selected ten information links from the directory of same-level governments, ten from that of affiliated departments, nine from that of lower-level governments and six from that of public enterprises and institutions on every website. Also, two information links in the directory provided by each of the five local authorities responsible for supervising food safety—bureaus of health, bureaus of agriculture, bureaus of quality and technology supervision, administrations of industry and commerce, and food and drug administrations—were randomly selected. For county-level and district-level governments, three departments were randomly selected and three information links of each department were verified. For public enterprises and institutions, three of them were randomly selected and two information links of each were verified.

Overall, the validity rate of same-governments' directory was slightly higher than that in 2009, the rate of lower-level governments' directory was the same as that in 2009, while the rates of affiliated departments' and public enterprises and institutions' directory were slightly lower than those in 2009 (see Fig. 4.2).

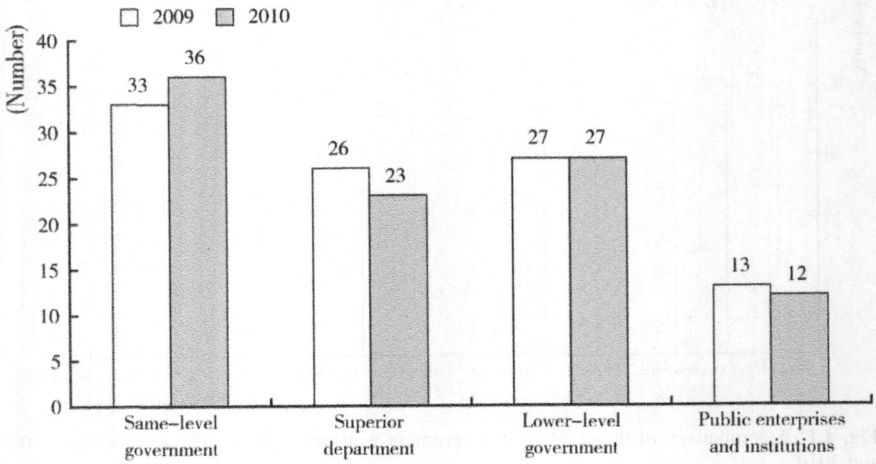

Fig. 4.2 A comparison of the number of local governments with all information links valid between 2009 and 2010

As for the departments under the State Council, ten information links were randomly selected by the Project Team for verification (See Fig. 4.3). The number of departments under the State Council with 4–6 information links valid was 0.

The 2010 evaluation found that 17 local government websites classified information in the directory based on genres, themes, objects and institutions to facilitate public search, compared with three in 2009. Twenty departments under the State Council did so.

In terms of the search functions provided for the directory, local government websites performed worse than they had done in 2009. In 2010, 23 local government websites were equipped with a simple search function. Among them, only those of 18 websites were functional. However, 21 provided the function in 2009 and all were effective. In 2010, 15 local government websites provided multiple search functions (including searching by using keywords in title, keywords in main body of the document, issuing department, document number). Among them, those of ten websites were functional. However, 18 provided the functions in 2009. In 2010, 12 local government websites provided combined search functions. Among them, those of nine websites were functional. However, 13 provided the function in 2009 and 12 of them were effective.

The performance of the departmental under the State Council was significantly better than that of local governments. Among the departments under the State Council, 36 provided a simple search function and those of 32 were functional; 28 provided multiple search functions and those of 24 were all valid; 30 provided combined search functions and those of 26 were functional (See Fig. 4.4).

When examining whether the information on the homepage of government websites was included in the directory, the Project Team found that the departments under the State Council performed significantly worse than local governments. By

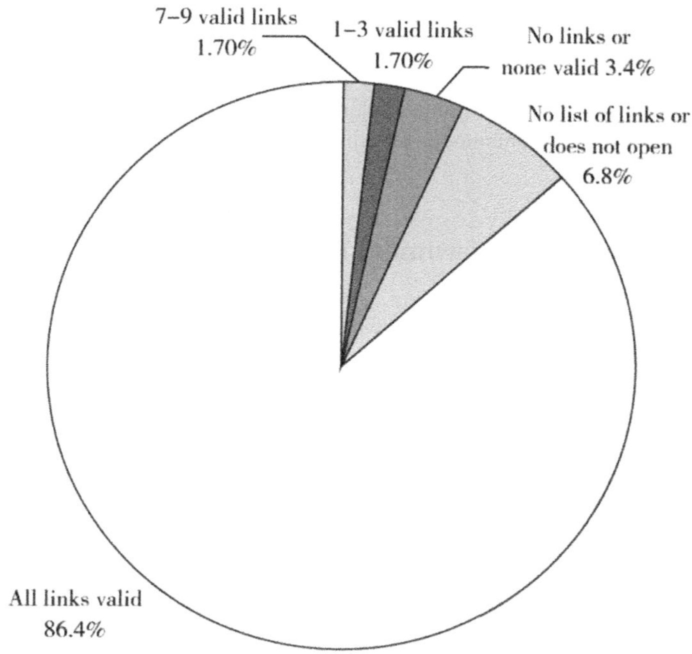

Fig. 4.3 The validity of information links of the departments under the State Council in 2010

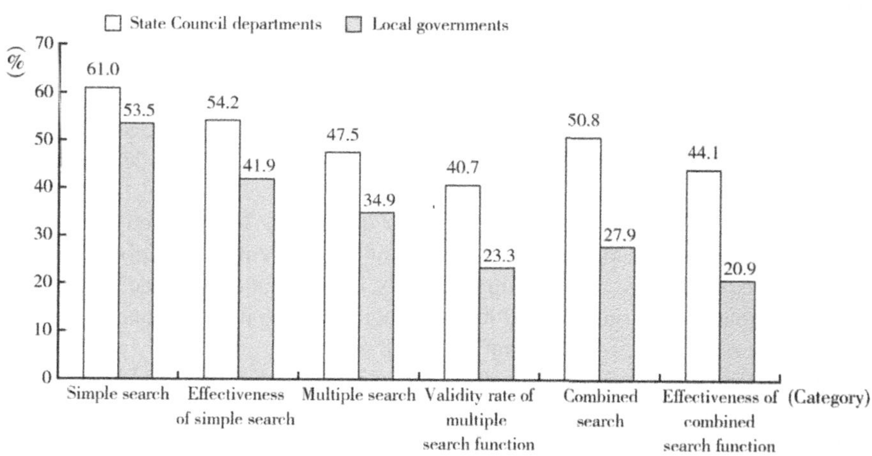

Fig. 4.4 A comparison of search functions between the departments under the State Council and local governments in 2010

randomly searching in the directory the main information provided on the homepage, the number of local governments where information could not be found in the directory was 20, accounting for 46.5% of all the local governments websites evaluated, while the number of the departments under the State Council was 42, accounting for 71.2% of all the departments under the State Council evaluated.

4.3 Guidelines on Government Information Disclosure

In 2010, the Project Team continued to examine the validity of the guidelines, though the standards applied were stricter than those in the 2009 evaluation. For example, if the contact number of the government agency responsible for the work of government information disclosure or in charge of accepting requests was not provided in the guidelines but elsewhere, it would be considered as the contact number not provided.

The Project Team evaluated the full text of guidelines provided by departments under the State Council and local governments. Among the 43 local government websites, 39 provided the guidelines in full or the guidelines could be found by using search engines, accounting for 90.7%, showing an upward trend compared with 31 in 2009. Among the websites of 59 departments under the State Council, 53 provided the guidelines or the guidelines could be found by using search engines, accounting for 89.8%.

The number of local governments and the departments under the State Council that provided the address of the agency responsible for the work of government information disclosure or the agency in charge of accepting requests was 28 (30 in 2009) and 51 respectively. Only 2 of the departments under the State Council provided the location maps or public transport options of the agency, while none of the local governments did so. The number of the departments under the State Council and local governments that provided specific office hours was 47 and 23 (same as in 2009) respectively.

Among the 43 local government websites evaluated, 36 provided the contact number of the agency responsible for the work of government information disclosure or the agency in charge of accepting requests in their guidelines, accounting for 83.7%, compared with only 29 in 2009. Among the 59 departments under the State Council, the number was 46, accounting for 78%.

Judging from the verification results of the contact number provided in the guidelines in 2010, the performance of local governments was slightly better than that of 2009. Most of the staff members in local governments answering the phone responded to the consultations in an active and detailed manner. However, as for the departments under the State Council, some calls were not answered and sometimes the person answering the phone was quite arrogant. To ensure the objectiveness of the verification, the Project Team made calls using the contact number provided by local governments and departments under the State Council in the name of an ordinary citizen. And the period during which the calls were made was from 9:00 am to 11:30 am and from 2 pm to 4:30 pm on Monday to Friday. During the calls made to the departments under the State Council, the project team inquired about the ways to obtain budget information of the department and qualifications for requesting the disclosure of the information. During the calls made to local governments, the project team inquired about the ways to obtain information about food safety and qualifications for requesting the disclosure of the information. The focuses of the verification were whether the contact number was valid, whether the line was busy for a long time or with no answer, whether the person answering the call was responsible for government information disclosure work, and he/she could respond to the consultations. Considering that the number of staff responsible for information disclosure work in local governments and departments under the State Council was quite limited and, the Project Team designed a one-week verification time period for each agency to ensure the objectiveness of the verification. During the period, for those lines which were busy or with no answers, calls would be made for at most six times, with the interval time between two calls being over 30 min.

In terms of the email address of the agency responsible for the work of government information disclosure or the agency in charge of accepting requests provided, Among the 43 local government websites, 27 provided the email address in the guidelines, accounting for 62.8%, more than 23 in 2009. Among the 59 departments under the State Council evaluated, 36 provided the email address in their guidelines, accounting for 61% and the rate was slightly lower than that of local governments. To verify whether the email address was valid, whether any reply would be made for the emails received, how long would it take to receive a reply, the Project Team sent emails to the departments under the State Council to inquire about the ways to obtain budget information of the department and qualifications for requesting the disclosure of the information and to local governments to inquire about the ways to obtain information about food safety and qualifications for requesting the disclosure of the information.

Among the 43 local government websites, 37 provided a description of the forms of voluntary disclosure in their guidelines, accounting for 86%, more than 31 in 2009. Among the 59 departments under the State Council evaluated, 51 provided a description in their guidelines, accounting for 86.4%. As for the relations between voluntary disclosure and request-based disclosure, The 2009 evaluation found that many local governments confused the relations, falsely claiming that citizens could only request to disclose the information that did not fall within the scope of voluntary disclosure. This was still the case for the local governments evaluated in 2010. And the problem also existed in the departments under the State Council. Some departments even falsely claimed that "voluntary disclosure plays a major part while request-based disclosure is an effective supplement". This exposed a fundamental misunderstanding of the information disclosure system.

Among the local governments evaluated, 35 provided the procedures for requesting information disclosure, accounting for 81.4%. The number was slightly higher than 33 in 2009. However, only nine used flowcharts in their guidelines (accounting for 20.9%), and another eight used flowcharts in the sections for request-based disclosure (accounting for 18.6%). Twenty used flowcharts either in their guidelines or in the sections for request-based disclosure in 2009. The difference in the number between the two years was mainly because the standards applied in the 2009 evaluation was less strict than those in 2020—using flowcharts in the guidelines was not required in 2009. Also, the links of the flowcharts provided in some guidelines in 2010 could not be opened. Among the departments under the State Council evaluated, 42 provided the procedures in words, accounting for 71.2%; though only three used flowcharts in their guidelines, while four provided a description in flowcharts in their sections for request-based disclosure, accounting for 5.1% and 6.8% respectively.

In terms of the supervisory mechanism, 17 local governments provided the address of the supervision agency in their guidelines, compared with only four in 2009. Same as in the 2009 evaluation, no public transport option or location map of the agency was provided in 2010. Among the departments under the State Council, 18 provided the address, and none provided public transport option or location map either. Among the local governments, 22 provided the contact number of the supervision agency, while six provided the email address, compared with 20 and five respectively in 2009. Among the departments under the State Council, 19 provided the contact number, while nine provided the email address. Also, 27 local governments provided methods of government assistance (same as in 2009), while 26 departments under the State Council did so. None of the local governments mentioned to which agency administrative reviews should be submitted or to which court administrative proceedings should be filed. Among the departments under the State Council, only the Ministry of Transport, the State Administration for Industry and Commerce and the State Administration of Quality and Technical Supervision clarified how to apply for administrative reviews.

4.4 Request-Based Disclosure

The evaluation found that local governments outperformed the departments under the State Council on the establishment of request platforms, especially online ones. Requests can be filed on the online request platforms of most local governments, while most departments under the State Council still required the public to submit requests via emails, or some even restricted it to only by mailing or in person.

Among the local governments, 40 set up a special section for request-based disclosure on their websites, accounting for 93% (same as in 2009). However, the section of two in 2009 could not be opened compared to none in 2010. Among the departments under the State Council examined, 49 provided the section, accounting for 83.1%.

Most government websites provided request forms. Among the local governments, 30 provided the forms in downloadable and editable formats (e.g. WORD); five in printable-only formats (e.g. Web Pages); the forms provided by four could not be downloaded or copied; and four failed to provide any forms. The corresponding number in 2009 was 28, three, one and 11. Also, the corresponding number of the departments under the State Council in 2010 was 44, two, five and eight.

When the establishment of online request platforms was considered, local governments acted significantly better than the departments under the State Council. Among all the local governments evaluated in 2010, 34 established special online request platforms, accounting for 79.1%; one received submissions via email; while eight failed to provide either of the aforesaid two methods. In 2009, the corresponding number was 33, one and nine. In contrast, among the departments under the State Council, 15 established online request platforms, accounting for 25.4%; 26 received submissions via email; while 18 failed to provide either of the aforesaid two methods.

In the name of an ordinary citizen, the Project Team filed requests with all the government agencies that provided online request platforms. In the requests, local governments were asked to disclose information about the annual law-enforcement inspection of food safety in 2010, while the departments under the State Council were asked to disclose information about the number of people travelling abroad for business and expenses from the beginning of 2010 to the time when the evaluation was conducted. The name and ID number of the applicants filled out the request forms were all virtual, their occupation was unemployed or student, email address was different from those used in the verification of the validity of the email address provided in the guidelines on the government agencies, and the purpose of requests was for study, research or writing theses.

The results showed that the excessive collection of applicants' personal information during request-based disclosure became increasingly popular instead of being curbed. During the evaluation, for those websites where providing workplace, ID number, gender or age of the applicant was not necessarily required, the Project Team attempted to send requests without providing such information first, and if the information was mandatory, then it would be filled out. Therefore, the Project Team was able to verify whether such personal information was mandatory. The evaluation found that among the local governments, 32 required part of all of the aforesaid information, accounting for 74.4% (compared with 30 in 2009). Among the departments under the State Council, 39 did so, accounting for 66.1%. Some websites even required applicants to upload a copy of their ID card and other identity document in a specific file format (e.g. specific image file format). Many would also verify the authenticity of the applicant's ID number online, while some asked the applicant to provide a copy of their ID card by email or fax after they had received the request forms.

Applicants were also commonly asked to provide the purpose of their requests. During the evaluation, for those websites where providing the purpose was not explicitly indicated, the Project Team attempted to send requests without providing the information first, and if it was mandatory, the information would be filled out. Therefore, the Project Team was able to verify whether such information was mandatory. The evaluation found that among the local governments, 21 required the purpose of requests, accounting for 48.8%, compared with only 15 in 2009. Among the departments under the State Council, 35 did so, accounting for 59.3%. Unlike in 2009, it was quite common for government agencies to require the purpose of requests in 2010. Some required applicants to upload documents online to prove their purpose, while some others asked applicants to provide via fax or other channels the document issued by a relevant authority stamped with the official seal of it to prove their purpose. Some even required applicants to declare that they will not abuse the information requested. When communicating with the staff of relevant government agencies, the Project Team learned that the main legal basis for government agencies to falsely claim that applicants shall provide their purpose of requests were the *Opinions on Some Issues Concerning the Regulations of the People's Republic of China on the Disclosure of Government Information* (No.36 [2008] of the General Office of the State Council) and the *Opinions of the General Office of the State Council on Doing a Good Job in Request-based Disclosure* (No. 5) [2010] of the General Office of the State Council). Based on the documents, many believed that the information requested shall be directly and closely related to the applicant, otherwise, the request shall not be accepted and information will not be disclosed.

The Project Team also found that the unreasonably designed online request platforms of some government agencies and technical difficulties there have caused extra difficulties and cost for the public to request information. Some required applicants to register in real name before filing a request. The allowed length of characters in the fields on some was shorter than the length of a typical email address, making it impossible to fill in an effective email address. In the field for contact number on some websites, only a fixed line number was allowed and mobile number was not accepted. What's more, the number, without any instructions, could only be in the format of "010-××××××××", not in "010××××××××". When errors occurred, some provided no instructions on which information filled out was wrong, leaving the applicant confused. Some required applicants to download, print and sign the request form, then scan and send it as an email attachment. Some stated on their request platforms that they did not accept certain email service providers. All of these caused inconvenience for filing request, and increased the time and cost needed, which went against the purpose of facilitating government information disclosure and establishing a service-oriented government.

To verify the validity of online request platforms, the Project Team filed requests with all the government agencies by which the platforms were provided. Among the 15 departments under the State Council that provided the platforms, requests to eight were successfully sent and a case number or receipt was provided; requests to six were successfully sent but no receipt was provided; and submission to one was failed. Among 26 departments under the State Council that only accepted requests submitted via email, the emails to 22 were successfully sent but no receipt was provided; the email to one was failed; and requests filed with another three were failed as no request form was provided. Among the 34 local governments that provided request platforms, requests to 17 were successfully sent and a case number or receipt was provided; requests to 11 were successfully sent but no receipt was provided; submission to six was failed. As for the only one local government that simply accepted requests submitted via email, the email was sent but no receipt was provided.

After verifying the online tracking function provided on government websites, the Project Team found that local governments outperformed the departments under the State Council on providing such functions as tracking requests and the real-time number of requests being handled on their websites. Among the departments under the State Council, nine equipped their websites with the function of tracking the status of requests online (15.3%); one listed the real-time number of requests being handled (1.7%); nine provided the function of tracking the results of requests (15.3%). By contrast, the corresponding number among the local governments was 18 (41.9%), eight (18.6%) and 20 (46.5%), compared with 20, nine and 22 respectively in 2009. The performance of local governments in 2010 was slightly poorer than that of 2009, mainly because two failed to update timely the information though they did provide the functions of tracking the status and results of requests online. In addition, the real-time number of requests being handled shown on another one website in 2010 was same as that in 2009. The functions of both of the aforesaid two websites were considered invalid.

Judging from the replies to requests provided by the government agencies, the Project Team found that the difficulties and obstacles impeding the public to obtain government information were still huge. Most government agencies failed to reply within the statutory period. The requirements of some brought about extra difficulties to applicants. Although some did provide replies, the content of the replies was empty and evasive. Eighteen departments under the State Council replied within the statutory period, accounting for 30.5%; while ten local governments did so, accounting for 23.3%. The content of the replies varied: (1) disclosing the information required or informing the applicant of ways of obtaining the information; (2) refusing to disclose the information required; (3) refusing to accept the requests; (4) asking to supplement documents required. The number of the departments under the State Council that provided the four kinds of replies were four, four, three and seven respectively, while the number of the local governments was two, zero, seven and one respectively. Three departments under the State Council explained the reasons for refusing disclosure (most of them being information involving secrets or information falling out of the scope of disclosure as stipulated by the Regulations). Also, some government agencies, based on the *Opinions of the General Office of the State Council on Doing a Good Job in Request-based Disclosure* (No. 5) [2010] of the General Office of the State Council), falsely claimed that only information that made through official documents fell into the scope of disclosure. As for further required documents, Some asked applicants to supplement ID number, workplace, and purpose of the requests via email or fax. Some even further required applicants to submit documents issued by a relevant authority stamped with its official seal to illustrate their purposes. Among the local governments that replied by disclosing the information required or informing applicants of the ways of obtaining the information, some, despite their knowledge that the applicant was faraway in another city, asked the applicant to come and check the information in the agency, claiming that the amount of the information about food safety was huge and was unable to disclose online. Although some departments under the State Council provided formal replies, the content of the replies were quite empty and evasive. For example, the reply of one was simply "the number of people travelling abroad for business and expenses were strictly following relevant state rules and reported to upper-level discipline inspection and supervisory authorities".

The 2020 evaluation found that many government websites provided the service of requesting information online, especially established online request platforms, which have improved the efficiency of public request. After receiving the requests from the Project Team, staff members of some government agencies managed to actively communicate with applicants to know more about the information requested, the purpose of requests, and the contact details of applicants. Some agencies managed to reply within the statutory period, while some also called to further explain the content of the replies.

4.5 The Annual Report on Government Information Disclosure

This section mainly evaluated whether departments under the State Council and local governments published the 2009 annual report as required by the Regulations, whether the full text of the report was accessible, and whether voluntarily disclosed information, information about request-based disclosure and applications for administrative complaints and administrative proceedings in respect of government information disclosure was included in the annual report.

In general, the work in this respect could be further enhanced, as both some departments under the State Council and some local governments failed to release their 2009 annual report in accordance with the requirements of the Regulations. In 2010, 37 local government websites provided the section for annual report (32 in 2009) and the full text of the 2009 annual report (34 in 2009), accounting for 86%. Meanwhile, 51 departments under the State Council provided the section for annual report on their websites, and 55 provided the full text of the 2009 annual report, accounting for 86.4% and 93.2% respectively. To ensure objectiveness and impartiality of the evaluation, for those websites that did not provide the section for annual report or the full text of the 2009 annual report was not included in the section, the Project Team search repeatedly by various means to check if they were provided somewhere else. As none was found on the websites of four departments under the State Council and six local governments, they were considered as failed to provide the section and the annual report.

Among all the governments evaluated, 48 departments under the State Council and 37 local governments provided overall data on voluntary disclosure in their annual reports, accounting for 81.4% and 86% respectively. Forty departments under the State Council and 31 local governments provided the data categorized by forms of voluntary disclosure, accounting for 67.8% and 72.1% respectively. The corresponding number of local governments did so in 2009 was 32 and 33 respectively.

According to the evaluation, the performance of the departments under the State Council on providing data on request-based disclosure in their annual reports was slightly better than that of local governments. The overall performance of local governments in 2010 was poorer than that in 2009. Generally speaking, the data on request-based disclosure provided by government agencies in their annual reports was not detailed enough. Among the departments under the State Council, 33 provided the total number of requests they had received in the previous year (55.9%); 25 provided the items with top requests (42.4%); 23 provided the number of requests categorized by different submission methods (39%); 44 provided the number of requests that had been reviewed and accepted (74.6%); 27 provided information categorized by content of replies (such as to be disclosed, not to be disclosed or to be partially disclosed) (45.8%); eight provided information categorized by the reasons why the request had been refused (such as involving state secrets or personal privacy) (13.6%); and 49 provided data on administrative proceedings, administrative reviews, and complaints involving government information disclosure (83.1%) in their annual reports. Meanwhile, among the local governments, 13 provided the total number of requests they had received in the previous year (30.2%, 14 in 2009); 14 provided the number of requests received in the previous year categorized by same-level government, lower-level and affiliated departments(32.6%, 11 in 2009); four provided the data on the governments that received top requests (9.3%) and the number in 2009 was 16, 17 provided information about the items with top requests (39.5%, 20 in 2009); 20 provided the number of requests categorized by different submission methods (46.5%, 19 in 2009); 30 provided the number of requests that had been reviewed and accepted (69.8%, 33 in 2009); 25 provided data categorized by the content of replies (such as to be disclosed, not to be disclosed or to be partially disclosed) (58.1%, 28 in 2009); 14 provided data categorized by the reasons why requests had been refused (such as involving state secrets or personal privacy) (32.6%, 17 in 2009); and 35 provided data on administrative proceedings, administrative reviews, and complaints involving government information disclosure (81.4%, 32 in 2009).

4.6 Information Disclosure in Specific Areas of Management

To further verify the implementation of the government information disclosure system, the Project Team selected several specific areas to evaluate the disclosure of information by relevant government agencies. The selected sub-indicator for the departments under the State Council was the disclosure of financial budgets, while that for local governments were both the disclosure of information on housing demolition and food safety management.

The Regulations stipulates that financial budgets are one of the key aspects of information that shall be disclosed. The *Guiding Opinions on Further Promoting the Disclosure of Financial budgets* issued by the Ministry of Finance of the People's Republic of China in 2008 and the *Guiding Opinions on Further Improving the Work on the Disclosure of Financial budgets* in 2010 propose requirements on the parties, content, and methods of disclosure. What's more, the *Opinions of the State Council on Strengthening the Construction of a Rule-based Government* issued in 2010 proposes that all government revenues and expenditures shall be included in budget management, and that information about the budgets management and implementation of public expenditures, infrastructure expenditures, administrative expenses, and the revenues and expenditures of government-managed funds and operational budgets for state capital shall be open and transparent. In earlier 2010, some government agencies disclosed their budgets, which attracted high attention from the public. Therefore, the Project Team conducted a special evaluation on the disclosure of financial budgets of the departments under the State Council, to examine whether a section for the disclosure of financial budgets was provided on their websites, and whether information about the overall budgets, the financial appropriation budgets, and the non-financial appropriation budgets in 2010 was disclosed.

Information on food safety management is closely related to the vital interests of the public and the disclosure of it is also an important measure to strengthen food safety supervision. As required by the rules including the Regulations, the *Food Safety Law of the People's Republic of China* and the *Administrative license Law*, information about administrative license, administrative punishment, food production standards, and the enforcement of law related to food safety shall be voluntarily disclosed. Hence, the sub-indicator selected for local governments herein was the disclosure of information on food safety, including the concentration of the information disclosed, business licenses of food safety production (food production licenses, food circulation permits and catering service licenses), food safety supervision and inspection, food safety credit, popularization of knowledge of food safety, and early-warning of food safety emergencies.

To evaluate and verify the performance of local governments on disclosing information about housing demolition and food safety, the Project Team also reviewed the websites of local departments in charge of housing demolition and food safety (including health administration organs, bureaus of quality and technical supervision, industrial and commercial administrative departments, and food and drug administration departments) and dedicated websites for disclosing information about housing demolition and food safety.

According to the evaluation, the performance of the departments under the State Council on disclosing financial budgets disclosure was less than satisfactory, mainly because the information disclosed was both inadequate and not detailed. Among the 59 departments under the State Council, only 27 set up a section for the disclosure of financial budgets on the homepage or in the related directory of their websites, accounting for 45.8%; 43 disclosed the information about financial budgets of the previous year in varied ways(72.9%)—17 in the special section for financial budgets, four in the directory, information of another nine were found by searching on their portals while information of another 13 was found by using search engines to search on other websites. In addition, of all the departments that disclosed their financial budgets, 41 disclosed information on financial appropriation budgets, and none of them disclosed that on non-financial appropriation budgets. None of the 59 departments under the State Council provided a detailed description of their budgeting standards for revenues and expenditures. Only three provided in their information about overall financial budgets a description of the items whose budgets changed significantly compared with the previous year, and one of them only made brief explanations. Two provided in their financial appropriation budgets the items whose budgets changed significantly compared with the previous year, and one of them made brief explanations.

The evaluation found that the performance of local governments on the disclosure of housing demolition information did not show much improvement compared with 2009, as such problems as poor disclosure, unconcentrated information and difficulties in accessing information were still very prominent.

In 2010, 32 local governments set up a section for the disclosure of information about housing demolition on their websites (27 in 2009), accounting for 74.4%. Among them, the section of 29 could be opened (27 in 2009). In the section of six, information on both housing demolition announcements and normative documents such as demolition regulations was provided, while in the section of 21, only one of the two kinds of information was provided, compared with eight and 19 respectively in 2009. Among all the departments in charge of housing demolition, 24 set up a valid section for the disclosure of information about housing demolition on their websites, compared with 23 in 2009. Among them, in the section of 15, information on both housing demolition announcements and normative documents such as demolition regulations was provided, while in the section of seven, only one of the two kinds of information were provided, compared with ten and 13 respectively in 2009. The evaluation also found that, among the 43 local governments, six had not only established the website for the department in charge of housing demolition but also a dedicated website for disclosing information about housing demolition. Some of them were specifically for work related to housing demolition, while some others were the websites of the internal institution responsible for specific housing demolition work in the departments in charge of housing demolition.

After searching on the official websites of local governments, the websites of the departments in charge of housing demolition, and the websites specifically for disclosing information about demolition, the Project Team found that 26 provided valid demolition announcements, compared with 25 in 2009. Also, only seven local governments provided core information such as demolition location in the title of demolition announcements, others only provided the issuing number of demolition announcement. Only three provided demolition location maps in the announcements, compared with two in 2009.

In 2010, 20 local governments provided demolition compensation standards on their websites, slightly fewer than 23 in 2009; five presented the demolition procedures in both Texts and Flowcharts, and nine only in either Texts or Flowcharts, compared with five and eight respectively in 2009.

In 2010, 14 local governments provided qualifications of demolition companies, compared with 13 in 2009; 13 provided qualifications of demolition appraisal companies, same as the number in 2009. In terms of resettlement houses, only four local governments in 2010 provided information about the location of the houses on their websites (nine in 2009), while four provided information about the prices (three in 2009).

As for the disclosure of food safety information, some local governments managed to publish relevant food safety supervision information through their government portals and the websites of competent departments. The evaluation found that 15 local governments set up a section for the disclosure of food safety information on their portals, and 27 set up a dedicated food safety information website to concentratedly disclose the food safety supervision information of various departments. Nevertheless, some problems were also identified herein.

First of all, the websites were poorly operated. The websites of many bureaus of quality and technical supervision, industrial and commercial administrative departments, and food and drug administration departments could not be opened, or little information was disclosed in the special sections. Although dedicated websites for publish information on food safety was set up by some local governments, the websites could not be opened either.

Second, a large amount of information about food safety could not be accessed online. The evaluation found that the local websites of bureaus of quality and technical supervision of only 22 local governments provided information about food production business licenses they generated, the websites of industrial and commercial administrative departments of only five provided information about food circulation permits and the websites of food and drug administration departments of only ten provided information about catering service licenses. And the number of the aforementioned three kinds of departments that provided information about food safety supervision and inspection, and special campaigns in 2010 was only 30, 30, and 31 respectively, while the number of the departments that provided information about food safety credits of food producers and traders was ten, ten and nine respectively. Thirty-six local governments provided information about food safety popularization on any of the websites of local government, food safety information, sanitary administration departments, bureaus of quality and technical supervision, industrial and commercial administrative departments, or food and drug administration departments and the number of local governments that provided information about food safety emergency early-warning or the exposure of food safety problems was 31.

Third, information about food safety lacked timely updates. The information on many local governments' websites had not been updated for a year or two. The relevant sections or even the whole websites were inactive, which was particularly the case for the food safety information websites in some places. One example was that only 23 local governments updated the information about food safety popularization to 2010 on any of the websites of local governments, food safety information, sanitary administration departments, bureaus of quality and technical supervision, industrial and commercial administrative departments, or food and drug administration departments.

Lastly, information was not concentratedly disclosed, which might be the result of lacking information sharing among different departments. As mentioned earlier, only 15 local governments set up a section for food safety information on their portals, and only 27 set up a dedicated food safety information website. However, even for those that have established a dedicated website, the information they provided still lacked concentration. Taking supervision and inspection information as an example, the number of the websites of bureaus of quality and technical supervision, industrial and commercial administrative departments, and food and drug administration departments that provided the information was 30, 30, and 31 respectively. However, only 11, ten and nine disclosed the aforementioned information on their special website for publishing information on food safety. As for information about the food safety credits of companies, the number of the websites of bureaus of quality and technical supervision, industrial and commercial administrative departments, or and food and drug administration departments was only ten, ten and nine respectively.

Generally speaking, by verifying the disclosure of financial budgets, housing demolition, and food safety, the Project Team found that difficulties for the public to access government information was still the core issue that needed to be tackled in promoting government information disclosure. The main causes of the issue were: (1) some departments failed to disclose relevant information according to law; (2) the establishment of e-government of some departments was less than satisfactory, leading to poor website operation; (3) information was not effectively shared among different departments; (4) huge gaps existed between expectations on government information disclosure and the actual implementation of the work, as many government agencies failed to update information to keep pace with real situation, leading to such problems as delayed information disclosure or updates.

4.7 Recommendations

The 2010 evaluation identified several highlights of the performance of both the departments under the State Council and local governments. However, many problems were also discovered, and gaps existed as for meeting the growing public demands for information and fully implementing the government information disclosure system. To implement the system and improve the transparency of governments at all levels, work in the following aspects should be strengthened.

First, government agencies at all levels, especially organs in charge of government information disclosure, shall understand correctly the related systems of government information disclosure. According to evaluation, misunderstandings or misapplications of many essential issues such as the role and function of government information disclosure system, the scope of government information, the relations between system of disclosure upon request and that of voluntary disclosure, as well as applicant qualifications and the procedures of disclosure upon request, was widespread in related government agencies. This will definitely become a major obstacle in the implementation of government information disclosure system in China in the coming years. Unless the misconceptions on such issues are corrected in government at all levels, especially the ones in charge of government information disclosure, the work of government information disclosure in China cannot be smoothly advanced, or even worse, it could eventually be a failure.

Second, job training of staff engaged in government information disclosure shall be enhanced. The evaluation conducted in the past two years have found that some government staff still have a low awareness of government information disclosure, lack understanding of the meaning of the government information disclosure system, are not clear about the procedures of information disclosure, and have little understanding of specific compilation standards of the directory, guideline, and annual report. Therefore, to further promote the implementation of the government information disclosure system, it is necessary to carry out in-depth training for the staff of government agencies at all levels, to enhance their awareness of and ability for the disclosure. Also, it is urgent to develop clear operational standards based on the rules and regulations of government information disclosure to guide their routine work.

Third, the performance evaluation mechanism of establishing e-government and implementing government information disclosure system shall be improved. The 2010 evaluation revealed that the problems such as poorly operated websites, repeatedly constructed platforms and some information that has been disclosed could not be accessed by the public conveniently are still prominent. In recent years, government agencies at all levels have invested heavily in establishing e-government and promoting government information disclosure. However, the large amount of capital investment is not proportional to the condition of government websites and the level of convenience for the public to obtain information. Therefore, it is necessary to strengthen the performance evaluation of the investment of government agencies in these two aspects and the actual outcome of such investment so as to improve the efficiency of capital use.

Fourth, make the public instead of the government as the central focus of further establishing a centralized and comprehensive information disclosure system. The evaluation found that although many evaluation objects have set up varied special sections on their websites, the information published in some was overlapped and some material information is not placed in a prominent place. As a result, even though the information has been disclosed as it appears, it is difficult for the public to obtain it. Therefore, government agencies at all levels have to further identify the starting point and goal of the work, considering whether the public can obtain government information effectively as the most important criterion for evaluating the performance of their work.

Fifth, the non-institutional barriers to public access to information shall be removed. In the information era, some people are excluded from sharing the fruits of the development of information technology due to information gaps. Therefore, special attention should be paid to eliminate the technical barriers to public access to information in implementing the work of government information disclosure. During the disclosure, government agencies should leverage advanced technology to improve the effectiveness of government information disclosure and to facilitate public access to information. However, the problems such as the increased time and cost for the public to obtain information brought by the use of technological means should be avoided, especially the one that some cannot share the benefits of government information disclosure due to their lack of familiarity with information technology or related information means.

Sixth, the accountability mechanism for government information disclosure shall be more carefully designed and implemented. The Regulations has already defined the legal liability of not fulfilling the responsibility of government information disclosure according to law. However, judging from the actual implementation of the work, the responsibilities related to publishing the directory, guideline and annual report have not yet been fully and effectively fulfilled, let alone that of disclosure upon request. The problems are caused as the responsibilities and liabilities are not specific and detailed enough, and also the relevant authorities failed to evaluate the work and hold underperformances to account according to law. In the future, in order to further promote government information disclosure, it is recommended that the implementation standards of the government information disclosure system be further clarified, the elements of legal liability of not fulfilling the responsibilities according to law be refined, and the implementation of accountability mechanism be strengthened.

Seventh, the practice of some authorities to limit and reduce the scope of government information disclosure shall be corrected. Both the *Opinions on Some Issues Concerning the Regulations of the People's Republic of China on the Disclosure of Government Information* (No.36 [2008] of the General Office of the State Council) and the *Opinions of the General Office of the State Council on Doing a Good Job in Request-based Disclosure* (No. 5) [2010] of the General Office of the State Council) have strictly limited the qualifications of government information disclosure applicants and "government information" is restricted to a extremely limited scope. This goes far against the provisions of the Regulations, the ever-increasing public demands for information, and the principle that "disclosure is a routine procedure while non-disclosure is an exception". If the problem continues to exist, the Regulations will definitely lose its meaning. Therefore, it is suggested that the relevant departments conform to the trend of social development, redefine the starting point of the work, to bring the implementation of government information disclosure system back on track.

Chapter 5
The 2011 Evaluation of China's Government Transparency

5.1 Overview of the Work of Government Information Disclosure in 2011

The 2011 evaluation found that steady progress was made in all aspects of government information disclosure.

First of all, the work of government information disclosure was highly valued by government agencies. In 2011, facing the problems occurred during the implementation of work by government agencies at all levels, the state issued a series of policy papers, including the *Notice of the General Office of the State Council on Further Strengthening the Administration of Government Websites* (Letter No. 40 [2011] of the General Office of the State Council), the *Notice of the General Office of the State Council on Forwarding the Opinions of the National Government Openness Leading Group on Conducting the Trial Work of Promoting the Openness of Government Affairs and Government Services of County-level Governments by Leveraging E-government Platforms* (Letter No. 99 [2011] of the General Office of the State Council) and the *Opinions on Further Promoting Open Government and Enhancing Government Services* (No. 22 [2011] of the General Office of the CPC Central Committee issued by the General Office of the CPC Central Committee and the General Office of the State Council. The publication of these documents further promoted the implementation of the Regulations and enhanced the constant construction of a transparent government.

Second, breakthroughs were made in the disclosure of information in key areas, and openness and transparency became an important means of supervising the government's rule-based administration and improving the quality of government management and services. In 2011, further attention was paid to the disclosure of information about budgets and public spending on government cars, overseas trips and official receptions—collectively known as "three types of public expenditures". Many government agencies disclosed the information. The evaluation also found

Y. Lv and H. Tian, *Evaluation on Government Transparency Index in China (2009–2016)*, Understanding China, https://doi.org/10.1007/978-981-16-5032-1_5

that the disclosure of information about environmental protection was standardized, which was partially due to the early implementation of the *Measures for the Disclosure of Information about environmental protection (for Trial Implementation)*.

Third, the implementation of the Regulations was improved. In 2011, the most obvious progress in government information disclosure was made in the release of the annual report. As of March 31, 2011, the percentage of government agencies that had published the annual report of the previous year in accordance with the Regulations increased significantly. Only a very few failed to release the annual reports in time. Great improvements were also made in the validity of information links. These achievements illustrated the government information disclosure system could be well implemented when government agencies attached enough importance to it.

Fourth, obvious progress was made by many government agencies in government information disclosure. The 2011 evaluation showed that obvious improvements were made by both the departments under the State Council and large-city governments in some or all aspects of their work on government information disclosure. This was undoubtedly directly related to their increased emphasis on the work.

Fifth, the number of requests filed for the disclosure of government information showed an upward trend. Statistics in the 2010 annual reports issued by government agencies revealed that six of the 59 departments under the State Council received over 100 requests, among which the State Administration for Industry and Commerce received as many as 7538. Eight of the 26 provincial-level governments received over 10,000 requests, among which Zhejiang Provincial Government received as many as 32,033. Twelve of the 43 large-city governments received over 1000 requests, among which Guangzhou Municipal Government received as many as 1,098,041. This showed that the number of requests filed by the public was increasing as the Regulations started to be implemented and citizens were more familiar with the government information disclosure system. The increased public participation would also contribute to the implementation and continuous improvement of the government information disclosure system.

Nevertheless, the 2011 evaluation also revealed some problems in the work of government information disclosure, which should be taken seriously in implementing the work in the future.

First of all, public awareness of government information disclosure needed to be improved. To have a better understanding of public awareness of government information disclosure, the Project Team conducted a questionnaire survey in Beijing, Sichuan, Shandong, Hebei, Tianjin, Jilin, Gansu, Anhui, Liaoning, Zhejiang, and Jiangxi in 2011. During the survey, 850 questionnaires were distributed and 793 valid questionnaires were collected. In the survey, 457 of the respondents were males, 323 were females and 13 refused to reveal their gender; 32 with an education background of junior high school or below, 94 with an education background of senior high school, 229 with an education background of junior college, 364 with a bachelor's degree, 72 with a degree of postgraduate or above, and two refused to reveal their education background. According to the results of the survey, public awareness of the government information disclosure system was less than satisfactory. Among all the respondents, only 6.4% said they would file requests with government agencies for the information they need, 35.7% said they would search on the Internet; while 44.2% said they would like to learn about the information via radio, television and newspapers. Only 58.4% knew what the Regulations was; 27.4% said that they had no idea that they could search the information they need on government websites; 31.7% said they did not know that they could file a request; and only 12.2% had an experience of filing requests for information disclosure. By analyzing the number of requests for government information disclosure in the 2010 annual report, the Project Team found that the number of requests accepted by many local governments was still limited. This reflected to some extent that the public's knowledge and utilization of the system still needed to be improved. To achieve such improvement, government agencies should enhance their efforts to popularize the government information disclosure system.

Second, the performance of a few government agencies on the work of government information disclosure was unstable. The Project Team found that the all or some aspects of the performance of a few government agencies showed a backward trend in 2011 compared with that of 2010.

Third, the websites of some government agencies were still poorly operated. The portals of some government agencies or those of their affiliated departments could not be opened or some sections on the websites could not be opened. Many information links provided on some websites were invalid.

Some websites were unstable and the sections on the websites could sometimes be opened while sometimes not. Some websites provided complete sections and valid information links during the evaluation, but after the evaluation, the problem of lacking sections or invalid links was found. Some claimed that a few sections were under revision, but the process lasted for a very long time, which imposed a negative impact on public access to information.

Fourth, some government agencies still considered the work of government information disclosure as a mere formality. Although more sections were developed on some websites after revision, information disclosed in the sections was seldomly enriched. Some government agencies focused more on providing news reports and officials' schedules and little information related to the production and life of the public or the functions of the government agencies was disclosed. Some failed to update the information for quite a long time and the obsolete information made the websites useless in this respect. All the websites established and work of government information disclosure conducted by government agencies by investing huge amount of manpower and physical resources became a mere formality.

Fifth, the barriers to public request for the disclosure of information were not eased. To start with, some government agencies confused the relations between voluntary disclosure and disclosure upon request. They refused requests on the grounds that the information that fell within the scope of voluntary disclosure could not be requested. Also, identity of applicants was checked based on no legal grounds. The problem of illegally collecting applicants' ID number and name of their workplace has been existing since the implementation of the Regulations. The 2011 evaluation found that some government agencies also verified the authenticity of the applicant's ID card and a failure of verification could lead to denied access of information. For example, Guangdong Provincial Government and its subordinate municipal governments verified the identity of applicants, and claimed that all the non-local Guangdong residents could not submit requests via online platforms, instead, they could only use conventional methods such as mailing and face-to-face submission. Such practice not only violated the Regulations but also went against the object of establishing an e-government to serve the public. Then, applicants were required to provide the purpose of their requests without any legal grounds. An increasingly number of government agencies tended to use this as a way to restrict requests. Some would life to spend an immense amount of time and manpower to ask applicants to provide the documents to prove the purpose of their requests, rather than provide them with the information that would not concern any secrets, do any harm to the rights and interests of other people, or have any negative influence on the functions of the government agencies. Finally, some still brought about extra cost for applicants by leveraging technological difficulties, such as submitting documents in specific formats.

5.2 The Directory for Government Information Disclosure

The evaluation found that 57 departments under the State Council (55 in 2010), 26 provincial-level governments, and 43 large-city governments (41 in 2010) developed a special section for the directory on their websites. Some also emphasized the results of government information disclosure. For example, the information provided by the Ningbo Municipal Government on its website was not only presented in texts but also could be read out. This provided convenience for people with special needs and embodied the concept of providing people-oriented services.

However, some problems in this respect were also revealed in the evaluation.

First, the performance of government agencies on developing the directory was less than satisfactory, which was mainly manifested in two aspects. For one thing, some failed to develop the directory. Two departments under the State Council failed to develop a section for information disclosure on their websites. Twenty-four provincial-level governments developed the directory for their affiliated departments; 23 developed the directory for their lower-level local governments; and only five developed the directory for the public enterprises and institutions. Thirty-nine large-city governments developed the directory for affiliated departments (42 in 2010); 37 developed the directory for district-level and county-level governments (40 in 2010); and 26 developed the directory of the public enterprises and institutions (31 in 2010). For another, information in the directory was not equipped with links directed to information details. Some only provided a list of information summary in the directory, without any links directed to detailed information, which failed to provide the public with easy access to the information. Among the government agencies that developed the section, six departments under the State Council failed to provide any information links; two provincial-governments failed to provide information links

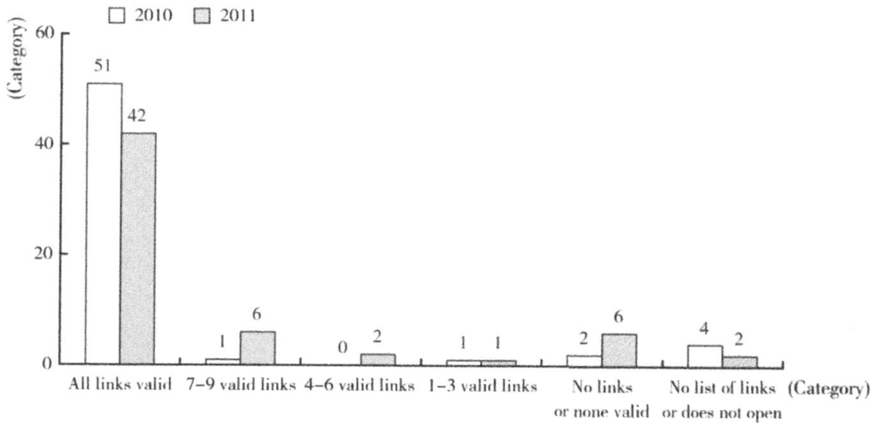

Fig. 5.1 A Comparison of the validity of information links in the directory provided by departments under the State Council in 2010 and 2011

in the directory for their affiliated departments; three provincial-governments failed to provide the links in the directory for their lower-level governments; two failed to provide the links in the directory for their public enterprises and institutions. All of these problems made the directory a mere formality.

Second, information links in the directory were of poor validity. By randomly selecting the information links provided by the government agencies, the Project Team found that invalid information links and webpages that could not be opened still existed. For example, when verifying the validity of information links provided by the departments under the State Council, the Project Team randomly selected ten information links on the website of each department and found that the information links of 42 were all valid, accounting for 71.2%, which was lower than that of 2010. (See Fig. 5.1).

When verifying the validity of information links provided by the provincial-level governments, the Project Team randomly selected ten information links in the directory for the same-level government; ten in the directory for affiliated departments; nine in the directory for lower-level governments; and six in the directory for public enterprises and institutions. The affiliated departments chosen were provincial bureaus of health, bureaus of agriculture, bureaus of quality and technology supervision, administrations of industry and commerce, and food and drug administrations. Two information links were selected from the directory for each of them. According to the results of the verification, the number of provincial-level governments with all of the information links in the directory for same-level governments, affiliated departments, lower-level governments and public enterprises and institutions valid was 25, 12, 15 and three respectively.

As for the large-city governments, the same verification was conducted. The affiliated departments chosen were also local bureaus of health, bureaus of agriculture, bureaus of quality and technology supervision, administrations of industry

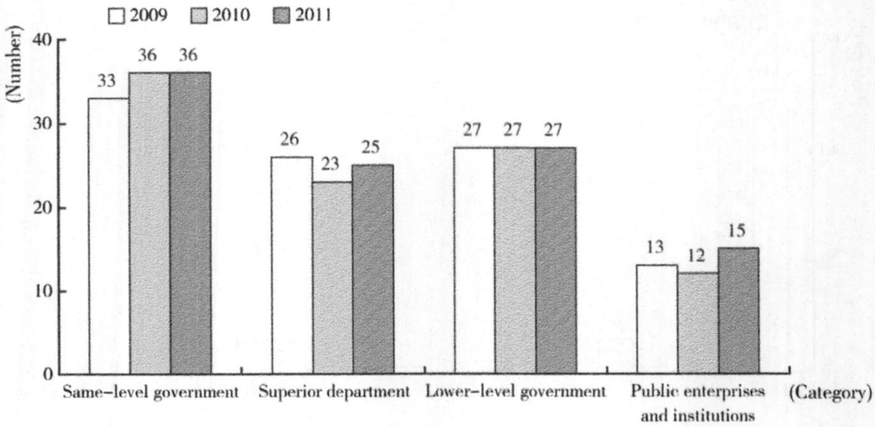

Fig. 5.2 A comparison of the number of large-city governments with all information links in each directory valid from 2009 to 2011

and commerce, and food and drug administrations. According to the results of the verification, the number of large-city governments with all of the information links in the directory for same-level governments, affiliated departments, lower-level governments and public enterprises and institutions valid was 36, 25, 27 and 15 respectively (See Fig. 5.2).

Third, the information in the directory was inconvenient for the public to access. This was mainly due to the uneven quality of the search functions provided by different government agencies on their websites. Among all the departments under the State Council evaluated, 34 provided the function of cross-database search (simple search), of which the functions provided by 27 were valid; 27 provided multiple search functions, of which the functions provided by 15 were valid; and 27 provided combined search functions (advanced search), of which the functions provided by 19 were valid. The corresponding number of the provincial-level governments was 18, 14, 11, eight, 13 and nine respectively. he corresponding number of the large-city governments was 26, 23, 19, 15, 19 and 12 respectively (See Fig. 5.3). As shown by the statistics, many government agencies failed to equip the directory with search functions. Even for those that managed to provide search functions, most of the functions were useless. In addition, the search functions provided by some could only be displayed after a random piece of information was opened, which was not what a typical search function should be.

Fourth, information update delays still occurred. Thirty-five departments under the State Council, 24 provincial-level governments and 39 large-city governments managed to update the information to one month before the time this evaluation was conducted. The Project Team found that the information provided by some large-city governments was only updated to 2009, and the relevant sections on the websites or the entire websites were not updated anymore. Information update delays have

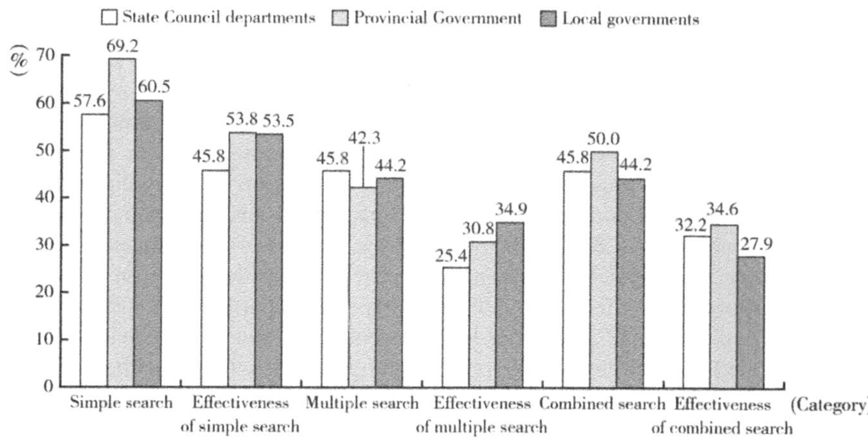

Fig. 5.3 A comparison of the search functions provided in the directory on the websites of the departments under the State Council, provincial governments and local governments in 2011

undoubtedly caused the stagnation of government information disclosure work and made many government websites a mere formality.

Fifth, information disclosed in the directory was not comprehensive. To be more specific, information contained in the directory was not consistent with that published in other sections, and the problem that information in other sections was not included in the directory was quite common. Forty-nine departments under the State Council, all of the provincial-level governments, and 41 large-city governments were faced with the problem.

5.3 The Guidelines on Government Information Disclosure

Significant improvements were made on the release of guidelines on government information disclosure. In 2011, all of the 59 departments under the State Council (53 in 2011) and 26 provincial-level governments provided the guidelines in full on their websites. The number of large-city governments that provided the guidelines in full on their websites or their guidelines could be found by using search engines was 39 (39 in 2010). Most government agencies placed their guidelines in specific sections, but the guidelines of some others were randomly placed. For example, the guidelines of Tangshan Municipal Government were mixed with the guidelines of other departments, which were difficult to be found. In addition, some local governments shared the same guidelines with the offices of same-level governments, and the problem that the guidelines were a mere formality still existed. The guidelines of some departments were adapted from the templates provided by their higher-level authorities, with some parts of the templates being empty when published. For instance, the fields for charging standards and complaints hotline in the guidelines provided by Zhengzhou Municipal Government and Luoyang Municipal Government were empty.

The performance of government agencies on providing basic information about the department responsible for government information disclosure or the agency in charge of accepting requests in the guidelines was improved. Fifty-eight departments under the State Council (51 in 2010), 23 provincial-level governments and 31 large-city governments (28 in 2010) provided the address of the competent department. Fuzhou Municipal Government also provided detailed location maps and public transport options in the guidelines. Forty-nine departments under the State Council (47 in 2010), 12 provincial-level governments and 24 large-city governments included detailed hours of service in the guidelines. Others either failed to provide the information or just gave general information. Fox example, the "consultation time" stated in the guidelines of Fujian Municipal Government was "office hours from Monday to Friday, excluding public holidays"; that in the guidelines of Shanxi Provincial Government was "office hours"; and that in the guidelines of Inner Mongolia was "office hours (Monday to Friday)". Fifty-two departments under the State Council (46 in 2010), 23 provincial-level governments, and 32 large-city governments (36 in 2010) provided the contact number of the competent department. Also, 44 departments under the State Council (36 in 2010), 15 provincial-level governments, and 26 large-city governments (27 in 2010) provided the email address of the competent department.

Fifty-eight departments under the State Council (51 in 2010), 25 provincial-level governments, and 39 large-city governments (37 in 2010) described the forms of voluntary disclosure in the guidelines. As was mentioned in the 2010 evaluation, some government agencies confused the relations between voluntary disclosure and disclosure upon request. This problem still existed in 2011.

In 2011, 56 departments under the State Council (42 in 2010), 23 provincial-level governments, and 37 large-city governments (35 in 2010) described the procedures of request-based disclosure in the guidelines. Four departments under the State Council (three in 2010), seven provincial-level governments, and eight large-city governments (nine in 2010) included flowcharts in the guidelines. However, the links directed to flowcharts in some guidelines were invalid.

Information about the supervisory mechanism for government information disclosure provided in the guidelines was not comprehensive. Eleven departments under the State Council (18 in 2010), nine provincial-level governments, and 17 large-city governments (same as in 2010) managed to provide the address of the supervision agency. Only Fuzhou Municipal Government also provided a location map and public transport options. Only one department under the State Council ad seven large-city governments provided information about the hours of service of the supervision agency. The information provided by others was too general. For example, the office hours provided by Nanchang Municipal Government was simply "excluding public holidays". Eighteen departments under the State Council provided the contact number of the supervision agency (19 in 2010), and seven provided the email address of the supervision agency (nine in 2010). The corresponding number of provincial-level governments that provided the aforesaid information was ten and six, and the number of large-city governments was 22 (same as in 2010) and six (same as in 2010) respectively. Some also provided an online platform for filing a complaint.

Thirty-three departments under the State Council (26 in 2010), 20 provincial-level governments, and 37 large-city governments (27 in 2010) provided relief channels. Among them, only three departments under the State Council (same as in 2010) and one large-city government (none in 2010) indicated the methods and authorities for applying for administrative reviews, namely, the Ministry of Transport, the State Administration for Industry and Commerce, the State Administration of Quality and Technical Supervision, and Fuzhou Municipal Government.

5.4 Request-Based Disclosure

The 2011 evaluation found that improvements were made in the operation of online request platforms compared with that of 2010. After receiving requests, the staff at some government agencies could contact the applicants in time to confirm the information requested, the purpose of requests or the contact details of applicants.

The overall performance on developing a special section for request-based disclosure on their websites among the departments under the State Council, provincial-level governments and large-city governments showed little difference. However, differences existed in the performance in specific areas. For example, Nearly two-thirds of the large-city governments and over half of the provincial-level governments provided an online request channel on their websites, but one-fourth of the departments under the State Council managed to do so. Nearly half of the departments of the State Department limited the method of request to just via emails, while others only receive either submissions in person or via mailing, or some even failed to provide any channels at all.

The evaluation showed that the performance of government agencies on developing the special section for request-based disclosure on their websites was generally satisfactory. All of the provincial-level governments managed to develop the section, while some of the departments under the State Council and large-city governments failed to do so. Among the departments under the State Council evaluated, 53 developed the section, accounting for 89.8% (51 in 2010). Among the large-city governments evaluated, 36 developed the section, accounting for 83.7% (93.7% in 2010).

The departments under the State Council performed better than in 2010 on providing request forms. To be more specific, 49 departments provided the form in downloadable and editable formats, such as Word; two provided the forms in a Webpage format, which could only be printed; the forms provided by three could not be downloaded or copied; and five failed to provide any forms. However, the situation went worse among large-city governments compared with 2010. Twenty-five large-city governments provided the form in downloadable and editable formats, such as

Word; two provided the forms in a Webpage format, which could only be printed; and 16 failed to provide any forms. The performance of the provincial-level governments showed positive results. Twenty-three provincial-level governments provided the form in downloadable and editable formats, such as Word; one provided the forms in a Webpage format, which could only be printed; and only two failed to provide any forms.

As for providing an online request platform, large-city governments performed significantly better than the departments under the State Council and the provincial-level governments. No obvious improvements were made by the departments under the State Council in this respect. Among the departments under the State Council evaluated, 15 provided an online request platform, accounting for 25.4% (15 in 2010); 27 limited the request method to via emails (26 in 2010); and 17 did not provide any of the two channels (18 in 2010). Thirty-one large-city governments provided an online request platform (34 in 2010); two limited the request method to via emails (one in 2010); and ten did not provide any of the two channels (eight in 2010). Fifteen provincial-level governments provided an online request platform; six limited the request method to via emails; and five did not provide any of the two channels.

In the name of an ordinary citizen, the Project Team filed requests with government agencies to evaluate their performance on request-based disclosure. In the 2011 evaluation, the Project Team asked the evaluation objects to disclose information about the amount of the funds used for constructing government websites and for conducting the work of information disclosure (including the total amount, the amount for purchasing and maintaining hardware facilities, website technical maintenance, and website construction outsourcing, etc.), the personnel for website construction and the personnel for information disclosure in 2011. For those that provided a valid online request platform, requests were submitted online; for those that provided the email address but without an online platform, requests were submitted via emails; and for those that only provided the mailing method, requests were sent in hard-copy through the China Post Express (EMS). The requests filed with Guangdong Provincial Government and its affiliated municipal governments, such as those of Guangzhou, Shenzhen and Shantou were also submitted through the China Post Express (EMS), as the online request platform of these governments was only open to local residents of Guangdong.

In terms of the validity of the online request platform, all the submissions to the 15 departments under the State Council and 14 of 15 provincial-level governments were successful. The requests filed with Guangdong Provincial Government were not submitted through the online platform as an ID card of a local resident in Guangdong was required. Submissions to 26 of the 31 large-city governments were also successful. In terms of the validity of the email address, the submissions to three of the 27 departments under the State Council were returned due to problems occurred in the email system, while all of the submissions to six provincial-level governments were successful and the submissions to two large-city governments were returned.

The evaluation results revealed that the accessibility of an online request platform was quite low. Even though some provided an online request platform or email address, requests still could not be submitted successfully. Also, a few government agencies only accepted face-to-face submissions. These problems all failed to facilitate public access to government information.

It was still common for government agencies to excessively collect applicants' personal information and the purpose of requests. Among all the 51 departments under the State Council to which requests were successfully sent, 15 required applicants to provide extra personal information besides legally required information in request forms, and 13 required applicants to provide the purpose of requests. For the other 36 departments under the State Council that did not explicitly state that applicants shall provide such information as their workplace, ID number, gender, age, and the purpose of requests, the Project Team submitted the forms without filling in these fields. However, 12 departments under the State Council informed by phone calls or via emails of the applicants to supplement the aforementioned information. In addition, 12 departments under the State Council failed to reply after receiving the requests, and only ten replied to the requests without asking for more personal information.

Among the 22 provincial-level governments to which requests were successfully sent via emails, 14 required applicants to provide extra personal information besides legally required information in request forms, and nine required applicants to provide the purpose of requests. For the other five provincial-level governments that did not explicitly state that applicants shall provide such information and the purpose of requests, the Project Team submitted the forms without filling in these fields. Four replied to the requests without asking for more personal information while one failed to provide any replies.

Among the 29 large-city governments to which requests were successfully sent via emails, 23 required applicants to provide extra personal information besides legally required information in request forms, and 13 required applicants to provide the purpose of requests. For those that did not explicitly state that applicants shall provide such information and the purpose of requests, the Project Team submitted the forms without filling in these fields. However, two asked the applicants to further provide their ID number and the purpose of requests.

After verifying the search functions provided on government websites, the Project Team found that the performance of the departments under the State Council on providing such functions as tracking the status and the result of requests online was slightly inferior to that of local governments. However, the departments under the State Council performed significantly better than provincial-level governments and large-city governments on providing the function of tracking the real-time number of requests being handled. As for the function of tracking the status of requests online, 11 departments under the State Council provided the function, accounting for 18.6% of the all the departments under the State Council evaluated and 26.3% of the 42 departments that provided an online platform or email address for submitting requests; the corresponding figures for provincial-level governments were seven, 26.9% and 33.3% respectively; and the corresponding figures for large-city governments were 12, 27.9% and 37.5% respectively. As for the function of tracking the result of requests, 11 departments under the State Council provided the function, accounting for 18.6% of all the departments under the State Council evaluated and 26.2% of the 42 departments that provided an online platform or email address for submitting requests; the corresponding figures for provincial-level governments were seven, 26.9% and 33.3% respectively; and the corresponding figures for large-city governments were nine, 20.9% and 28.1% respectively. As for the function of tracking the real-time number of requests being handled, 23 departments under the State Council provided the function, accounting for 39% of all the departments under the State Council evaluated and 54.8% of the 42 departments that provided an online platform or email address for submitting requests; the corresponding figures for provincial-level governments were five, 19.2% and 23.8% respectively; and the corresponding figures for large-city governments three, 7% and 9.4% respectively.

The evaluation found that most government agencies failed to provide any replies to the requests within the statutory period. Even some did provide a reply, the content of their replies was irrelevant to the information requested or applicants could not access the information through the channels provided in the replies. Some even delayed the disclosure on the grounds that the staff responsible for information disclosure was away on a business trip or permissions needed to be sought from their superiors first.

The evaluation found that the response rate of none of the three types of evaluation object exceeded 25 percent. Only 14 departments under the State Council, seven provincial-level governments, and seven large-city governments managed to reply within the statutory period.

Only an extremely few of government agencies disclosed all the information requested. Most of them chose not to provide the information requested or just disclose part of it. Although some informed the applicants of the channels to obtain the information that had been disclosed voluntarily, no information could be found through the channels. Nine departments under the State Council, three provincial-level governments and three large-city governments disclosed all the information requested. This result was far from achieving the goal of promoting government information disclosure and building a service-oriented government. Although some departments under the State Council replied in written forms, the content of the replies were quite empty and evasive. For example, some replies were just "the information does not exist" or "no funds invested". Some government agencies did not provide any written replies, instead, they informed the applicants of the refused disclosure by calling them or briefly told them the information requested. Some even required the applicants to go to the government service hall to request the information in person.

The evaluation also revealed that a few government agencies still faced the problem of causing barriers and increased cost for the public in the process of requesting for the disclosure of government information. For example, the unreasonable design of some online request platforms and some technological means and tools used there have brought about extra difficulties and cost for applicants. Some websites required applicants to register in their real name before they could file a request. In the fields for filling in contact number on some websites, only fixed line number was allowed. Some websites required applicants to download, print and sign the request form, then scan it in an image format as an email attachment of the request.

All of these caused inconvenience to public request, and increased the time and cost needed. Also, all of these problems had been identified in the 2010 evaluation, and no improvements were made in 2011.

5.5 The Annual Report on Government Information Disclosure

In this section, the performance of government agencies on the release of the annual report and the elements of the annual reports are mainly evaluated. Given that there was a statutory period for publishing the annual report, the Project Team conducted the evaluation from March 15 to April 20, 2011.

In 2011, most government agencies managed to release the annual report for the previous year in time. The evaluation found that all of the 59 departments under the State Council managed to release the 2010 annual report without delay. By contrast, four had failed to do so even by the end of 2010. Thirty-seven out of the 43 large-city governments managed to do so (same as in 2010). As of the end of this evaluation, one more large-city government released its annual report. Twenty-five of the 26 provincial-level governments released their annual reports in time.

However, the performance of government agencies on developing a special section for the annual report on their websites was less than satisfactory. Some failed to develop the section while others failed to release the annual report in the section developed on their websites. This impeded public access to the annual report and negatively affected the effectiveness of the disclosure. Fifty-five departments under the State Council developed the section for the annual report, two of which failed to publish the 2010 annual report in the section. Forty large-city governments managed to develop the section on their websites, two of which also failed to publish the 2010 annual report in the section. Twenty-four provincial-level governments managed to develop the section on their websites and all of them published the 2010 annual report in the section. Another problem was that some government agencies only managed to publish the 2010 annual report in the section, not those of previous years. Three departments under the State Council and two large-city governments failed to provide the annual reports of 2009 and years before.

The problem that the content of the annual report was evasive and empty was barely changed, and the preparation standards needed to be refined. The annual reports of some government agencies just reported generally on what achievements had been made while concealing the problems existed in the agencies, which failed to provide effective data based on which the public can supervise their work on government information disclosure. This was particularly the case in the information disclosed both voluntarily and upon request. What's worse, in 2011, a number of government agencies simply used the annual reports of previous years as the one of 2010.

Compared with 2010, the performance of government agencies in 2011 on providing data on voluntary disclosure in the annual report showed both experienced ups and downs. On the one hand, the number of government agencies that provided overall data on voluntary disclosure increased, as 53 departments under the State Council (48 in 2010), 39 large-city governments (37 in 2010) and 26 provincial government managed to provide the data. On the other hand, the number of government agencies that provided the data on voluntary disclosure categorized by the forms of disclosure saw a slight decrease, as only 31 departments under the State Council (40 in 2010), 20 large-city governments (31 in 2010) and 14 provincial-level governments managed to do so.

The disclosure of data on request-based disclosure is still less than satisfactory. Overall, the related data provided by governments in their annual reports was not detailed enough, and some just jumped over or briefly described the core elements of request-based disclosure.

Among the departments under the State Council evaluated, 34 provided the total number of requests they had received in the previous year (same as in 2010), 28 provided the items with top requests (same as in 2010), 21 provided the number of requests categorized by different submission methods (23 in 2010), 56 provided the number of requests that had been reviewed and accepted (44 in 2010), 23 provided data categorized by the content of replies (such as to be disclosed, not to be disclosed or to be partially disclosed) (27 in 2010), 11 provided data categorized by the reasons why the request had been refused (such as concerning state secrets or personal privacy) (eight in 2010), and 56 provided data on the number of administrative proceedings, administrative reviews, and complaints involving government information disclosure (49 in 2010).

Among the large-city governments evaluated, 11 provided the total number of requests they had received in the previous year (13 in 2010), ten provided the number of requests received in the previous year categorized by same-level government, lower-level governments and affiliated departments (14 in 2010), five provided the information about the departments that received top requests (four in 2010), 24 provided the items with top requests (17 in 2010), 23 provided the number of requests categorized by different submission methods (20 in 2010), 40 provided the number of requests that had been reviewed and accepted (30 in 2010), 23 provided data categorized by the content of replies (such as to be disclosed, not to be disclosed or to be partially disclosed) (25 in 2010), nine provided data categorized by the reasons why the request had been refused (such as involving state secrets or personal privacy) (14 in 2010), and 41 provided data on the number of administrative proceedings, administrative reviews, and complaints involving government information disclosure (35 in 2010).

Among the provincial-level governments evaluated, 12 provided the total number of requests they had received in the previous year, 15 provided the number of requests received in the previous year categorized by same-level government, lower-level governments and affiliated departments, five provided the information about the governments that received top requests, 18 provided the items with top requests, 14 provided the number of requests categorized by different submission methods, 24 provided the number of requests that had been reviewed and accepted, 18 provided data categorized by the content of replies (such as to be disclosed, not to be disclosed or to be partially disclosed), seven provided data categorized by the reasons why the request had been refused (such as involving state secrets or personal privacy), and 26 provided data on the number of administrative proceedings, administrative reviews, and complaints involving government information disclosure.

After reviewing the annual reports provided by the departments under the State Council, the provincial-level governments and the large-city governments, the Project Team found that the preparation standards of the annual reports were confusing, and types of elements contained were mixed. Taking the disclosure of data on request-based disclosure as an example, some governments just provided the data of the same-level governments, some provided the data of both the same-level governments and of the affiliated departments, while some others provided the data of the same-level governments, affiliated departments and the lower-level governments. Also, many governments failed to provide comprehensive data. These problems all illustrated that the preparation of the annual reports needed to be standardized.

5.6 Normative Documents

The term "normative documents" referred to the generally binding decisions, orders, and administrative measures other than administrative regulations and rules formulated by the departments under the State Council and their internal offices. As its definition suggested, the main authorities of the preparation of these documents were the departments under the State Council and their internal offices. They were typically released in the names of "announcement" or "notice" instead of "regulation" or "measure", or "executive order". Some normative documents might only apply to the internal offices of administrative agencies. However, a large number of normative documents in reality directly or indirectly affected the administrative counterpart, defined rights and obligations of the administrative counterpart or had a material impact on their rights and obligations. Hence, the scope of application of normative documents would not be taken into consideration in the evaluation and the normative documents published by all the government agencies would be evaluated.

According to the evaluation, the performance of government agencies on the disclosure of normative documents varied. Many released their normative documents in an organized and clear manner. However, a few just had a vague understanding of normative documents and related information in the sections was in a mess.

First of all, sections for normative documents were randomly developed. Most government agencies developed more than two sections for normative documents on the homepage of their websites, titled "Laws and Regulations", "Policy Documents", "Notices and Announcements" or "Normative Documents". Information contained in the sections was poorly organized and no clear boundaries were set among the sections. The evaluation found that 53 government agencies developed more than two sections for normative documents. This indicated to a certain extent that the definition of normative documents was not clear enough. Also, there was a lack of uniform criteria and standards, both theorical and practical, to define what kinds of documents were normative ones and what kinds of documents were not.

Second, the sections developed by the same government agency in different places on their websites were inconsistent. Most government agencies developed two normative document sections: one on their homepage and one in the directory for government information disclosure. However, the problems that the two sections were inconsistent and the information contained in the section was not synchronized were commonly seen. Among the 58 government agencies that provided normative document sections, the two sections of 47 were inconsistent and the information contained was not synchronized. This brought about difficulties for the public to access information.

Third, the normative documents were randomly placed. This problem was also prominent. For example, some government agencies put normative documents in the section for rules and regulations or for news and events. This illustrated that some government agencies lacked standards on information release and they might also lack an appropriate understanding of normative documents.

Fourth, normative documents were of poor accessibility. Most government agencies did not have their normative documents categorized. Among the 58 government agencies that provided sections for normative documents, only four had their sections categorized by items, and none was categorized by departments.

Fifth, normative documents were not updated in time. The normative documents provided by some governments were outdated, and some even were just updated to 2009. Among the 58 government agencies that provided sections for normative documents, 13 failed to publish the normative documents in 2011 in the sections. Among the 30 government agencies that provided sections for the interpretation of normative documents, 15 failed to update the information to half year before the time when the evaluation was conducted.

Sixthly, performance on disclosing the preparation process of normative documents was less than satisfactory. Only 25 government websites provided valid sections dedicated to releasing the drafts of normative documents and to gathering public opinions on the drafts. Only 22 provided no less than three valid drafts of normative documents, of which, 19 provided the drafts in their special sections, and three did not have such sections. Only 29 provided channels to solicit public opinions on the drafts of normative documents, of which, five did not have related sections and the channels were provided elsewhere on their websites.

5.7 Information About Environmental Protection

In this section, the evaluation objects were 26 provincial-level governments. Their performance on the disclosure of information about environmental protection showed positive results. The environmental administrations of the 26 provincial-level governments all had their own website. of which, the website of the Bureau of National Territory Recourse of Hainan concentratedly provided information about land management, environmental protection and geological and mining resources management. The websites of the provincial environmental administrations were generally equipped with necessary sections for publishing information. Information about environmental protection that needed to be disclosed as per relevant regulations was disclosed in the sections. For example, all the websites of environmental administrations evaluated provided normative documents developed by the department itself and its superior provincial government. In the normative documents, environmental protection standards (including water environmental protection standards, atmospheric environmental protection standards, environmental noise and vibration standards, soil environment protection standards, solid waste and chemical environmental pollution control standards, nuclear radiation and electromagnetic radiation environmental protection standards, ecological environmental protection standards, pollution prevention technology policies, and local environmental protection standards) were published. By randomly selecting five information links from each website, the Project Team found that all the links provided by 25 were valid. In terms of information on environmental quality, the websites of 24 environmental administrations provided information about water quality in their respective jurisdictions by releasing monthly reports, and 23 provided information about air quality by releasing daily reports. Twenty-five developed a section for the annual environmental protection reports, of which, 24 actually provided the reports in the section, and the 2010 report was also included. The positive outcomes were mainly a result of the implementation of the *Measures for the Disclosure of Information about environmental protection (for Trial Implementation)*. The Measure refined the requirements of the Regulations on voluntary disclosure, and specified the information that environmental administrations shall disclose voluntarily.

However, some problems were also identified, namely, the failure of disclosing some information, the random arrangement of the information disclosed on the websites, failure of obtaining information due to invalid information links and failure of update information without delay, etc. These problems have seriously affected the effectiveness of the disclosure of information about environmental protection, resulting in some information not being disclosed, or some disclosed information not accessible to the public.

First, the disclosure of some information about environmental protection was less than satisfactory. Article 11 of the *Measures for the Disclosure of Information about environmental protection (for Trial Implementation)* defined the types of information about environmental protection that environmental administrations shall disclose voluntarily to the public as long as it was within the scope of its functions and responsibilities. However, the evaluation found that the requirements of the Article were not fully implemented. For example, some information about environment quality could seldomly be found on the websites, including the issuance of pollutant discharging licenses, the types and amount produced and the disposal of solid waste in large and medium-sized cities, environmental administrative punishment, the list of enterprises that had serious environmental pollution accidents or incidents and the list of enterprises that refused to comply with the effective decisions on environmental administrative punishment. In terms of information about environmental quality, only five environmental administrations provided information about noise quality by releasing monthly reports. In terms of information about solid waste, 21 environmental administrations failed to provide information about solid waste types, 22 failed to provide information about the amount of solid waste produced, 16 failed to provide information about solid waste disposal, and none of the administrations provided information about the issuance of solid waste discharge licenses. Also, in terms of information about environmental administrative punishment, six failed to set up a special section for disclosing information about environmental administrative punishment; the section links of one department were invalid; only 13 provided the list of enterprises that had serious environmental pollution accidents or incidents; and only one provided the list of enterprises that refused to comply with the effective decisions on environmental administrative punishment.

Second, some information links were invalid. The sections provided by some environmental administrations were empty, or some information links were invalid, resulting in failure to access information. Also, the sections for environmental administrative punishment developed by some administrations were empty. Some provided many detailed standards in the section titled "Scientific and Technological Standards". However, most of the links directed to standards were invalid.

Third, the problem of information update delays was prominent. The information disclosed by many environmental administrations on their websites was not updated in time and some of the information only updated to the end of 2008. Only five environmental administrations updated the information about the amount of solid waste produced or disposed to less than three months before the time when the evaluation was conducted. Only 13 updated the results of environmental administrative punishment to less than six months before the time when the evaluation was conducted. The information in the "Administrative Punishment" section on the website of an environmental administration had not been updated since 2009, with the information about complaint cases only updated to November 30, 2010. The information in the section for solid waste on the website of another environmental administration was just update to 2010.

Fourth, information was randomly arranged, resulting in disordered, repeated, and unconcentrated disclosure. Although some environmental administrations developed related sections, information was still randomly placed on the websites, and could be found sometimes in the sections and sometimes not. Fox example, the "Pollutant Charge Management" section of an environmental administration was placed in the "Financial Disclosure" section, but information related to pollutant charge was also disclosed in the "Notice and Announcement" section. Also, the information contained in these two sections was inconsistent.

Although the disclosure of information about environmental protection could not replace environmental law enforcement, it was undoubtedly an important aspect of environmental law enforcement, and an important means to promote environmental law enforcement and supervise environmental administrations. Therefore, although some achievements were made on the disclosure of information about environmental protection thanks to the implementation of the *Measures for the Disclosure of Information about environmental protection (for Trial Implementation)*, the aforesaid problems have to be tackled to advance the course of environmental protection.

5.8 Food Safety Information

In this section, the performance of 43 large-city governments on disclosing food safety information was evaluated. The focus of the evaluation was the disclosure of information about the catering services license and its implementation. Evaluation objects were the websites of the departments in charge of catering services, and the indicators included the disclosure of information about the policy regulations and normative documents, approval of the catering services license, supervision of catering services, business credit of catering services companies, the warning of food safety risk, and food safety measures.

As per the *Food Safety Law of the People's Republic of China*, since June 1, 2009, the food and drug supervision agencies replaced the health supervision agencies to supervise catering services, and the catering services license replaced the food hygiene license. To renew the catering services license, the State Food and Drug Administration had issued a special notice requiring that, from June 1, 2009, catering service supervision agencies at all levels shall issue the catering service license in strict accordance with the requirements of the *Food Safety Law of the People's Republic of China* to those catering service operators who apply for new, changed, extended, and reissued licenses. However, the evaluation found that the supervision authority of catering services in many municipalities, such as Wuxi, Chengdu, Hangzhou, Luoyang, Haikou, Xiamen, and Fuzhou, was not fully handed over. Therefore, for these municipalities, the Project Team evaluated both the websites of the food and drug supervision agencies and those of the health supervision agencies. And for some other large cities, though the authority had been handed over, the information about catering service management has not been disclosed on the websites of the food and drug supervision agencies. For example, the related information of Guiyang was disclosed on local government portals, the information about catering services in Xuzhou was provided by the Food Safety Website, and the authority of food safety supervision in Shenzhen was still the Shenzhen Market Supervision and Administration.

Judging from the results of the evaluation, which focused on evaluating the supervision of catering services, some achievements on the disclosure of food safety information were made while some problems were also identified. The main achievements were: the food and drug supervision agencies as well as departments in charge of supervising catering services all established their websites; the supervision agencies of all but two large cities provided a description of their own internal offices and respective responsibilities on their websites; 41 local food and drug supervision agencies provided the contact number or email address on their websites, to which complaints and opinions could be sent; 40 provided related laws and regulations and normative documents on their websites; and 40 provided the information about the supervision and inspection of catering services.

However, several major problems were also identified and should be taken seriously.

First, the disclosure of food safety information lagged behind public demands for food safety information and the requirements of strengthening food safety regulation. As of the end of the evaluation, among the 43 large-city governments evaluated, the review and approval of the catering services license of 32 was conducted by the local food and drug supervision administrations, that of ten was conducted by the local bureaus of health, and that of one (Shenzhen) was conducted by the Shenzhen Market Supervision and Administration. However, the work of disclosing information about the catering services license was not adjusted accordingly after the hand-over of the authority in some large cities. In these cities, of all the information disclosed by the local food and drug administrations, the major part was about drugs, and little about food safety. Fox example, in the section for food safety information on the websites of the food and drug administration of some large cities, information about medication safety other than food safety was provided; complaints hotlines were just for the management of drugs; and no hotline or email address was provided for the public to make complaints about food safety. Also, the food and drug administrations of some cities claimed for a long time to develop a section titled "Food Safety Credit File for Catering Service Providers", but none has been established yet. In addition, the amount of related information disclosed in the sections was small, and some websites disclosed less than five pieces of information in their sections for normative documents.

Second, some information that was legally required to be disclosed was not published. After repeated searches, the Project Team found that only the government agencies of 28 large cities provided the procedures for applying for the catering services license; 24 provided related guidelines; 29 listed the documents to be submitted; and 19 published the results of applications. In terms of supervision and inspection, only ten released the investigation and punishment results of illegal acts, and three developed a section titled "Food Safety Credit File of Catering Service Providers"; 17 provided information about the early-warning and warning food and drugs safety risks, and 27 provided basic knowledge about food safety. Therefore, it could be seen that the disclosure of information about catering services supervision as required by such laws and regulations as *Food Safety Law of the People's Republic of China* was not well implemented.

Third, the validity rate of information links was low. The Project Team randomly selected five information links of normative documents disclosed by the catering services supervision agency of each large city to verify their validity. The links of only 27 were all valid. Also, the information links of food safety provided by the food and drug administration of one city were invalid. The links of institutional functions provided by the administration of another city were invalid either.

Fourth, the problem that information was arranged disorderly was prominent, which imposed a negative impact on public access to information. To start with, the websites of some governments failed to have their sections set properly. For example, the website of one food and drug supervision agency was not equipped with a "Policies and Regulations" section and information about food safety supervision was disclosed in the sections such as "Official Documents" and "Notices and Announcements". Also, information was placed in a random and disorder manner. Fox example, the normative documents on local food safety supervision provided by one food and drug supervision agency was disclosed in the sections where national laws and regulations were published. Then, information was disclosed in an inconsistent and unsynchronized manner, which often occurred when the same information was disclosed in different sections. For example, the normative documents disclosed by some food and drug supervision agencies in different sections on their websites were different and inconsistent, resulting in confusion.

Fifth, information update delays occurred. In the 2010 evaluation, only 23 local governments managed to provide information about food safety popularization and knowledge (including information in 2010) on any of the websites of local government, food safety information, sanitary administration departments, bureaus of quality and technical supervision, industrial and commercial administrative departments, or food and drug administration departments. And in the 2011 evaluation, by applying a stricter method, the Project Team examined the disclosure of information within the three months before the evaluation was conducted. According to the evaluation, 35 government agencies managed to disclose supervision and inspection information about catering services in recent three months; only eight disclosed the inspection and punishment results of illegal activities in the same period; and seven disclosed information about the early-warning and warning of food safety risks. Therefore, it could be seen that the problem of outdated information or failing to update information was quite common. Information disclosure has not yet met the demands for food safety supervision or maintaining public well-being.

5.9 Information About Administrative Approval

The term "administrative approval" refers to the activity of administrative authorities (including other organizations with the authority of administrative approval), upon the application of the administrative counterparts, to approve them to engage in specific activities, recognize its qualifications, confirm specific civil relations or confirm its specific capacity for civil rights and capacity for conduct. The authority of administrative approval is part of state power, and it is an important power for governments at all levels to organize and manage public affairs according to law. The *Opinions on Further Promoting Open Government and Enhancing Government Services* (No. 22 [2011]) issued by the General Office of the CPC Central Committee and the General Office of the State Council emphasizes the importance of the government service center in promoting the reform of the administrative approval system and requires to further enhance the disclosure of information about administrative approval. Therefore, the Project Team decided to focus on the construction of government service center as an indicator to evaluate the performance of large cities on disclosing information about administrative approval.

The evaluation found that most of the large cities managed to set up dedicated websites to disclose information about administrative approval. Among the 43 large cities evaluated, 39 managed to establish a physical government service center, and those without the physical ones were Wuhan, Zhengzhou, Nanjing, and Xiamen; 41 managed to establish dedicated websites for administrative approval, and the two without the websites were Shijiazhuang and Jilin. In other words, among all the large cities evaluated, 37 established both physical a government service center and an administrative approval website; two only had a physical center; and four only had a dedicated website.

A large number of governments disclosed related information on their administrative approval websites. First of all, the basic information provided on the websites facilitated public access to government services. To make it easier for the public to conduct related activities and make consultations, the administrative approval websites of most governments provided related information of government service centers in a detailed and specific manner, such as their functions, address, transport options (including self-driving guides and public transport transfer options), contact number, email address, location maps and office hours, which not only offered convenience to the public, but also greatly improved the level of service and efficiency of administrative approval. Second, many local administrative approval websites managed to provide detailed information about approval. According to the evaluation, many websites provide the names of offices for administrative approval, the list of items subject to approval, approval guidelines, approval procedures, as well as contact details for service consultations in the government service center. Finally, to make it easier for the public to keep track of the items subject to approval, some websites provided dynamic disclosure of the items under examination. Many also developed a section titled "Dynamic Information about Items Subject to Approval" to provide a channel for tracking the status and results of administrative approval.

Nevertheless, some problems were also identified in this respect. There still existed a gap between administrative approval performance and the requirements of the reform of the administrative approval system and the construction of a service-oriented and transparent government.

First of all, the performance on constructing a dedicated website for administrative approval was less than satisfactory. According to the evaluation, two large cities failed to set up the government service center, let alone administrative approval websites. The administrative approval websites of some governments were operated poorly, with problems such as webpages could not be opened, could only be opened in a very slow manner, or some related functions were useless frequently occurring. For example, the "Items Subject to Approval", "Results of Approvals", "Monthly Ranking" and "Pending Consultations" sections on some websites could not be opened, while the links to the "Individual Application Guidelines" "the Enterprise Application Guidelines" were directed to the homepage of related government websites instead of the place where applications could be made.

Second, some administrative approval websites failed to have their sections well established and the information contained in the sections was poor in validity. The government service centers shall set up a section for disclosing internal regulations to inform the public and to strengthen public supervision. However, according to the evaluation, among the 41 administrative approval websites evaluated, only 32 provide the section and nine failed to do so. Among the 32 websites that were equipped with the section, 28 could have up to five information links opened and four could only have less than five information links opened. Also, to make it easier for the public to apply for administrative approval, the websites shall provide the list of items subject to approval and guarantee the validity of related information links. However, according to the evaluation, three of the 41 websites failed to provide such a list, and the list provided by one could only be opened after applicants have registered on the websites and have their identity verified.

Third, information provided on different websites was inconsistent. In the evaluation, information disclosed on the administrative approval websites was compared with that on government portals, as most large cities disclosed information on both websites. However, according to the evaluation, most of the information was inconsistent. To be more specific, by randomly selecting ten information links on administrative approval provided by 37 governments, the Project Team found that the information of only five cities was consistent, namely, Wuxi, Jinan, Tangshan, Haikou and Suzhou.

Fourth, related information was not fully provided. According to the evaluation, either the contact details of the government service center, or approval guidelines, or dynamic information of items subject to approval, were not fully provided, which was mainly manifested in the following three aspects:

To start with, contact details provided was insufficient. To offer convenience to the public, the basic information of government service centers, such as their functions, address, transport options (such as self-driving guides and public transport transfer options), contact number, email address, location maps and office hours (business days and hours) shall be provided on the administrative approval websites. However, of the 41 large cities with such websites, six failed to describe their functions, 14 failed to provide the address, 32 failed to provide transport options (either self-driving guides or public transport transfer options), nine failed to provide contact details, 16 failed to provide email address, 30 failed to provide location maps, and 30 failed to provide their office hours. Only two managed to provide all the aforesaid information.

Then, the information about administrative approval items was not fully disclosed. To offer convenience to the public, information such as the basis for administrative approval, approval conditions, application documents, approval procedures, approval duration, office address, and the contact number shall be provided. Of the 41 administrative approval websites evaluated, 38 provided a list of approval items, among which, the number of websites with up to five information links that could be opened was 37. By randomly selecting ten piece of approval information links on each of the 37 websites, the Project Team found that only 25 had all their links provided the basis for administrative approval, 24 had all their links provided application documents, 23 had all the links provided approval procedures, 29 had all the links provided approval duration (either statutory or contractual). Only three had all the links provided all the aforementioned information about administrative approval.

In addition, the dynamic information about items under approval was incomplete. To facilitate the public to keep track of their applications, related information such as information about offices in charge of the service, items under approval, application time, approval status (e.g. under approval or approval completed) shall be disclosed. According to the evaluation, only 35 of the 41 administrative approval websites provided related dynamic information, among which, only 25 provided information about offices in charge of the service, 31 provided information about items under approval, 18 provided application time, and only 29 provided approval status.

5.10 Recommendations

According to the 2011 evaluation, the following improvements need to be made to advance the work of government information disclosure.

First, the emphasis on the work of government information discourse shall be constantly increased. By comparing the results of the 2011 evaluation with those of the 2010 evaluation, the Project Team found that most of government agencies that had lagged behind in some respects made significant progress. This showed that the results of work of government information disclosure depended on whether the government agencies were willing to do it well and whether enough attention was paid to it.

Second, the misconceptions of government information disclosure systems at all levels of government agencies and their staff shall be promptly corrected. The intentional or unintentional misunderstanding of the system by relevant departments and their staff was the fundamental problem hindering the implementation of government information disclosure. Therefore, for one thing, the system and mechanism that violated the basic principle of the government information disclosure system and failed to meet the needs of social development shall be revised as soon as possible. For another, the training of staff responsible for the work of government information disclosure shall be conducted and facilitated to improve staff awareness of the work.

Third, the performance on voluntary disclosure shall be improved. According to the evaluations conducted in recent years, poor performance on voluntary disclosure was a major problem. Therefore, it needs to be guaranteed that the information that shall be voluntarily disclosed in accordance with the law can be disclosed in an accurate, comprehensive, timely, and effective manner, and that enough importance shall be attached to information disclosure work related to the vital interests of the public and to law-based government administration, with special attention paid to the effectiveness of information disclosed, such as the operation of websites, the validity of information links and the timely update of information.

Fourth, the work of government information disclosure shall be standardized as soon as possible. In recent years, though the number of requests for government information disclosure did not show an explosive increase trend, it was increasing year by year. This will definitely bring challenges to governments at all levels. Therefore, government agencies at all levels shall attach more importance to their work on request-based disclosure and improve their capabilities accordingly. Governments shall also keep an eye on the information that is widely requested, and disclose it voluntarily in a timely manner, thus reducing the cost of public access to information and the pressure on governments to deal with requests. In addition, governments at all levels shall also standardize the procedures such as replying with information at a time, to ensure the application of the principle of "one item, one request" and to improve the service level of request-based information disclosure.

Fifth, the cost of public access to government information shall be reduced. The construction of government websites shall be strengthened and the operation and the ability to provide online information of the websites shall also be improved to facilitate public access to information online. Also, some unnecessary processes such as identity verification and data provision shall be eliminated to facilitate public access to information. Instead of setting barriers to public access to information, government agencies shall focus on how to provide convenience to the public.

Sixth, clear standards for conducting the work of government information disclosure shall be perfected as soon as possible. Relevant departments shall further refine the standards for developing the directory, preparing the guidelines and the annual report, so as to eliminate the arbitrary behavior of government agencies in implementing the work, and to enhance the overall effectiveness of the work.

Seventh, the practice of relevant departments to limit the scope of government information disclosure should be corrected. Both the *Opinions on Some Issues Concerning the Regulations of the People's Republic of China on the Disclosure of Government Information* (No.36 [2008] of the General Office of the State Council) and the *Opinions of the General Office of the State Council on Doing a Good Job in Request-based Disclosure* (No. 5) [2010] of the General Office of the State Council) provided strict limitations on the qualifications of government information disclosure applicants and "government information" is restricted to a very limited scope. This goes far against the provisions of the Regulations, the ever-increasing public demands for information, and the principle that "information disclosure shall become a regular government practice and non-disclosure only happens in exceptional cases". If the problem continues to exist, the Regulations will definitely lose its meaning. Therefore, it is suggested that the relevant departments conform to the trend of social development, redefine the initial intentions and ultimate goals of their work, to bring the implementation of government information disclosure system back on track.

Chapter 6
The 2012 Evaluation of China's Government Transparency

6.1 Overview of the Work of Government Information Disclosure in 2012

The 2012 evaluation found that the overall government transparency showed an upward trend as progress was made in implementing the government information disclosure system by government agencies at all levels.

First, government agencies attached great importance to the work of government information disclosure. In response to the deficiencies of the work identified in the previous year and public demands for information, the *Major Work Arrangements for Government Information Disclosure in 2012* issued by the General Office of the State Council, pointed out work priorities in 2012, identified key aspects of the work, and assigned tasks to different departments. Local governments also developed their work priorities of the year. Some further improved the related laws and regulations, an example of which was the publication of the *Interim Measures for Government Information Disclosure of the Government* by Zhejiang Provincial People's Government.

Second, gradual improvements were made in the implementation of the Regulations. This was most significantly reflected in the release of the annual report. In the evaluation, only a very few government agencies failed to release the 2011 annual report in a timely manner. The validity of the information links and the consistency of information voluntarily disclosed on government websites were also greatly improved. The performance on providing channels for requesting information and replying to requests improved markedly. In addition, the websites of many government agencies managed to provide the information requested by the Project Team.

Third, the number of requests accepted by government agencies was increasing, as shown by the data published in the annual report. According to the 2011 annual report issued by various departments, the number of the government agencies that received no request decreased obviously while that of the requests accepted by government agencies showed significant increase in the past year. This trend indicated that the

Y. Lv and H. Tian, *Evaluation on Government Transparency Index in China (2009–2016)*, Understanding China, https://doi.org/10.1007/978-981-16-5032-1_6

government information disclosure system was being applied in people's production and life, and playing an active role in meeting public demands for information, which, of course, brought about huge pressure on government agencies and prompted them to further strengthen their law-based administration and improve the level of management.

Nevertheless, some problems were also identified in the work of government information disclosure and more attention should be attached to them.

First, the awareness of disclosure should be improved. According to the evaluation, the awareness of the staff of many government agencies varied, and many still regarded the work as a burden. Some were reluctant to do the work and reflected their mood in their attitude towards applicants. Also, some only considered how they could complete their work easily, without thinking about whether it would be convenient for people to access information. For example, the replies provided by many government agencies to the Project Team in the evaluation were quite general. Also, some chose to use express delivery on a freight forward basis for the sake of tracking package status instead of using registered mail which would be much cheaper. All of these illustrated that the awareness of the staff of government agencies should be improved.

Second, the performance on establishing a special department for government information disclosure was less than satisfactory. Although nearly five years have passed since the implementation of the Regulations, some government agencies still did not manage to set up a special department or assign dedicated staff to conduct the work. This imposed g a negative effect on the effectiveness of disclosure. In the evaluation, the Project Team found that staff of a few agencies were temporarily arranged to deal with the requests received. However, as they were unfamiliar with the work and lacked related expertise, they generally showed a not-so-well attitude and poor professionalism. This could not meet public demands for information and the staff were not competent to conduct the increasingly complex and arduous work.

Third, the performance on establishing government websites and disclosing information through the websites was less than satisfactory. The problems such as no government websites, non-functional websites, and non-updated information on the websites still existed. Some might have functional websites and comprehensive information was disclosed in a timely manner, but the work of some of their affiliated departments was far from satisfactory. Although local economic development might be a factor affecting the performance, it was not an essential factor, nor was the level of the governments. All in all, the performance of the work depended on whether the government agencies and the staff attached enough importance to it.

Fourth, a few government agencies performed poorly on voluntary disclosure. When voluntarily disclosing government information through websites, they faced the problems such as the information that should be disclosed according to law was not published; the information disclosed was not comprehensive; some information links were invalid; it was difficult to find related information; update delays occurred; information was randomly arranged on the websites; and information disclosed in different sections was consistent. Also, some still regarded the work as a mere formality. Some redesigned their websites with more information sections established, however, the information contained in the sections was hardly enriched. Some focused on publishing news reports and officials' schedules on their websites instead of the information related to people's production and life and functions of the government agencies themselves. The problem of unclear and inconsistent information disclosure standards was particularly prominent as for the disclosure of information about environmental protection, food safety and normative documents. All these problems made the tremendous financial and human resources invested by government agencies on the work of establishing government websites and government information disclosure a mere formality.

Fifth, the problem of unnecessary barriers to public access to government information seldomly changed. Reasons for refusing disclosure varied, including the failure to prove the applicant's identity as a "Chinese Citizen" since no identity information was provided, the failure to prove the purpose of the request, violation of the "one item, one request" rule, government agencies not responsible for compiling and processing the information requested, the information requested being internal or confidential data. Some even delayed the reply when the request time limit was about to expire, by the excuse of additional request information required or extension needed.

6.2 The Directory for Government Information Disclosure

The evaluation found that the performance on the directory in 2012 experienced obvious improvements compared with that of 2011, with the validity and convenience of the information links in the directory increased, too.

First, the construction of the directory was greatly improved. All evaluation objects has set up a special section for the directory on their websites, with increasingly enriched information contained. Among them, all large-city governments had the directory with information links contained. Fifty-six departments under the State Council and 25 provincial-level governments did so. The State Administration of Foreign Exchange did not have the directory in 2011, but in 2012 its directory was quite complete. The directory of some was more comprehensive and reasonably designed. For example, the China Meteorological Administration, the Ministry of Finance, and the China Earthquake Administration all named the directory as "request-based disclosure directory", which illustrated the function of the directory and facilitated public access to government information. The directory of the Ministry of Housing and Urban–Rural Development was more reasonably designed, as information on the homepage was linked to that in the directory, with the information on the homepage of the website being consistent with that in the directory, ensuring information accuracy and consistency.

Second, the performance on the validity of information links improved. By randomly selecting ten information links disclosed in the directory, the Project Team found that, the information links provided by 48 departments under the State Council were all valid, accounting for 81.4% (42 in 2011, 71.2%); the number of large-city governments was 42, accounting for 97.7% (36 in 2011, 83.7%).

Third, the directory was more accessible. The number of government agencies with multiple classifications of their directory increased significantly. For example, the number of the departments under the State Council with multiple classifications of their directory grew from 16 to 25. Also, the search functions of the directory were better equipped. In 2012, 39 departments under the State Council, 22 provincial-level governments, and 32 large-city governments provided the "simple search" function (34, 18, and 26 in 2011). Among them, the function provided by 36, 18, and 27 respectively was functional (27, 14 and 23 in 2011).

Fourth, less information update delays were found. For example, the Ministry of Housing and Urban–Rural Development website was able to update the information on the same day or the day before it was collected or produced.

Fifth, more attention was paid to details when constructing the directory. The 2012 evaluation found that the functions of the directory were constructed by many government agencies in a more careful and user-friendly way. The China Banking Regulatory Commission (CBRC) provided a "Information Search" function in the directory, through which information could be found by entering the issuing number of documents (for example, Order No. X [Year] of the China Banking Regulatory Commission or No. X [Year] of the China Banking Regulatory Commission). The National Energy Administration of China provided a "Search Help" function, which could facilitate users to understand the meaning of keywords quickly. The State Electricity Regulatory Commission (SERC) established a special website for disclosing electricity information, through which related government information of SERC, local SERCs and electric power enterprises was published and the design of the website was user-friendly. The State Administration of Foreign Exchange designed a "Correlation Comparison" function to promote the accuracy of search results.

Nevertheless, the major problems revealed in this respect were as follows.

First, some government agencies still did not develop the directory on their websites yet. Three departments under the State Council (the National Tourism Administration, the Ministry of Railways and the Ministry of Human Resources and Social Security) and one provincial-level government (Shandong Provincial Government) failed to provide the directory for same-level governments. One provincial-level government did not develop the directory for affiliated departments, two did not develop that for lower-level governments, and only two provided the directory for public enterprises and institutions. Among the large-city governments, one did not provide the directory for affiliated departments, three did not provide that for lower-level governments, and only 19 provided that for public enterprises and institutions. In addition, a few government agencies still just provided a list in the directory without developing any links directed to the information, which made the directory a mere formality. The directory developed by these government agencies failed to publish the full range of information or to facilitate public access to government information online.

Second, some sections were unreasonably designed. Some government agencies established sections titled "Openness of Government Affairs" and "Disclosure of

Government Information" at the same time, and some even established a special website for disclosing government information. However, due to a lack of coordination among different sections, information could not be disclosed at one web address. Fox example, SERC established both the directory for same-level government information disclosure on its websites and the directory on the dedicated website for disclosing electricity information. But the two directories lacked coordinated management, causing information inconsistency.

Third, the validity of information links contained in the directory needed to be improved. Some links were still invalid. For example, the links provided by eight departments under the State Council could not be all opened. As for the provincial-level governments, the Project Team randomly selected ten, ten, nine and six information links respectively from the directory of their same-level governments, affiliated departments, lower-level departments and public enterprises and institutions, to verify their validity. The affiliated departments whose information links were selected were local bureaus of health, bureaus of agriculture, bureaus of quality and technology supervision, administrations of industry and commerce, and food and drug administrations. Two information links were selected from each. According to the evaluation, the information links of the same-level governments of 22 provincial-level governments were all valid; those of the affiliated departments of 16 were all valid; those of the lower-level departments of 16 were all valid; and those of the public enterprises and institutions of one were valid (See Fig. 6.1). In addition, the sections of four departments under the State Council and one large-city government were empty.

The same verification was conducted on large-city governments. The affiliated departments whose information links were selected were also local bureaus of health, bureaus of agriculture, bureaus of quality and technology supervision, administrations of industry and commerce, and food and drug administrations. According to

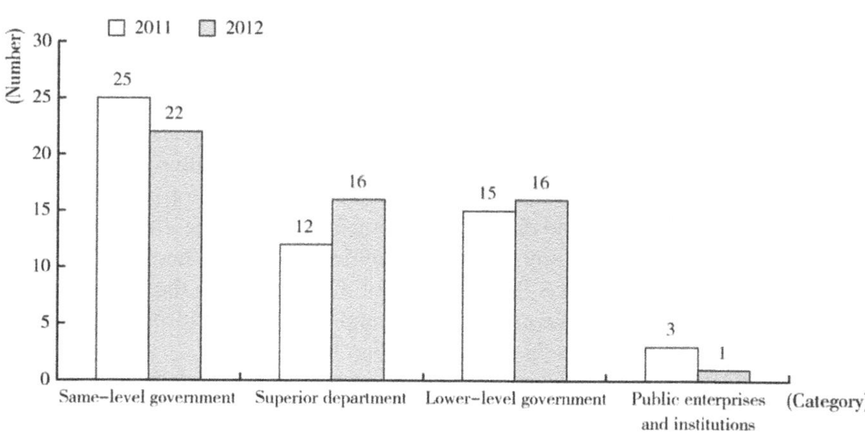

Fig. 6.1 A comparison of the validity of information links continued in the directory of provincial-level governments between 2011 and 2012

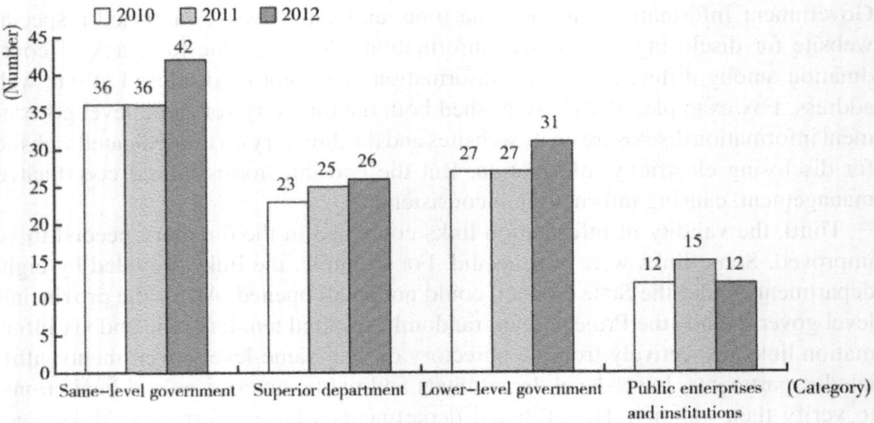

Fig. 6.2 A comparison of the validity of information links continued in the directory of large-city governments among 2010, 2011 and 2012

the evaluation, the information links of the same-level governments of 42 large-city governments were all valid; those of the affiliated departments of 26 were all valid; those of the lower-level departments of 31 were all valid; and those of the public enterprises and institutions of 12 were valid (see Fig. 6.2).

Fourth, the accessibility of the directory needed to be improved. For one thing, the problem of unreasonable classification of information was still prominent. Only 25 departments under the State Council, eight provincial-level governments and nine large-city governments provided multiple classifications in the directory with information contained in each one. The directory of others was either roughly or unreasonably classified, with some information being uncategorized while some other was repeatedly categorized. For another, the search functions of the directory were not well designed. The number of the departments under the State Council that provided the "Simple Search" function was 39 and those of 36 were valid; the corresponding number of provincial-level governments was only 22 and 18; and the corresponding number of large-city governments was only 32 and 27. The number of the departments under the State Council that provided multiple search functions was 38 and those of 22 were valid; the corresponding number of provincial-level governments was 21 and 13; and the corresponding number of large-city governments was 29 and 19. The number of the departments under the State Council that provided combined search functions was 38 and those of 17 were valid; the corresponding number of provincial-level governments was 17 and 7; and the corresponding number of large-city governments was 24 and 15 (see Fig. 6.3).

Fifth, the information contained in the directory was incomprehensive. The information contained in the directory of many governments was far from consistent with that disclosed on the homepage of their websites, and much of the information disclosed through the homepage was not included in the directory, making the directory less useful. According to the evaluation, 57 departments under the State

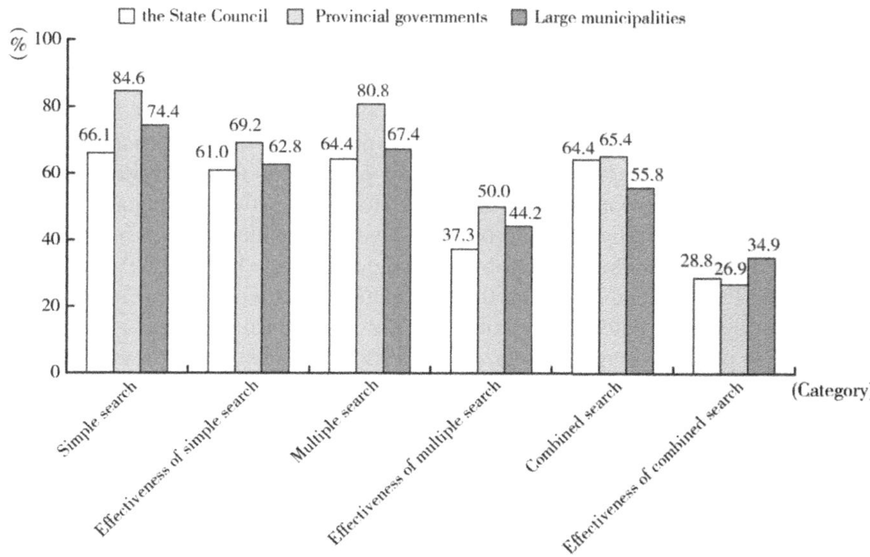

Fig. 6.3 A comparison of the search functions of the directory provided by the departments under the State Council, provincial-level governments and large-city governments in 2012

Council, 25 provincial-level governments and 36 large-city governments encountered the problem.

Sixth, information was randomly arranged. Due to the unreasonable or repetitive establishment of the sections and the directory, the information in the directory and that on the homepage of the websites were severely inconsistent. For example, instead of putting some information in the sections for normative documents, statistics, information about human resources where it should be, the information was put into the sections for news and events or notices and announcements. The messy arrangement of information inevitably led to the inconvenience of accessing information. even though some government agencies already provided the information, the effectiveness of disclosure was negatively affected as it was difficult to find the information.

6.3 Government Gazettes

The government gazette is a serial publication published by government agencies. It is mainly used to publish various government documents such as laws, guidelines, policies, and information on human resources. The *Law on Legislation of the People's Republic of China* stated that the government gazette is an important carrier for the publication of laws and regulations. The Regulations also considered it as a crucial platform for disclosing government information.

The evaluation found that the performance on releasing the government gazette was generally satisfactory. To begin with, government agencies at all levels highly valued the compilation and publication of government gazettes in recent years. As we have entered the information society, many also provided e-gazettes on their websites, which not only reduced cost but also facilitated public access to information. All of the 26 provincial-level governments provided e-gazettes on their websites and most of the websites were equipped with a special section for the government gazette. Also, the e-gazettes provided by all the provincial-level governments could be copied or downloaded. After a random selection and verification of the links of the government gazettes, the Project Team found all the information links were valid. Finally, many government agencies paid great attention to the accessibility of the e-gazette. Not only did they publish government gazettes in different stages, but also set up special search functions for government gazettes to facilitate public access to information.

Nevertheless, several problems in the release of the government gazette were identified.

First, some provincial-government agencies delayed publishing government gazettes. The government gazette is an official carrier for government documents and its publication plays an essential role in the timely release of government decisions. However, the evaluation found that some government gazettes were not released in a timely manner. For example, five out of the 26 provincial-level governments did not publish the government gazette of the previous month of the time when the evaluation was conducted.

Second, it was difficult to retrieve information from government gazettes. As the government gazette was published on a monthly basis, there might be hundreds of them on one website and it was both time-consuming and labor-intensive to check them one by one to retrieve information. Some technological means would be necessary to facilitate public access to information. However, the evaluation found that the performance on designing search functions for government gazettes was still less than satisfactory. Only the websites of 12 government agencies provided a search function for searching the title of the government gazette and those of nine were effective. Only the websites of nine provided a search function for searching the content of the government gazette, and those of only seven were effective.

Third, particular reading software was required to read the government gazette provided by a few governments, hindering public access to information. The publication of the government gazette was to facilitate public access to government information such as laws and regulations, guidelines and policies, as well as human resources information. Hence, the most suitable methods for public access needed to be employed. The government gazettes provided by some provincial-level governments were downloadable, in a PDF format, and well-designed. However, those of some others were just looking good and were difficult to be accessed by the public. Some were in a not commonly used CEB format in a very large file. Even though theirs looked good with both texts and pictures, particular reading software was needed to read. Also, the slow download speeds caused a waste of time.

6.4 Work Information

Work information is a reflection of government work and the disclosure of such information offers the public an opportunity to know the general situation, organization structuring, duties and responsibilities, and execution of duty of government agencies. It is also necessary to facilitate public access to government services, state guidelines and policies and effective supervision. The evaluation found that all the departments under the State Council managed to basic work information online to facilitate public access. To start with, most departments under the State Council managed to provide information on their officials. Seventeen provided complete information on their officials, including the names of the head and deputy leaders, their resumes, and their job responsibilities. Also, all departments managed to provide basic information about the responsibilities of the departments, their internal offices and lower-level departments. Finally, some managed to provide the work summary of the previous year, the work summaries of previous years, the key points of work of the year and the annual work plans of previous years (seven, 12, 13 and 17 respectively). Among them, seven departments under the State Council provided complete information on their annual work, namely, the Ministry of Science and Technology, the State Bureau of Religious Affairs, the General Administration of Quality Supervision, Inspection and Quarantine of the People's Republic of China, the State Intellectual Property Office, the State Administration for Industry and Commerce, the China Banking Regulatory Commission and the Ministry of Water Resources. Some also provided information about the development of the corresponding industries. For example, the State Intellectual Property Office compiled the annual developments of the intellectual property industry and provided survey information about the status quo of intellectual property protection in China, which imposed a positive effect on comprehensively promoting intellectual property protection in China. Developing and publishing work summaries and work plans to received public supervision was an act that took much courage. It was also a reflection of the high awareness of information disclosure of these departments.

Nevertheless, some problems that created the gap between the current situation and the construction of a transparent government were also identified in this respect.

First, work information was randomly arranged on the websites, making it difficult to be found. The work information on many websites was not gathered at one place on the homepage or was not categorized in a special section. Instead, it was scattered in different sections such as sections for government information discourse, agency profile and contact information. This led to the messy arrangement of work information, imposing a negative impact on public access to information, consultation and supervision.

Second, information about officials was not comprehensive. One department under the State Council does failed to provide a full list of its head and deputy leaders, five failed to provide the resumes, four just provided some of the resumes, 30 failed to provide job responsibilities, and 11 only provided the job responsibilities of some officials. Also, the Project Team was unable to find any information about its officials on the website of the Ministry of Railways.

Third, the performance on publishing the responsibilities of some departments was less than satisfactory. The disclosure of department responsibilities is conducive to strengthening the sense of responsibility of the staff, raising the level of work and service, standardizing work on supervision and management, and facilitating public access to government services. However, six departments under the State Council failed to provide any information on their responsibilities on their websites, namely, the Ministry of Agriculture, the Ministry of Human Resources and Social Security, the National Population and Family Planning Commission, the General Administration of Sport of China, the State Administration of Cultural Heritage and the State Tobacco Monopoly Bureau.

Fourth, information about division of labor of the internal offices of some departments was not comprehensive. Providing information about the structuring of their internal offices and divisions of functions was necessary for government agencies to facilitate public access to government services and was necessary for them to understand the working mechanism of government agencies. Three departments under the State Council failed to provide any information about the responsibilities of their internal offices at all, while 12 provided partial information; 14 failed to provide any information about the structuring of their internal offices, while 15 provide partial information; and only seven provided all the information about the divisions of responsibilities of their internal offices. In addition, to facilitate public consultation and better serve the public, government agencies shall provide information about the staff in charge of the internal offices and their contact details (contact number, email address, etc.) on their websites. However, only 20 provided the information about the person in charge of their internal offices, only 16 provided the contact number of their internal offices, and only one provided the email address of their internal offices.

Fifth, little information about public enterprises and institutions under the State Council was disclosed. As many government agencies has set up affiliated public enterprises and institutions, the disclosure of their basic information was also necessary for building a transparent government. However, among the 59 departments under the State Council, except for the China Insurance Regulatory Commission, the National Bureau of Letters and Calls and the National Bureau of Corruption Prevention, which did not have any directly affiliated enterprises and institutions, only 53 of the remaining departments provided a list of their affiliated departments. The departments without a list were: the Ministry of Foreign Affairs, the State Administration of Work Safety and the State Administration of Foreign Exchange. Of all the departments that provided the list, only 14 provided a description of the responsibilities of their affiliated agencies, while none of them provided comprehensive contact information (including contact number and email address) of their affiliated agencies. Even some managed to provide a list of their affiliated agencies, the links to the agencies were incomprehensive or some of them were invalid. The links of only 16 were all valid.

Sixth, insufficient attention was paid to the disclosure of annual work information. Information about annual work includes the annual work summary and the annual work plan. The annual work summary is a review and analysis of the work conducted in the past year. In the summary, experience and lessons were drawn and developed into regularities to guide future work and practical activities. A work plan can help identify the tasks and purposes of work, avoid blindness in work, make gradual and manageable work schedule, and it is an important guarantee for improving work efficiency and successfully completing the work. For a long time, such information was not allowed to be disclosed, and citizens could provide objective evaluation and supervision of government performance as they did not have access to the details of the work conducted by government agencies. In the evaluation, only seven departments managed to provide comprehensive annual work information, while many failed to provide such information, or the information provided was not well-organized, or provided the information occasionally, or some did not have a special section for the disclosure of annual work information, making it difficult to find such information.

6.5 Normative Documents

The evaluation found that the performance of different agencies on releasing normative documents varied. On the plus side, governments at all levels performed relatively well in setting up sections for normative documents, updating normative documents, guaranteeing the validity of links to normative documents, and filing normative documents of local governments.

First, most government websites established a special section for normative documents. According to the evaluation, only one department under the State Council failed to do so.

Second, the performance on the update of normative documents was satisfactory. Most government agencies issued the normative documents in 2012 on their websites, 33 departments under the State Council, 16 provincial-level governments, and 34 large-city governments to be exact.

Third, most information links directed to normative documents were valid. To verify the validity of information links, the Project Team randomly selected ten normative documents on the website of every government agency, all the information links provided by 53 departments under the State Council (same as in 2011), 25 provincial-level governments and all large-city governments were valid.

Fourth, the performance of local governments on filing normative documents was relatively satisfactory. Most local governments disclosed information about the filing of normative documents either on their government portals or on the websites of their legal departments, 23 provincial-level governments and 22 large-city governments to be exact.

Nevertheless, some problems should also be acknowledged.

First, in terms of information disclosure itself, three major problems existed: the websites were not operating well, the sections for normative documents were constructed in a mess, and information was difficult to obtain.

To start with, the websites of some local legal departments were in poor operation. According to the evaluation, the websites of some local legal departments were operated in a very slow, unstable manner, and some of them were sometimes inaccessible. What's worse, some governments even did not have a website for legal departments, such as the ones in Anshan, Datong and Fuzhou.

Also, sections for normative documents were randomly established. Most government agencies developed more than two sections on the homepages of their websites, including sections for laws and regulations, policy documents, notices and announcements, and normative documents. The information listed in the sections was in disorder and misleading, with no clear boundaries set. The evaluation found that 56 departments under the State Council, 26 provincial-level governments and 43 large-city governments developed more than two sections for normative documents. This also indicated that the definition of normative documents was not clear enough, and there was a lack of uniform criteria and standards to define what kinds of documents were normative ones while what kinds of documents were not.

Then, information published in different sections on the same website was inconsistent. Most websites provided sections for normative documents both on the homepages and in the directory for government information disclosure. However, the information disclosed in the two sections was not synchronized nor consistent. This problem occurred on the websites of 52 departments under the State Council, 19 provincial-level governments, and 38 large-city governments, hindering public access to information.

In addition, the accessibility of normative documents was poor. Normative documents published on the websites of most government agencies were not categorized. Only five departments under the State Council and one provincial-level governments categorized normative documents by items. None of the large-city governments did so. Only two provincial-level governments categorized normative documents by departments. None of the departments under the State Council or large-city governments did so. This seemingly trivial act of categorizing documents was easily conducted by government agencies. However, it played an important role in enabling people to find the information they need quickly and accurately.

Second, the disclosure of the preparation process of normative documents was less than satisfactory. In recent years, significant improvements have been made on the disclosure of the preparation process of laws and regulations. However, that of the normative documents was still relatively less than satisfactory. This was mainly manifested in the fact that not many drafts of normative documents were released, not so many channels for gathering public opinions were provided, and a very limited number of responses were given to the public opinions solicited. Only 27 departments under the State Council, 11 provincial-level governments and 12 large-city governments provided a valid special section for publishing the public opinions gathered. Twenty departments under the State Council, eight provincial-level governments and seven large-city departments provided channels for gathering public opinions in the other sections on their websites though they did not have a special section. Only 27departments under the State Council, 12 provincial-level governments and11 large-city governments provided up to the drafts of three normative documents with valid information links contained. Among all the government agencies evaluated, only one provincial-level government provided responses on the public opinions solicited. In addition, the drafts of normative documents and channels for gathering public opinions provided on many government portal websites or local legal departments websites were about their affiliated agencies or lower-level government instead of that about the same-level governments.

Third, interpretations of important normative documents were generally were generally lacking. Some normative documents were as closely related to public interests and complicated as many legal documents such as regulations and laws. Hence, the necessary explanations for the purpose of development, guiding concepts, and how to understand and implement the related important systems should be provided by government agencies to facilitate the public to understand the relevant systems and implement them. However, the performance on disclosing such information was far from satisfactory. Many government agencies failed to provide a section for interpretations and related information on their websites. Only 38 departments under the State Council, 16 provincial-level governments and 24 large-city governments developed a section for normative documents interpretations with valid information links contained. Only 12 departments under the State Council, seven provincial-level governments and nine large-city governments provided interpretations of normative documents in other sections with valid information links contained. Also, Also, some interpretations were not disclosed in time. Only 21 departments under the State Council, 15 provincial-level governments and 22 large-city governments managed to provide interpretations of normative documents with valid information links for the previous six months.

Fourth, the disclosure of information about the abolishment and modification of normative documents was far from satisfactory. A regular removal of the normative documents that have been published and disclosure of information about the abolished, modified or currently effective normative documents was conducive for the public to know the basis for obtaining relevant government services. It could also contribute to standardizing government agencies' law-based services and was an essential part of constructing a law-based and transparent government. However, the performance of many governments was less than satisfactory. Only 37 departments under the State Council, 22 provincial-level governments and 37 large-city governments provided information about the abolishment of normative documents. Only five departments under the State Council, three provincial-level governments and 13 large-city governments provided the information of 2012. Only eight departments under the State Council, six provincial-level governments and 14 large-city governments provided information about the modification of normative documents. Only one department under the State Council, two provincial-level governments and seven large-city governments provided the information of 2012.

6.6 Information About Environmental Protection

In the 2012 evaluation, besides the 26 provincial-level governments, 43 large-city governments were also evaluated. The release of the information about air quality, water quality, the regulation of solid waste, radiation safety, environmental impact assessment on construction projects and environmental administrative penalty results was evaluated.

The evaluation revealed huge differences between the performance of provincial-governments and large-city governments in this respect. Based on the overall evaluation scores, provincial-level governments performed well while large-city governments generally performed poorly on the disclosure of information about environmental protection. In general, the following highlights were worthy of recognition.

First, the websites of environmental administrations were generally well constructed. All the evaluation objects established websites for environmental administrations. Also, all the websites except those of three large-city governments could be opened.

Second, comprehensive information was disclosed by the environmental administrations of provincial-level governments. eighteen out of the 26 provincial-level governments provided information on the air quality of the regions within their jurisdiction on a daily basis; 24 provided information water quality of the major rivers of the regions within their jurisdiction on a monthly basis; 24 provided the information about hazardous waste business licenses; 25 provided the information about issuance of radiation safety permits. The number of provincial-level governments that provided the information about the acceptance of the examination and approval of environmental impact assessment of construction projects, the information about environmental impact assessment of projects constructed in 2012 prior to the approval of the projects, and the information about environmental impact assessment of projects constructed in 2015 after the approval of the projects was 20, 21 and 22 respectively. Seventeen provincial-level governments provided the information about environmental protection inspection and acceptance of construction projects completed in 2012 prior to the approval and 23 provided the information about protection inspection and acceptance of construction projects completed in 2015 after the approval. Twenty-two provided the information about the institution undertaking environmental impact assessment of construction projects.

Third, the air quality disclosure system provided by some government agencies was effective, practical and understandable. For example, not only did the air quality report was provided on a daily basis but also in real time. Some also provided air quality tendency chart of a specific period in their air quality disclosure systems. The systems of some employed satellite maps, making it quite easy for users to understand.

Fourth, some government agencies provided detailed monthly reports on the quality of drinking water. Some governments not only provided monthly reports on water quality of major rivers within their jurisdiction, but also weekly reports.

Some provinces, Guizhou for example, provided two kinds of monthly reports on water quality, namely, the monthly water quality report of urban centralized drinking water sources and that of rural centralized drinking water sources. The information provided by both was comprehensive.

Nevertheless, the following problems were revealed in the evaluation.

First, sections were unreasonably established and information was randomly arranged. The evaluation found that, instead of developing special sections for solid waste management, radiation safety management, environmental impact assessment of construction projects, environmental protection inspection and acceptance upon the completion of construction projects, related information was placed in the sections of notices and announcements or news and events by many government agencies. And due to the complexity of information in these sections, it was difficult for the public to find the information they needed quickly.

Second, some information that should be made public was not disclosed. Among all the environmental administrations of provincial-level governments, only nine provided forecast information about the air quality of the regions within their jurisdiction (34.62%); only ten provided a monthly report of the water quality of the major rivers of the regions within their jurisdiction (38.46%); only 11 provided information about examination and approval of the qualifications of the application for trans-provincial transfer of hazardous waste or disposal of waste electrical and electronic products (42.31%); only 12 provided all the information about the acceptance of environmental impact assessment for construction projects, the information about environmental impact assessment of projects constructed in 2012 prior to the approval of the projects, and the information about environmental impact assessment of projects constructed in 2012 after the approval of the projects (46.15%); only nine provided the information about the acceptance of application for environmental protection inspection and acceptance upon the completion of construction projects in 2012 (34.62%); only six provided all the information about the acceptance of application for environmental protection inspection and acceptance upon the completion of construction projects, the information about environmental protection inspection and acceptance of construction projects completed in 2012 prior to the approval, and the information about protection inspection and acceptance of construction projects completed in 2012 after the approval (23.08%). The performance of the environmental administrations of large-city governments was even poorer, with the data corresponding to the aforementioned indicators of the provincial government being 11 (25.58%), 20 (46.51%), 13 (30.23%), 15 (34.88%), six (13.95%) and four (9.30%) respectively.

Third, some failed to continuously disclose information about environmental protection. Among all the environmental administrations of the 43 large-city governments, only 14 provided continuous air quality forecast information on the day of the survey and kept all the precious information online; only three provided the monthly reports of water quality in major rivers of the previous six months; and only eight provided the monthly reports of drinking water quality evaluations of the previous six months.

Fourth, information update delays occurred. Among all the environmental administrations of the 43 large-city governments, only 19 provided information about hazardous waste management licenses of the previous six months before the day the evaluation was conducted; only five provided information about approval of disposal qualification of discarded electronic products of the same period; and only nine provided information about approval of radiation safety licenses of the previous six months before the day the evaluation was conducted. Also, among all the environmental administrations of the provincial-level governments, only 21 provided information about hazardous waste management licenses of the previous six months before the day the evaluation was conducted; only seven provided information about approval of the application for trans-provincial transfer of hazardous waste of the same period; and only 21 provided information about approval of radiation safety licenses of the previous six months before the day the evaluation was conducted.

Fifth, some of the information disclosed was overly simplified. The purpose of the disclosure of information about environmental protection was to enable the public to obtain relevant information and to promote public participation in environmental protection. However, if the information provided was overly simplified, this goal could not be achieved. When disclosing information about the acceptance of application for environmental protection inspection and acceptance upon the completion of construction projects, the information about environmental protection inspection and acceptance of construction projects completed in 2012 prior to the approval, and the information about protection inspection and acceptance of construction projects completed in 2012 after the approval. many environmental administrations did not provide a brief version of the reports which could be easier understood by the public. Some just provided the information of the past month or months in a list, with only some brief information such as time of approval, approval number and file name in it, without providing a detailed description of the construction project and environmental impact assessment. Also, he information about protection inspection and acceptance of construction projects completed in 2012 after the approval provided by some departments contained only a title "Reply to XXX Project", and no content was included.

Sixth, the work of disclosing information about environmental protection was not taken seriously. For example, in a list titled "Approved projects for acceptance" provided by one municipal environmental administration, it showed that three pieces of information was disclosed 15 days after the investigation was conducted and in another list titled "Approved construction projects", it also showed that the release time of one piece of information was March 22nd, 2013, both of which were impossible. Another example was that same monthly report on the water quality of the major rivers was provided both in the "Environmental Quality" section and in the "Environmental Monitoring" section on the website of one provincial environmental administration. However, the information in one was disclosed two months earlier than that in another. In addition, the monthly report on the water quality of the major rivers should be a summary of the water quality in a month. However, the release time of one report in the "Environmental Quality" section on the website of one provincial environmental administration was at the beginning of the month.

6.7 Information About Food Safety

In the evaluations of the previous two years, the focus was the disclosure of information about catering services license and related law enforcement of large-city governments. However, in the 2012 evaluation, the focus changed into the disclosure of information about food safety regulation by the bureaus of quality and technical supervision of large-city governments. The indicators included food safety policies and regulations, food production licenses (including licensing procedures, guidelines and issuance of licenses), filing of entrusted food processing of food manufacturing enterprises (including filing procedures, guidelines and filing information), food safety supervision and inspection, qualifications of food production enterprises and basic knowledge about food safety disclosed by the bureaus of quality and technical supervision of large-city governments.

According to the evaluation, the following aspects of food safety information disclosure were worthy of recognition.

First, great importance was attached to the release of policies and regulations. The bureaus of quality and technical supervision of 39 large-city governments provided policies and regulations on food safety, accounting for 90.7%. Those of 26 large-city governments provided normative documents on food safety regulation applied to their own cities with valid information links.

Second, significant attention was to the disclosure of information about food safety regulation. The bureaus of quality and technical supervision of 37 large-city governments provided application guidelines for food production licenses; those of 24 provided the results of food production licenses; 21 provided the guidelines for filing of entrusted food processing of food manufacturing enterprises; 30 provided spot check results of food safety supervision; and 32 provided basic knowledge about food safety.

Third, information accessibility was highly valued. For example, Guangzhou Municipal Quality and Technical Supervision Agency provided scene-based services in the administrative approval process, which facilitated public access to government services. Also, the information provided by the agency in the "Announcement on the Spot Inspection Results of Food Safety" section on a regular basis contained corresponding food safety knowledge and consumer advice.

Nevertheless, the overall performance of the bureaus of quality and technical supervision of large-city governments on the disclosure of information about food safety was still less than satisfactory and the following problems should be acknowledged.

First, websites should be better constructed. The website of Haikou Municipal Quality and Technical Supervision Agency was still under construction. The websites of some others either could not be opened sometimes or were just a mere formality with no valid information provided.

Second, the performance on the disclosure of importance information about food safety regulation was less than satisfactory. This was mainly manifested in the following aspects.

The first aspect was the disclosure of normative documents on food safety regulation. To meet the regulatory requirements, local governments formulated some normative documents applicable locally according to the requirements of the related laws at the higher level, and the disclosure of these documents was the premise for regulation. However, only 26 bureaus of quality and technical supervision published the normative documents related to local food safety regulation on their websites, accounting simply for 60.5%.

The second aspect was the disclosure of information about food safety administrative approval. The bureaus of quality and technical supervision of five local governments failed to provide guidelines for applying for food production licenses, and only five provided comprehensive information about food production licenses (including various procedures such as issuing new licenses, reissuing, changing, correcting, and revocation). Only 21 provided guidelines for filing of entrusted food processing of food manufacturing enterprises and only nine provided comprehensive guidelines (including the basis for administrative approval, the office, office locations, contact details, documents to be submitted, services procedures and time limit). The results of administrative approval were vitally important for the public to know the qualifications of food production enterprises. However, the disclosure of such information was still less than satisfactory. Only the bureaus of quality and technical supervision of 24 local governments provided the results of the issuance of food production licenses, and only five disclosed the results of filing of entrusted food processing of food manufacturing enterprises.

The third aspect was the disclosure of spot check results of food production supervision. The disclosure of such information not only indicated that regulatory authorities were functioning properly, but also enabled the public to keep abreast of current food safety situation. However, according to the evaluation, only the bureaus of quality and technical supervision of 30 local governments provided such information and only ten of them provided information updated to one month before the evaluation was conducted.

The fourth aspect was the disclosure of information about food safety credit files of food production enterprises. Strengthening the integrity management of food safety is both a statutory duty stipulated by the *Food Safety Law of the People's Republic of China* and an important means of innovating food safety regulation. However, only 16 bureaus of quality and technical supervision provided food safety credit files of food production enterprises, and even fewer provided detailed information about the enterprises. Fox example, only the bureaus of quality and technical supervision of Xuzhou, Ningbo and Changchun provided comprehensive information about food production enterprises, and only the agencies of Hangzhou, Nanjing, Ningbo and Xiamen provided the records of illegal behaviors of the enterprises.

The fifth aspect was the disclosure of basic knowledge about food safety. The disclosure of basic knowledge about food safety enables to raise public awareness of food safety and their self-protection, and is also an important supportive means for food safety regulation. However, according to the evaluation, the bureaus of quality and technical supervision of 11 large-city governments failed to provide any basic knowledge about food safety. Also, for those that did provided related information, the amount of information provided was quite limited.

Third, information was randomly arranged. Many websites were not equipped with a special section for food safety information, and the information was scattered everywhere, often leading to invalid search and inquiry. The main manifestations of this problems were: the laws, regulations and policy documents on food safety were just placed together with many other polices and regulations without being categorized; the results of spot check of food safety supervision was just scattered in the "Notices and Announcements" section where hundreds or even thousands pieces of information were listed; no special section for basic knowledge about food safety was set, and related information was placed in sections such as the "Consumer Guidelines" section; and the guidelines for application for food production licenses and filing of entrusted food processing of food manufacturing enterprises were not put in the sections such as the "Application Guidelines" section, where they could be easily found.

Fourth, information update delays occurred. Many websites had not been updated for a long time, and the information disclosed was seriously lagging behind the actual situation. Among all the bureaus of quality and technical supervision evaluated, only 12 issued the application results of food production licenses within half a year; only four disclosed information about the filing of entrusted food processing of food manufacturing enterprises within six months, namely, Nanjing, Zhengzhou, Guangzhou and Shenzhen; only ten provided the results of spot check of food supervision within the last month; none provided information about credits files of food safety within one month; and only 13 provided basic knowledge about food safety within six months.

Fifth, information was inconsistent. By conducting a spot check on the food safety information disclosed on the municipal government portals and that on the websites of the bureaus of quality and technical supervision, the Project Team found that the problem of inconsistent information occurred everywhere.

6.8 Information About Administrative Approval

In 2012, the Project Team continued to assess the disclosure of information about administrative approval by local governments and. The evaluation objects were 26 provincial-level governments and 43 large-city governments. According to the evaluation, the following aspects of disclosure were worthy of recognition.

First, administrative approval websites were well constructed. Most local governments managed to set up a dedicated administrative approval website, equip them with different sections and disclose information about administrative approval through it. All of the 43 large-city governments established physical government service centers. Although eight of them did not have websites for their service centers, four established dedicated websites for online examination and approval, and three developed the "Online Service" section on their government portals. Among the 26 provinces and municipalities, ten established physical government service centers, of which nine established websites for their service centers, and one developed the "Online Service" section on its government portal. In comparison, among 16 provinces and municipalities that did not have a physical government service center, seven constructed dedicated websites for online approval and nine developed the "Online Service" section on their government portals.

Second, the performance on the release of basic information about physical service centers was satisfactory. These websites were often equipped with a "Center Profile" section on their homepage, providing such information as general introduction to the center and specific contact details including the address, traffic routes (for both self-driving and public transport options), location map, contact number, email address and office hours. The information provided was quite clear, and people could obtain related information just by a click of their mouse. It also made it more convenient for the public to gain government services and improved the efficiency of governments work on administrative approval.

Third, comprehensive information about items subject to approval was provided. Many administrative approval websites managed to provide the list of categorized items subject to approval. For example, they might be categorized by the competent departments, service users, and services scenarios to facilitate public access to government services in a targeted way. Also, information about items subject to approval provided by most websites was quite comprehensive, with the list of items subject to approval, procedures, guidelines, online consulting and frequently asked questions included.

Fourth, the performance on the disclosure of dynamic information about administrative approval was quite satisfactory. The special section set up by many websites showed scrolling dynamic information, while some websites even set up special section for tracking items, enabling the public to keep track of the processes and results of their applications.

However, some problems were also identified, and there still existed a gap between administrative approval performance and the requirements for reforming the administrative approval system, transforming government functions and establishing a service-oriented and transparent government.

First of all, improvements needed to be made on the construction of administrative approval websites. According to the evaluation, although all the 43 large-city governments established physical government service centers, Fushun Municipal Government still did not have any administrative approval website. Among the ten provincial-level governments that established physical government service centers, only nine equipped the centers with corresponding websites. The Project Team found that the governments with a physical service center performed better on the disclosure of such information, as they had a specialized department to handle with items subject to approval concentratedly, while those that did not have one performed poorer.

Second, administrative approval websites were unstably operated. For example, the websites of a municipal government service center and a provincial online government affairs hall sometimes could not be opened. The new version of the websites of one provincial government affair hall was poorly coordinated with its old version, and the section for items subject to approval could not be opened.

Third, sections were not well developed on administrative approval websites and some information links were invalid. The section for internal regulation on administrative approval websites enables the public to understand the rules and regulations of the government service center, strengthening public supervision. However, only four provincial government service center websites provided the section for internal regulations with up to five information links valid. Among the 29 government service center websites that provided the section, the number of those that provided up to five valid information links was 28. Also, the disclosure of the list of items subject to approval on the websites can enable the public to find corresponding guidelines much easier. The government service center websites or administrative approval websites of 40 large cities provided the list of the items, 39 of which had up to five valid links while one did not. Twenty-four provincial-level governments provided the list and all of them provided up to five valid information links.

Fourth, information on administrative approval websites was randomly arranged. For example, instead of being placed in one specific section, contact information on some websites was scattered and fragmented, hindering public access to the information. Information about internal regulations on most websites was put in the section for laws and regulations. However, laws and regulations were just put into one section without being categorized, which made it hard for the public to find the internal regulations. Also, the dynamic information about the items subject to approval was both disclosed on the homepage of the websites and in the special section. However, as the information released in the two places was sometimes inconsistent, users needed to open the links to keep track of the items, which brought about unnecessary difficulties for the public.

Fifth, information about items subject to approval was inconsistent. A section for online services was developed on almost all portals of provincial-level and large-city governments, as well as on the websites of their affiliated departments. Most of the sections were for administrative approvals. By comparing the information about items subject to approval, the application guidelines on specific items and other information disclosed on these websites, the Project Team found that the problem of information inconsistency was widespread. For example, only four provincial-level governments and eight large-city governments provided consistent information about the list of items and the application guidelines on specific items.

Sixth, information related to administrative approval was incomprehensive. The evaluation revealed that the information provided on most websites was incomplete. To start with, contact information was incomplete. To facilitate public access to government services, basic information of the government service centers, such as address, contact number, email address, transportation routes (both drive routes and public transport transfer options), location map and office hours (specific opening hours) shall be provided on the administrative approval websites. However, only two of the large-city governments managed to provide all the aforementioned information, while none of the provincial-level governments did so. Also, information about administrative approval items was not complete. To facilitate public access, information such as the basis for administrative approval, approval conditions, documents to be submitted, approval procedures, approval duration, office address, and contact number shall be provided on the websites. By randomly selecting ten pieces of information disclosed on the websites, only ten provincial-level governments and five large-city governments managed to provide all the aforementioned information in their application guidelines. In addition, the dynamic information about items under approval was also incomplete. To enable citizens to keep track of their applications, information on competent departments, items under approval, application time, approval status (e.g. under approval or approval completed) shall be disclosed. According to the evaluation, 35 large-city governments developed a section for the dynamic information, four of which provided all the aforementioned information; 13 provincial-level governments provided the section, only two of which provided all the aforementioned dynamic information.

6.9 Request-Based Information Disclosure

In 2012, the evaluation of request-based information disclosure still focused on the validity of the online request platforms and government agencies' replies to requests.

In the evaluation, the Project Team filed requests with government agencies for the disclosure of information about officials' appointment and removal (including positions held by and the number of officials; gender ratios, academic qualifications and areas of experts of the officials newly appointed; and the number of officials disciplined, causes and types of punishments) from January, 2012 to the end of September, 2012. Neither the purpose of requests nor the identity of applicants was provided in the process. The requests were submitted through online request platforms. For those without an online request platform, requests were sent in hardcopy through China Post Express (EMS). In the meantime, the Project Team also filed requests with the finance departments or bureaus of 26 provincial-level governments through the China Post Express (EMS) for the disclosure of information about government procurement. To be specific, the two pieces of information were a complete commodity catalogue under the provincial government's procurement agreement of October, 2012, and the complete records of transaction under the agreements from January 1 to October 1, 2012. In this process, the copies of applicants' ID card, the purpose of requests issued by the Law Institute were provided. The two items were submitted separately, in case that some agencies would refuse to provide the requested information on the grounds that the requests did not comply with the requirement of "one request for one item".

In the evaluation, the following problems were identified, which should be taken seriously.

First of all, many government agencies still failed to provide a functional online request platform. Only 19 departments under the State Council (15 in 2011), 13 provincial-level governments (14 in 2011), and 23 large-city governments (26 in 2011) developed a valid online request platform. Thirty-two departments under the

State Council (27 in 2011), 13 provincial-level governments (six in 2011), and ten large-city governments (two in 2011) received requests submitted via emails. Two departments under the State Council explicitly indicated that they would not accept government information disclosure requests. One provincial-level government and three large-city governments did not have a valid online request platform yet.

Second, the staff's awareness and level of service at a few government agencies needed to be promoted. When contacting with the staff responsible for government information disclosure at some government agencies, the Project Team found them impatient, arrogant and they only cared about what was convenient for themselves. One at a local government verbally informed the applicant to search information on their portals, saying that he/she was too busy at work to handle the requests received. One at a department under the State Council verbally informed the applicant in one time of several documents to be further submitted, and repeatedly rejected the applicant's request for a written reply. One at a department under the State Council refused to send a "Notice of Supplementary Documents" to the applicant on the grounds that verbal reply was reasonable, provided delayed response by the excuse of too many requests received, and asked the applicant to further provide the copy of ID card to prove that the applicant was a Chinese citizen. One at a department under the State Council required the applicant to bear the postal cost (what in the envelope was the notice "the requested government information does not fall into the scope of disclosure"). The applicant's proposal of delivering it via registered mail to lower the cost was rejected on the grounds that registered mails could not be tracked to see if it has been delivered to the applicant and going to the post office was too troublesome. This was a practice only based on their own interests and let applicants pay for that and it went against with the efforts of establishing a service-oriented government. One at a local government required the applicant to send some necessary documents to withdraw requests, so as to satisfy their "procedure needs".

The staff at some government agencies only made a perfunctory effort at work. The problem of buck-passing occurred among government agencies. Some replied to applicants saying "the information requested is possessed by other departments such as the CPC Organization Department, the Personnel Department, the State Bureau of Civil Servants or the Discipline Inspection Committee". Some responded that they could not provide the contact details of other departments as they did not have. In addition, some just did not take their work seriously, and the responses they sent to the Project Team were revised based on those to other applicants without deleting the original requests.

Third, the practice of excessively collecting applicants' personal information and asking for the purpose of requests showed an upward trend. The Project Team submitted requests via email to 57 departments under the State Council. Twenty-nine of them explicitly required in the request forms or in the guidelines that personal information shall be provided. One did not have explicit requirements, but the request could not be submitted without providing personal information. Nine informed the applicant by calls, emails or mailing that personal information should be further provided. As for another eight departments that did not contacted or responded to the applicant via any method, the Project Team was uncertain as to whether personal information was required. Also, 20 departments under the State Council explicitly required for the purpose of requests, 18 informed the applicant to supplement the purpose when they noticed that it had not been provided. Likewise, as for the eight departments that did not contacted the applicant, the Project Team was uncertain as to whether the purpose of requests was required. The Project Team successfully submitted requests to 25 provincial-level governments via email. Among them, 20 explicitly stated that personal information shall be provided, four asked the applicant to supplement personal information. The Project Team was uncertain as to whether one provincial-level government required such information. Six explicitly stated that the purpose of requests shall be provided, three asked the applicant to provide the purpose when they noticed that it had not been provided. Likewise, and the Project Team was uncertain as to whether one provincial-level government required such information. The Project Team also successfully submitted requests to 42 large-city governments via email. Among them, 24 explicitly stated that personal information shall be provided, three asked the applicant to supplement personal information, and the Project Team was uncertain as to whether six large-city governments required such information. Seventeen explicitly stated that the purpose of requests shall be provided, four asked the applicant to provide the purpose when they noticed that it had not been provided. Likewise, the Project Team was uncertain as to whether six large-city governments required such information.

Fourth, the performance on replying to requests was less than satisfactory. Many government agencies failed to reply within the statutory period. In the evaluation, 37 departments under the State Council, 20 provincial-level governments and 26 large-city governments managed to provide timely replies. Many replied to the Project Team long after the requests had been submitted via online platforms or the time when the EMS delivery was received. A few even replied on the last day of December 2012, falsely claiming that they had just received the requests, and it was obviously a consequence of their low work efficiency. Some did not inform the applicant that the replies were postponed or further documents needed to be submitted until the statutory period was about to expire. This revealed that they might abuse the system of statutory period. Some informed the applicant via telephone that further documents were needed just one or two days before the end of the statutory period, saying that it was necessary to postpone the replies. Some even informed the applicant via telephone one or two days before the end of the statutory period that the request had been transferred to another department, and replies would be provided after discussions. Hence, the time limit would be postponed to the next "15 working days". This practice of contacting the applicant when the time limit was about to expire greatly reduced work efficiency and caused inconvenience for applicants.

Fifth, the content of replies provided by government agencies was less than satisfactory. In the evaluation, the replies received from government agencies could be roughly divided into the following six categories.

(1) Providing the information requested. The Ministry of Science and Technology, the Civil Aviation Administration of China, and the State Bureau of Religious Affairs had classified the information before sending them to applicants.

Ningbo Municipal People's Government replied the applicant with the information about personnel appointment and removal that had been requested without classifying it.

(2) Informing applicants that the information requested had been voluntarily disclosed. Some government agencies informed applicants of instructions on where to find the requested information, while some others just informed that applicants should search the information on the websites of governments or on government gazettes. The project team found that sometimes no information could be found if applicants follow the instructions of some government agencies.

(3) Claiming that requests should be resubmitted separately to follow the principle of "one request for one item". Some government agencies claimed that the requests made were asking for many categories of information. Hence, requests should be resubmitted separately.

(4) Confusing the relations between voluntary disclosure and request-based disclosure. One example was that the staff at Lanzhou Municipal People's Government claimed that information that did not included in the directory of government information disclosure could not be requested.

(5) Claiming that the government agency did not have the information requested. The offices of some local governments claimed that the information about personnel appointment and removal was not possessed by them, and applicants should file requests with departments responsible for organizing, personnel and supervision, and the contact details of the relevant department were provided by a very few government agencies. The finance departments of some local governments informed that they did not have the information about the government agreement procurement system. Some claimed that they did not have the information as they had not compiled it.

(6) Refusing to disclose the information requested. Some refused to disclose the information about personnel appointment and removal on the grounds that they had not compiled and did not have the responsibility to do so. Some just claimed that the requested government information was out of the scope of disclosure as per the Regulations. Some claimed that the information requested was involving secrets without giving any explanations. Some claimed that the information about government procurement was trade secret. Some claimed that the information about personnel appointment and removal was involving personal privacy. Some even claimed that the information about personnel appointment and removal was only a type of internal information.

6.10 The Annual Report on Government Information Disclosure

According to the evaluation, the overall performance on the disclosure of the 2011 annual report was better than that of 2010.

First, most government agencies managed to carefully prepare the annual reports of the same-level governments in accordance with the Regulations and issue the reports within the statutory period. In the evaluation, the Project Team searched the annual reports on the websites of government agencies, on those of the superior governments, and on other websites. As of 24:00 on March 31, 2012, 57 out of the 59 departments under the State Council, all the 26 provincial-level governments and 43 large-city governments had released their annual reports for the previous year within the prescribed period. Only the National Corrupt Prevention Organization did not release the annual report in time, and the State Administration of Cultural Heritage only provided statistics on government information disclosure in 2011 instead of publishing an annual report.

Second, the annual reports of many government agencies were comprehensive and detailed. The annual reports of many provided a whole landscape of the work of same-level governments on government information disclosure in 2011. They contained detailed information about voluntary disclosure, request-based disclosure and related administrative reconsideration, proceedings, and complaints, identified the major problems of same-level government's work on information disclosure, and proposed corresponding measures for potential improvements.

Third, new forms of disclosing the annual reports were employed. For example, the annual reports of some government agencies were published in the form of e-magazines with comprehensive content and clear data contained.

Fourth, the performance of providing statistics about voluntary disclosure in the annual report was improved comparing with that of 2011. Fifty-four departments under the State Council (52 in 2011), 26 provincial-level governments (same as 2011) and 17 large-city governments (14 in 2011) provided the data on voluntary disclosure categorized both by the forms of voluntary disclosure and by the categories of items involved.

Fifth, more importance was attached by government agencies at all levels to the inter-organizational coordination of the release of the annual report. To facilitate public access to information, the General Office of the State Council concentratedly provided the 2011 annual reports disclosed by the departments under the State Council and provincial-level governments on the Central Government Portal (www.gov.cn). Also, some provincial-level governments and large-city governments released the annual reports of their affiliated departments and lower-level governments on their government portals. This significantly improved the performance on the disclosure of the annual report and also strongly facilitated the work.

However, some problems concerning the release and preparation of the annual reports were also revealed in the evaluation. For example, the work was not well regulated or relevant standards were missing.

First of all, some government agencies delayed releasing the annual reports. Although some government agencies released their annual reports as early as the beginning of January, most of them disclosed theirs almost at the end of March. Statistics showed that only three departments under the State Council, one provincial-level government, and 13 large-city governments managed to publish their annual reports before the 5th of March. By contrast, 32 departments under the State Council, 20 provincial-level government, and 18 large-city governments published theirs within six days before the deadline (from 26th to 31st of March).

Second, a very few government agencies failed to take the required deadline of releasing the annual reports seriously. For one thing, a very few departments arbitrarily changed the deadline. For example, as stated in the section for the annual report on the website of Jilin Provincial People's Government, the deadline shall be March 30, 2012, but the annual report had not been released even when the Project Team checked at 11:18 on March 31, 2012. For another, the deadline stated on the website of a few governments was not consistent with that stated in the annual reports. An example was that the deadline stated on the website of State Oceanic Administration was March 30, 2012, while that in the annual report was March 21, 2012.

Third, the performance on developing the section for the annual report was less than satisfactory. The construction of a section for the annual report enables to disclose the reports in one place and can facilitate public access to information. However, there were still some websites not equipped with the section. The websites of three departments under the State Council, namely, the National Tourism Administration, the State Administration of Foreign Exchange and the State Bureau of Cultural Relics, failed to develop the section. Their failure in developing a section for the annual reports made it impossible to search and find the reports in one place.

Fourth, the section for the annual reports failed to play its role in centrally disclosing annual reports. The section of some government agencies was randomly developed and was a mere formality. Some government agencies developed the section on their websites, but the reports were not put in the section. Some even put the same annual report repetitively in different sections. A department under the State Council failed to develop the section on its website and put the annual reports of recent years in the section for news and events as well as in the section for theoretical research. A provincial department put the report on the work of government in the section for the annual reports, while the annual report could only be found in the section for notice and announcement. The government of one large city (Handan) developed the section, but the annual reports were put in the section for integrated government affairs. Another large-city government also develop the section, but the annual reports were placed both in the section for policies and papers and in the section for normative documents. Some government agencies, the one in Fushun City for example, did not disclose the annual report on their own websites, instead, the annual reports were disclosed on the websites of superior governments or other websites, and some reports could not be found even by using search engines.

Fifth, the performance on the continuous disclosure of the annual reports needed to be improved. A few government agencies just had only the annual report of the previous year disclosed on their websites. Some deleted the previous annual report when they published a new one. Hence, the annual reports of previous years could not be found. Although some had developed the section for the annual reports, the reports of 2008 to 2010 could not be found. According to the evaluation, two departments under the State Council, one provincial-level government and one large-city government failed to provide the reports or 2008 to 2010 in the sections.

Sixth, information inaccuracy occurred when superior government agencies releasing the annual reports of lower-level ones. According to the evaluation, a few of the 2011 annual reports of the departments under the State Council and provincial-level governments centrally disclosed by the General Office of the State Council on the website of the Central People's Government (www.gov.cn) were inconsistent with those that were released on the respective websites of departments or local governments. For example, the annual report of Yunnan disclosed on the website of the Central People's Government was titled *Annual Report on the Government Information Disclosure of the Office of the People's Government of Yunnan Province in 2011*, but the one disclosed on the website of Yunnan Provincial People's Government was titled *Annual Report on the Government Information Disclosure of Yunnan Province in 2011*. Also, the annual report of Anhui published on the website of the Central People's Government was titled *Overview of data on the Government Information disclosure of Anhui Province in 2011*, while the one that was disclosed on the website of Anhui Provincial People's Government was titled *Annual Report on the Government Information Disclosure of the People's Government of Yunnan Province in 2011*.

Seventh, the performance on disclosing some core data of the government agency of the previous year in the annual report was less than satisfactory. This was mainly manifested in the following three aspects.

(1) The investment of personnel and capital was not included. The investment of personnel and capital in the work of government information disclosure of the previous year was not mentioned in the annual report of any government agency, and the proposed investment of 2012 was not included either.
(2) The number of requests received and that of requests accepted were confused. Most of the government agencies evaluated only disclosed either the number of requests they received or that of requests they accepted. Only an extremely few disclosed both. This illustrated that the information disclosed was not comprehensive.
(3) The performance on disclosing data on request-based disclosure was less than satisfactory. The quantity of data on request-based disclosure disclosed by the departments under the State Council has experienced a decline compared with that in the previous year. According to the evaluation, in the annual reports of all the departments under the State Council evaluated, 34 provided the total number of requests received in the previous year, which was roughly equivalent to the quality of data disclosed in 2012; 24 provided the items with top requests (28 in 2011); 21 provided the number of requests categorized by different submission methods (same as in 2011); 39 provided the number of requests that had been reviewed and accepted (56 in 2011); 23 provided data categorized by the content of replies (such as to be disclosed, not to be disclosed or to be partially disclosed) (same as in 2011); five provided data categorized by the reasons why the request had been refused (such as involving state secrets or personal privacy) (11 in 2011), 53 provided data on the number of administrative proceedings involving government information disclosure; 57

provided data on the number of administrative reviews involving government information disclosure and only ten provided data on the number of administrative complaints involving government information disclosure. In the annual reports of all the provincial-level governments evaluated, 13 provided the total number of requests received in the previous year (12 in 2011); none provided the number of requests received in the previous year categorized by same-level government, lower-level and affiliated departments, though 15 provided the requests received categorized by two of the three government agencies; six provided the data on the governments that received top requests (five in 2011); 18 provided the items with top requests (same as in 2011); 14 provided the number of requests categorized by different submission methods (same as in 2011); 22 provided the number of requests that had been reviewed and accepted (24 in 2011); 18 provided data categorized by the content of replies (such as to be disclosed, not to be disclosed or to be partially disclosed) (same as in 2011); eight provided data categorized by the reasons why the request had been refused (such as involving state secrets or personal privacy) (seven in 2011); 24 provided data on the number of administrative proceedings involving government information disclosure; 25 provided data on the number of administrative reviews involving government information disclosure and eight provided data on the number of administrative complaints involving government information disclosure. In the annual reports of all the large-city governments evaluated, 18 provided the total number of requests received in the previous year (11 in 2011); none provided the number of requests received in the previous year categorized by same-level government, lower-level and affiliated departments, though seven provided the requests received categorized by two of the three government agencies; six provided the data on the governments that received top requests (five in 2011); 26 provided the items with top requests (24 in 2011); 22 provided the number of requests categorized by different submission methods (23 in 2011); 36 provided the number of requests that had been reviewed and accepted(40 in 2011); 27 provided data categorized by the content of replies (such as to be disclosed, not to be disclosed or to be partially disclosed) (23 in 2011); ten provided data categorized by the reasons why the request had been refused (such as involving state secrets or personal privacy) (nine in 2011); 40 provided data on the number of administrative proceedings involving government information disclosure; 41 provided data on the number of administrative reviews involving government information disclosure and ten provided data on the number of administrative complaints involving government information disclosure. Only Datong Municipal Government announced in its annual report that no request had been received in 2011. However, after failing to submit requests via the online platform of Datong, the Project Team submitted successfully the request via email in 2011, but no reply was received as of March 31, 2012. If it was true that no request had been received in 2011, then the government information disclosure system of Datong was not working at all and was just a mere formality.

Eighth, the standards applied to the release of the annual report were inconsistent. According to the evaluation, a few local governments considered the annual report of the general office of same-level governments as that of the government itself. The statistical methods employed were also different. This was especially the case in publishing the data on request-based disclosure. For example, of all the provincial-level governments evaluated, the number of requests reviewed and accepted disclosed by Guangdong, Jiangsu, Hebei and Shaanxi was that accepted by their general office; that disclosed by Hubei and Hunan was the number accepted by its provincial-level governments and departments; and also the number disclosed by some other provincial-level governments was that accepted by the municipal governments across the province. This illustrated that governments at all levels lacked consistent standards for conducting the work. It was also an important reason for the large differences in the performance of disclosing data by various governments.

6.11 Recommendations

Based on the results of the 2012 evaluation, it is suggested that the following improvements should be made to promote the work of government information disclosure.

First, strengthen the establishment of competent departments responsible for government information disclosure. The promotion of the work and the growing public demands for government information disclosure have put forward increasingly higher demands on the professional level and timeliness of government information disclosure. The work of various government agencies needs to be arranged and conducted in an orderly manner, which cannot be achieved if there is no specific department and staff responsible for doing the job. Therefore, government agencies at all level should have a specific department and the professional staff that are equipped with related knowledge in management, law, information technology and other aspects of expertise to complete the work.

Second, raise the staff's awareness of government information disclosure. Awareness promotion is a long and subtle process, where targeted, systematical and long-term training should be conducted to different groups of staff, instead of just having meetings or reading related documents. The ultimate goal is to internalize the culture of government information disclosure into the work attitude and methods of the staff, and this also helps to avoid "lazy thinking" in government agencies.

Third, develop clear standards for government information disclosure. Explicit standards should be developed in terms of the establishment of related websites, the construction of the section for information disclosure, and the content of voluntarily disclosed information, the place and ways in which it should be disclosed, the definition of the information that does not fall into the scope of request-based disclosure, as well as key elements of the annual report. The development of these standards helps improve the level of government information disclosure and facilitate supervision and evaluation.

Fourth, reform the management model of government websites and government information disclosure. The management model should be shifted from the current decentralized pattern to a centralized one to reduce costs and improve management efficiency. Local governments at all levels should establish and operate their government portals well, and then integrate the information disclosed on various departments to the portals, thus changing the huge differences existed in the establishment of government websites.

Chapter 7
The 2013 Evaluation of China's Government Transparency

In 2013, China further stepped up its efforts on enhancing government information disclosure and government transparency. The General Office of the State Council issued some related documents including the *Opinions of the General Office of the State Council on Further Strengthening the Government Information Disclosure to Respond to Social Concerns and to Enhance Government Credibility* (No. 100 [2013] of the General Office of the State Council) and the *Notice of the General Office of the State Council on Printing and Distributing the Current Work Arrangements for Government Information Disclosure in Key Areas* (No. 73 [2013] of the General Office of the State Council) to guide the work of government agencies at all levels and to adapt to the current public demands for government information.

7.1 Highlights

7.1.1 The Following Four Highlights Were Revealed in the Evaluation

i .First, the directory for government information disclosure was developed in a more standardized manner.

The evaluation found that the directory was more standardized and it played an increasingly important role in centrally disclosing government information and improving the convenience for the public to obtain it. The directory was developed on most government websites. The government portals of all the 31 provincial-level governments were equipped with the directory and information links were put in the directory. Fifty-four out of 55 departments of State Council and 48 out of the 49 large cities developed the directory on their websites. Improvements could be seen in this respect compared with 2012. The Project Team randomly selected ten information links in the directory of each website to verify their validity. Among the departments

Y. Lv and H. Tian, *Evaluation on Government Transparency Index in China (2009–2016)*, Understanding China, https://doi.org/10.1007/978-981-16-5032-1_7

under the State Council, the links of 49 were all valid, accounting for 89.09 percent (48, 81.4 percent in 2012). Among provincial-level governments, the links of 28 were all valid, accounting for 90.32 percent (22, 84.62 percent in 2012). Also, the accessibility of the directory was increased. For example, the number of departments and local governments that provided multiple classifications of the directory was increased significantly. Compared with 2012, the number of the departments under the State Council that provided multiple classifications of the directory grew from 25 to 29; that of provincial-level governments from eight to ten, and that of large-city governments from nine to 18. In addition, the validity of combined search functions of the directory was improved. Twenty-one departments under the State Council, nine provincial-level governments, and 19 large-city governments provided valid combined search functions in 2013, compared with 17, seven and fifteen respectively in 2012.

Second, the results of voluntary disclosure in many fields were worthy of recognition.

For example, great improvements were made on the disclosure of the developing process of normative documents. In 2013, 13 provincial-level governments and 14 large-city governments developed a section for gathering public opinions on drafts of normative documents. Twenty-four departments under the State Council, 11 provincial-level governments and 13 large-city governments published information about drafts of normative documents. Thirty-six departments under the State Council, 15 provincial-level governments and 23 large-city governments provided channels for gathering public opinions on drafts of normative documents. All of these efforts were better than those in 2012. Another example was the disclosure of supervision information about food production safety. The bureaus of quality and technical supervision of 38 large cities provided application guidelines for food production licenses; 34 provided application results; 23 provided application guidelines for filing of entrusted food processing of food manufacturing enterprises; 31 provided spot check results of food safety supervision; and 35 provided basic knowledge about food safety.

Third, many government websites valued more on the accessibility of information.

Ningbo Environmental Protection Bureau had different sections for the public, enterprises, environmental protection to disclose information and provide services in a targeted manner. The information was disclosed in a simple and illustrated form. The website of Shaanxi Environmental Protection Bureau provided an online request platform for administrative license items for the public to enquiry the information about environmental impact assessment and acceptance of construction projects. The information about environmental impact assessment and acceptance of construction projects provided by the website of Dalian Environmental Protection Bureau was categorized by different districts. Some governments were more friendly to the public when disclosing normative documents and their drafts. For example, the General Administration of Customs and the Harbin Municipal Government issued the normative documents with relevant policy interpretation documents at the same time, the content of which were simple and user-friendly. The archival information of the normative documents of Hainan Provincial Government was disclosed monthly in a comprehensive manner. In Jilin, a website dedicated for supervising and managing normative documents was established to enable normative document sections to be better regulated and to provide easier access for the public to gain information.

Fourth, the annual report on government information disclosure was published in a more standardized manner.

Significant improvements were made in releasing the 2012 annual report.

To start with, most government agencies issued their annual reports within the statutory period. In the evaluation, the Project Team searched annual reports on the websites of government agencies evaluated. As of 24:00 on March 31, 2013, 58 of the 59 departments under the State Council (the access to the website of the Ministry of Railways was blocked due to institutional restructuring), 31 provincial-level governments and 46 of the 49 large-city governments had released their annual reports of the previous year in a timely manner (the annual reports of Handan and Urumchi were not found and the section for the annual report on the website of Jilin Municipal Government could not been opened until 3 April, 2013). Also, some government agencies, being efficient at work, such as the former Ministry of Health, the State Administration of Traditional Chinese Medicine, Xiamen, Fuzhou and Lhasa released their annual reports as early as in January.

Then, most annual reports disclosed were comprehensive and detailed. A majority of reports provided a whole landscape of the work of same-level governments on government information disclosure in 2012. They contained detailed information about voluntary disclosure, request-based disclosure and related administrative reconsideration, proceedings, and complaints, summarized the major problems of same-level governments' work on information disclosure, and identified objectives and measures for improvement. Among them, Fuzhou scored full marks in this respect as its annual report was both complete and systematic.

Lastly, more attention has also been paid to the forms of the annual reports and the readability of their content. The evaluation found that some government agencies emphasized the diversity and vividness of the forms of annual reports, while some others focused more on the readability of the content. For example, the annual reports of the governments of Beijing, Shanghai, and Chongqing were released in the form of Flash brochures with exquisite styles and complete content, being both creative and practical. Many government agencies provided detailed charts in their annual reports, which enhanced the visibility of reports and facilitated the public to understand the content. In some annual reports, comparisons were made between the performance of the very year and that of previous years, which not only enriched the content but also made it simple for the public to understand the information disclosed, maximizing public convenience.

7.2 Problems

Nevertheless, the following four major problems were also identified in the evaluation.

The Regulations and other relevant laws and regulations have provided clear requirements as to what kinds of government information shall be voluntarily disclosed by government agencies. However, in practice, the work on voluntary disclosure was far from achieving the target of complying with laws and regulations and meeting public demands for government information. A large amount of information that should have been voluntarily disclosed was either not disclosed, or not fully disclosed, or not disclosed in a timely manner, or disclosed in a way that was difficult to find. As for disclosure upon request, problems such as the normative documents that were confidentially reviewed was not been removed, government agencies' work on handling requests was not standardized, the procedures and standards of handling requests for government information disclosure among different government agencies differed significantly, and requests were sometimes been rejected by different and unreasonable excuses were identified.

First, the performance of disclosing government information through government websites remained to be improved.

To start with, the problem of no government websites or the unstable operation of websites still existed. For example, after institutional restructuring, the Ministry of Railways did not have an official website until January 2014; the government portal of Fushun was still under construction; Haikou Quality Supervision Bureau still had no website; the website of Jilin Quality Supervision Bureau could not be opened during the evaluation and Lhasa had no independent website for quality supervision. The websites of some environmental protection departments, such as those in Anshan and Xiamen, sometimes could not be opened. Furthermore, some websites, such as that of Xining Quality Supervision Bureau, were a mere formality, with serious problems identified in the completeness and validity of information. It was particularly noteworthy that despite that some provincial or municipal governments performed well on the construction of government websites and the disclosure of government information, the corresponding performance of some of their affiliated departments was still poor.

The construction of sections for information disclosure was unreasonable. Some government agencies set up such sections as "the Openness of Government Affairs" and "the Disclosure of Government Information" at the same time, which led to separate disclosure as the sections were repetitive. Another problem was that the directory of information disclosure on the websites of some local governments directed to the list of all the departments of the governments, while in the directory of information disclosure of the government office was the information about same-level government, which made it functioned as the directory of the government itself, for example, that of Anshan and Henan.

Also, there were still some government websites without a directory. Three provincial governments had no directory for affiliated departments while two had no directory for lower-level governments. The corresponding number of large-city governments was three and three respectively. Also, the directory of a few government agencies, such as those of Guangxi Zhuang Autonomous Region and Nanning, was not equipped with links to information, which made the directory a mere formality.

Then, the accessibility of the directory needed to be improved. The problem of not providing multiple classifications was widespread. In 2013, 21 departments under the State Council, 17 provincial-level governments and 26 large-city governments provided only one type of classification. Also, the search functions of the directory were not well designed. The problems included: the search functions of the directory of some were too simple, as information could not be searched by title and index number; the search functions of some were invalid or some even did not have search functions, which made it inconvenient for the public to search the documents they needed; although the combined search functions of some were well established and information can be searched by text number, index number, title, key words, content, time, etc., corresponding elements such as text number and key words were not provided in the documents, which made the combined search functions a mere formality. What's more, the search functions on some websites, such as the websites of National Bureau of Geographic Mapping and Hohhot Municipal Government were placed in the sub-section of the directory or the section for information disclosure and it was difficult for the public to find the function.

In addition, problems such as the information disclosed was randomly placed and sections on the websites were a mere formality still existed. The lack of reasonable design and classification of some government portals made it difficult for the public to access the information they needed effectively and easily. As for information arrangement, some information was placed in the sections where it should not be put. For example, basic knowledge and news were put in the section for policies and regulations and some put all information into the section for notices and announcements. As a result, many information sections failed to function effectively, adversely affecting or even misleading the public when they searched for information.

Lastly, information disclosed through different platforms tended to be inconsistent. These platforms included the government portals of local governments, the websites of their affiliated departments, and the dedicated websites in some fields such as administrative approval and food safety. As a result, it was likely that the information disclosed on different websites were inconsistent. For example, as for the disclosure of information about food safety, the information about food production licensing disclosed by only three large-city governments was consistent with the information on the websites of quality supervision bureaus, and for others, either the information was consistent or there was no such information disclosed. Similarly, only five large-city governments provided consistent guidelines for filing of entrusted food processing of food manufacturing enterprises. These problems would cause inconvenience to the public and enterprises and lead to increased cost of accessing government services.

Second, the performance on voluntary disclosure was less than satisfactory.

To begin with, the performance of many government agencies on the disclosure of basic position information was less than satisfactory. One manifestation was that the position information of department heads was incomplete and little progress was made in this respect compared with 2012. Four agencies failed to provide the resume of department heads on their websites, and two just provided that of some. Twenty-six failed to provide the distribution of responsibilities of their leaders and seven provided that of only some. Despite the fact that the disclosure of information about government agencies is conducive to improving the transparency of governments, offering convenience to the public when they search for services, easing the problem of buck-passing among different departments, and improving government's work efficiency on serving the public, the actual performance of government agencies in this respect was less than satisfactory. Although 53 government agencies provided the lists of their internal offices on their websites, few of them managed to provide the institutional responsibilities and contact details of the internal offices while even fewer managed to provide the lists and responsibilities of the divisions of their internal offices. According to the evaluation, 41 government agencies provided responsibilities of all their internal offices; 18 provided the contact number and email address of all their internal offices; 29 provided the list of the divisions of all their internal offices; and only five provided the responsibilities of the divisions of responsibilities of all their internal offices. Also, in terms of the information about the affiliated public enterprises and institutions of the departments under the State Council, the websites of eight government agencies still did not have such information.

Also, the performance of some local departments on the disclosure of the policies and regulations—issued by local governments—that were related to the departments themselves was less than satisfactory. Local people's congresses and local governments often issued detailed and enforced laws and regulations on relevant administration work. These laws and regulations were often the most direct bases for the relevant departments to conduct their work. Therefore, the disclosure of these laws and regulations was a basic requirement for improving transparency in administration. However, what the Project Team has found was that many local departments often only disclosed laws and administrative rules, while the relevant regulations issued locally were rarely disclosed. Taking information about food safety supervision as an example, only the websites of the quality supervision bureaus of 15 out of 49 large-city governments provided the regulations and policies for food production safety regulation issued by people's congresses, governments and relevant departments at the same level, accounting for merely 30.61 percent. Also, the performance on the disclosure of the internal regulations of some government service centers was less than satisfactory. Only three of nine provincial government service centers that had a dedicated website released their internal regulations. In addition, only 26 of the 41 large-city governments that had a dedicated website released their internal regulations on the websites.

Lastly, the performance on the disclosure of information about administrative approval was less than satisfactory. Only the bureaus of quality and technical supervision of two large-city governments provided the guidelines for all services (issuing new licenses, reissuing, changing, correcting, and revocation) related to food production licenses, and only these two provided complete information about how to access related services, including the basis for administrative approval, competent office, office address, approval conditions, documents to be submitted, approval procedures, approval duration.

Third, the information disclosed was not updated in a timely manner.

Although the Regulations clearly prescribed that information should be disclosed in a fixed period of time, the Project Team found that information update delays were still widespread in 2013. The quality and technical supervision administrations of only 14 large-city governments managed to disclose the results of the issuance of food production licenses within three months before the evaluation was conducted, while those of only two managed to publish the results of filing of entrusted food processing of food manufacturing enterprises during the same period of time. The same problem also existed in the disclosure of information about food safety spot check, qualifications of food production enterprises and basic knowledge of food safety. The problem was also identified in the provincial and municipal environmental administrations, with information update delays being even more severe in the latter. Among 49 municipal environmental administrations, the number of those that provided the information about hazardous waste management licenses, approval of the application for trans-provincial transfer of hazardous waste, radiation safety licenses, approval of environmental impact assessment of radiation projects, acceptance of the environmental impact of radiation projects and credits of environmental protection of enterprises within six months before the day the evaluation was conducted was 13, three, eight, six, six, and 13 respectively. Among 31 provincial environmental administrations, the number of those that provided the information about approval of the application for trans-provincial transfer of hazardous waste and credits of environmental protection of enterprises within six months before the day the evaluation was conducted was nine and three respectively.

Fourth, request-based disclosure should be more standardized.

In the evaluation, the requests filed with the departments under the State Council was to ask for the disclosure of the total number of staff and the number of civil servants, permanent staff, temporary employees, and loaned employees at the government agency.

Also, the requests filed with the local government was to ask for the disclosure of information about the disposal of local waste, including: (1) local waste disposal capacity, the construction of waste treatment facilities (including the current situation and construction plans of pollution-free disposal plants, sanitary landfills and waste incineration facilities), and annual amount of waste disposed (hereinafter referred to as the "first item"); (2) local regulations and status quo on waste and emissions reduction, and policy papers related to the recycling and packaging reduction (hereinafter referred to as the "second item"); (3) local regulations on waste charge, the amount charged in 2012 and related charge standards (hereinafter referred to as the "third item"); (4) local budgets and use of funds invested in the construction of waste disposal facilities, technological transformation, and government funding in 2012 (hereinafter referred to as the "fourth item").

In the requests submitted to local governments, the Project Team asked competent authorities to disclose the above-mentioned four items separately. The aforesaid four types of work in 24 provincial-level governments and 43 large-city governments were all in the charge of the same department, namely the Department of Housing and Urban–Rural Development, those in direct-controlled municipality were in the charge of municipal sanitation departments, and in others were assigned to different departments.

The evaluation revealed several major problems in disclosure upon request.

To start with, request channels were less than accessible. Taking online request platforms as an example, applicants were required by some to register before making a request. However, registration failures or webpage errors could occur, leading to request failures. Although it was stated in the guidelines of some government agencies that requests could be made online, when the applicant filled out the request form and submitted it, "wrong information submitted" would be displayed without specifying what was wrong. Whereas some did not state in their guidelines that requests could be made online, the window for making request online would just pop up on their government portals. The inconsistency of information obtained by applicants would make it difficult for them to choose which one to believe.

Also, the work process of request-based disclosure was less than standardized. Examples include: instead of notifying applicants to supplement documents and providing replies by a written instrument, some government agencies only completed the work by making phone calls; some got documents delivered to applicants on a freight forward basis without informing them in advance, let alone allowing them to choose a cheaper alternative; some refused to disclose the information requested without offering any reasons or government assistance methods to applicants. The Project Team also found that related staff members engaged in information disclosure at some local government agencies did not have the expertise required in their work, as some seemed to be quite unfamiliar with the process. One example was that a staff member at an urban-management bureau called the applicant who filed a request, falsely claiming that applicants should first need to send the request to the municipal government, and that the bureau could only disclose the requested information upon receiving the government's approval. Even the applicant tried to persuade him during the eight-minute phone call, the staff member still stuck to the practice.

Then, the performance on providing replies should also be improved. (1) the problem that requests could not be replied in a timely manner was prominent. In terms of the four above said items on waste disposal requested by the Project Team, 14 provincial-level governments and 26 large-city governments managed to reply to the request for the first item in a timely manner; 14 and 16 respectively for the second one; 14 and 19 respectively for the third one; and 14 and 16 respectively for the fourth one. Meanwhile, 37 departments under the State Council managed to do so too. (2) a relatively low portion of information requested was disclosed. In terms of the four above said items on waste disposal requested by the Project Team, 11 provincial-level governments and 25 large-city governments provided all the information requested in the first item; five and 11 respectively provided all the information requested in the second item; three and 18 respectively provided all the information requested in the third item, and five and 11 respectively provided all the information requested in the fourth item. Meanwhile, only two departments under the State Council provided all the information requested. The replies of many government agencies were evasive. For example, when asked for the number of public servants at the department under the State Council, some only provided the number of the personnel on the strength. However, "the number of the personnel on the strength" and "the number of actual permanent staff" are two entirely different concepts. (3) No standard was developed for disclosure refusals. When requesting information about the disposal of local waste, the Project Team found that a large number of local governments refused to disclosed the information requested by the excuse of "not responsible for collect, process or compile government information requested", and some refused on the grounds that the information requested was unclear. As for the requests for disclosing information about the personnel of the departments under the State Council, the reasons for refusal to disclose mainly were: information requested involving state secrets, being internal information, or the department being not responsible for processing and compiling government information for applicants, etc."

Lastly, confidentiality norms needed to be revised or re-formulated. When requesting for the disclosure of information about personnel of the departments under the State Council, the Project Team encountered for the first time the problem that requests were rejected by many departments on the grounds that the information requested was involving state secrets. The confidentiality norm on which the practice of these departments was based was the *Regulations on State Secrets and Specific Secret Classes in the Work of Personnel*, which was issued in the 1980s. In accordance with the regulation, the statistics and reports on the structure and personnel of party and government offices at all levels of government, public institutions and social organizations fall into the scope of classified information. However, this regulation was quite outdated and unable to keep pace with the existing policies and practices of promoting the disclosure of information about personnel by the state. Many local governments and some of the departments under the State Council had disclosed the information comprehensively. All of these revealed that confidentiality norms were urgently needed to be cleaned up and reviewed based on the actual situation.

7.3 Recommendations

Based on the results of the 2013 evaluation, it was suggested that the following improvements should be made to promote government information disclosure.

First, continue to enhance the construction of government websites. Generally, most government agencies have established their websites, which is a leap forward. In the future, besides continuing to urge a very small number of government agencies that have not built government websites to build their own websites as soon as possible, it is necessary to strengthen the work on disclosing government information online, improve the level of online services, and enhance government interactions with the public. Therefore, government websites, the main platform for government information disclosure, could be turned into a channel that is accessible for the public to gain government information. To this end, not only does the hardware need to be improved to increase the server level and network bandwidth so as to ensure the smooth operation of the websites, but also the design of websites should be enhanced to make the layout both beautiful and concise, and with sections reasonably arranged, it will be convenient for the public to find the information they need from a huge amount of government information displayed. Meanwhile, it is also suggested that a special guideline for the use of the government website be developed to inform the public in a concise manner of the sections, the functions of the sections and the efficient ways to obtain the information on the website.

Second, the work on voluntary disclosure should be strengthened. Voluntary disclosure is the key of performing well on government information disclosure. If the information that should be voluntarily disclosed is not released, not only the public's right to know would be negatively impacted, but also the burden on government agencies would be increased, and the credibility of government agencies may also be affected. Therefore, it is recommended that the work on voluntary disclosure be further strengthened. Government agencies are recommended to figure out the categories of information that should be disclosed voluntarily, disclosure methods, as well as disclosure time limit required by existing laws and regulations. Government agencies should try to disclose the information that shall be disclosed and make the disclosed information accessible to the public.

Third, the work process of request-based disclosure should be more standardized. It is recommended that relevant departments develop detailed and clear procedures for request-based disclosure based on the characteristics and development trends of government information disclosure requests in recent years. In the process, procedural rules should be clearly developed, related standards be specified, and the scope of non-disclosable information be clearly defined in accordance with laws. To this end, the training of the staff engaged in government information disclosure should be strengthened so as to familiarize them with the work procedures and enable them to give reasonable and legal reasons when they refuse to disclose the information requested.

Fourth, clean up the obsolete confidentiality norms. It is recommended that government agencies have a thorough review of all the confidentiality norms, revise and eliminate the obsolete ones based on the existing development of confidentiality and information disclosure.

Chapter 8
The 2014 Evaluation of China's Government Transparency

8.1 Overview of the Work of Government Information Disclosure in 2014

In 2014, government transparency generally showed an upward trend, with varying degrees of progress being made by both central and local governments on their implementation of the government information disclosure system.

First, government information disclosure was becoming a new means of governance. The disclosure of government information was not only a requirement for building a transparent government, but also an important means of governance, and it was an important aspect of the modernization of state governance capabilities. A number of regulations were issued in 2014 to further clarify that the disclosure of government information shall be an important means for government administration. Also, against the background of implementing the "streamlining administration and delegating power" policy, the *Interim Regulation on Enterprise Information Disclosure* proposed that enterprise information held by government agencies shall be disclosed to strengthen self-discipline of enterprises and to foster a market environment operated with integrity. The *Opinions on Disclosing the Information about Administrative Punishment Cases Involving the Production and Sale of Counterfeit and Substandard Commodities and the Infringement on Intellectual Property Rights according to law (for Trial Implementation)* stated that relevant information about administrative punishment cases involving the production and sale of counterfeit and substandard commodities and the infringement on IPR shall be disclosed. In the *Notice of the General Office of the State Council on Strengthening Environmental Supervision and Law Enforcement* (No. 56 [2014] of the General Office of the State Council), government information disclosure was also been considered as an important means to strengthen environmental supervision and law enforcement. All of these illustrated that "the disclosure of government information" has become a new method taken to transform the concepts and practices of government administration in 2014.

Y. Lv and H. Tian, *Evaluation on Government Transparency Index in China (2009–2016)*, Understanding China, https://doi.org/10.1007/978-981-16-5032-1_8

Second, top-down guidelines were offered to urge and promote the work of government information disclosure. According to the Regulations, the General Office of the State Council was the top department in charge of government information disclosure throughout the country and was responsible for advancing, guiding, coordinating, and supervising the work nationwide. In recent years, the General Office has promoted the nationwide work by issuing the arrangement on key work of government information disclosure or the key tasks in disclosing government information every year. The *Key Tasks in Disclosing Government Information in 2014* stated the key items that should be disclosed in the year in a comprehensive manner, providing a very clear guide for government agencies at all levels to conduct the work. Significant progress has therefore been made on the work of the disclosure and interpretation of government information in key fields. Based on the requirements of the Key Tasks, the General Office of the State Council carried out inspections, and administrative agencies at all levels disclosed the implementation of the key points of information disclosure in 2014 both on their own government portals and central government portals, to receive public review and supervision.

Third, great improvements were made on constructing government portals. In 2014, the portal of the Central People Government (www.gov.cn) was revised. The new website was equipped with eight sections, namely, "State Council", "News and Events", "Features", "Policies", "Services", "Discussing Politics", "Data" and "National Conditions". All the information on the website was arranged in the sections with clearer layout, fresh and simple design. It was more convenient for the public to search for information. Many administrative agencies had started to follow this practice.

Fourth, more attention was paid by government agencies to the interpretation of major policies and regulations. The interpretation of major policies and regulations was an important means for administrative agencies to proactively describe the background, legal basis, and specific management ideas behind the policies and regulations. It enabled the public to comprehensively and accurately understand the meaning of relevant policies and regulations, effectively protected their legitimate rights and interests, thus improving the implementation of polices and regulations. As great importance was attached to the interpretation, many administrative agencies developed a special section for the interpretation of policies and regulations on their websites. Instead of just forwarding the interpretations of higher-level departments, many administrative agencies had their own interpretations of the major policies and regulations issued by the agency itself or by other local governments. Facing the problems of decentralized disclosure of the basis for administrative approval for enterprises to obtain government services and the inconvenience for them to search for related information, Ningbo developed a section titled "Search Platform for Enterprise Policies in Ningbo" and attached a sub-section titled "Policy Interpretation" to each policy and regulation issued by the agency itself and its affiliated departments. What's more, to facilitate enterprises to understand relevant policies and regulations, all policies and regulations were followed by other related policies as required, as well as the contact number of the competent department, so that enterprises can consult by calling the department. This manifested the careful work Ningbo did.

Fifth, the evaluation objects' performance on the work of government information disclosure showed an overall upward trend. According to the evaluation, despite the fact that the evaluation indicators became increasingly refined and the requirements stricter, the overall all scores and the scores in each category showed a significant rise. Although scores could not fully reflect the outcomes of the evaluation and there was still a gap between the work of government information disclosure and social development as well as public expectations, the increasing scores could show to some extent that the level of the work had been significantly improved. Such improvements could not be achieved without the top-down promotion of the work and the high attention that was paid by government agencies to the work.

However, the evaluation also revealed some problems in this respect, which should be taken seriously in promoting government information disclosure.

First, the problem that there was no dedicate department or professional staff for government information disclosure was widespread. Most government agencies failed to establish a special department or choose the staff to conduct the work. The department responsible for government information disclosure had no permanent staff. The staffs at other departments were required to conduct the work at the same time, or some personnel were loaned from other departments to conduct the work, making it difficult to guarantee the professionalism and continuity of the work.

Second, multi-channel management hindered the effectiveness of government information disclosure. This problem had a long history. The General Office of the State Council had integrated functions such as government information disclosure, openness of government affairs, government gazette management, and Weibo and WeChat management, and the effectiveness of government information disclosure had been significantly improved. However, multi-channel management was still a prominent problem both at the departments under the State Council and local governments. For example, at some administrative agencies, the work of government information disclosure was in the charge of the general office, while press conferences and Weibo and WeChat management were in the charge of news and publicity departments, government portals were managed by the information center, and responses to hot-spot issues were a responsibility for the publicity department or the dedicated department for public opinions monitoring. Some local governments had established multiple government portals, which belonged to the government office and publicity department of party committee respectively. For instance, Changchun had two municipal websites in operation, one's URL was http://www.changchun.gov.cn/, and it showed that the website was constructed by the CPC Changchun Municipal Committee and the Changchun Municipal People's Government while the other one's URL was http://www.ccszf.gov.cn, and it showed that this one was constructed by the Changchun Municipal People's Government. Multi-channel management and inconsistent policies not only failed to improve the effectiveness of government information disclosure, but also often led to increased internal cost in government information disclosure, and the inconsistent information disclosed severely affected government credibility.

Third, the quality of government information disclosure still needed to be improved. Statistics showed that a huge amount of information was disclosed by government agencies every year, but the quality of the disclosure was still less than satisfactory. To start with, little information demanded by the public was disclosed. Many government agencies were still focusing on publishing news, and more often the information about the whereabouts of their officials, while the information that the public really demanded was often not disclosed, not disclosed in a timely manner, or the information disclosed was difficult for the public to obtain. Then, there was a lack of consistency in information update. For example, as for the departments under the State Council, the Office of the Central Institutional Compilation Committee released the lists of items subject to administrative approval of various departments in early 2014, and many departments under the State Council just forwarded the list for themselves without updating the items on their portals accordingly. As a result, the list released on the portal of some departments under the State Council was still the information of 2011 and 2012, thus leading to information inconsistency. In addition, it was difficult for the public to figure out whether the normative documents disclosed were still effective or not. A huge number of normative documents was formulated and released by government agencies, and some of them were not effective anymore and some of them had been abolished or replaced by new ones, but it was difficult to figure out the effectiveness of normative documents based on the information disclosed. What's more, most administrative agencies removed old documents when they issued new ones, which also caused inconvenience for the public. Even though these documents were no longer effective, they were still of great significance for the public to have an understanding of the continuity of related polices or to resolve some historically controversial issues.

Fourth, the work of government information disclosure was still in a "Campaign-Style". The evaluation found that the work of many government agencies was still in a campaign-style and was not integrated into routine work. In many cases, the performance of government agencies on the work varied with the level of supervision of higher-level departments. If the supervision was strict, the performance would be better.

Fifth, improvements needed to be made on the construction and operation of government websites, as the poor performance in this respect had affected the effectiveness of government information disclosure. Some websites were poorly operated and sometimes could not be opened. For example, the government portals of the Xinjiang Uygur Autonomous Region and Shijiazhuang Municipal Government could not be opened for many times in the evaluation. Some local governments did not set up a website for their legislative affairs offices or the links of the website were invalid. For example, Anshan, Fuzhou and Tangshan failed to sect up the website, while the website of Changchun Municipal Legislative Affairs Office could not be opened. In addition, the search functions on the government portals of the National Energy Administration and the National Grain Administration were invalid, while there were no search functions provided on the government portals of the General Administration of Quality Supervision and Jilin Provincial Government. Some websites had compatibility problems. For example, the design of some websites required a screen resolution of 1024 × 768, leading to a screen display problem when users searched and read the items subject to administrative approval on the website, which went against the objective of building a government that serves the public. Finally, the characters (words) on some websites were overlapped, and the problem remained unchanged even when the Project Team viewed the websites on different computers, browsers and systems.

8.2 The Directory for Government Information Disclosure

In 2014, obvious progress was made on developing the directory compared with that of 2013. To be more specific, the construction of the directory on websites, the validity of information links in the directory, the accessibility of the directory, the validity of search functions, and the timelessness of information update in the directory all experienced improvements.

First, performance on the construction of directory was good. Most government websites were equipped with the directory. To be more specific, all of the 31 provincial-level governments developed the directory on their websites and information links were also provided. The websites of the 55 departments under the State Council were all equipped with a relatively complete directory, while those of 48 out of the 49 large-city governments did so. All of these represented further improvements compared with those of 2013.

Second, improvements were made on the validity of information links. By randomly selecting ten information links disclosed in the directory, the Project Team found that, the information links provided by 50 departments under the State Council were all valid, accounting for 90.91% (49 in 2013, 89.09%); those provided by 26 provincial-level governments were all valid, accounting for 83.87% (28 in 2013, 90.32%); and those provided by 42 large-city governments were all valid, accounting for 85.71% (40 in 2013, 81.63%).

Third, the accessibility of the directory was enhanced. To start with, the number of government agencies with multiple classifications of their directory increased significantly. For example, the number of the departments under the State Council with multiple classifications of their directory has grown from 29 in 2013 to 30 in 2014; while the corresponding number of provincial-level governments remained unchanged (10). Also, the validity of combined search functions of the directory was improved. In 2014, the directory of 33 departments under the State Council, 12 provincial-level governments, and 24 large-city governments were equipped with valid search functions. Among them, the combined search functions of 14 departments under the State Council (17 in 2012 and 21 in 2013), two provincial-level governments (seven in 2012 and nine in 2013), and nine large-city governments were valid (15 in 2012 and 19 in 2013).

Fourth, the number of local governments that provided the directory for public enterprises and institutions increased significantly. In 2014, eight provincial-level governments (four in 2013) and 28 large-city governments (22 in 2013) provided the directory for public enterprises and institutions.

Fifth, more information was updated without delay. Thirty-one departments under the State Council, 25 provincial-level governments and 34 large-city managed to provide the information of one week before the time when the evaluation was conducted.

Nevertheless, the following problems were identified in this respect.

First, the problem that some government websites did not have the directory or information links were invalid still existed. For example, the information links on the government portal of Hohhot Municipal Government were invalid. A very few government agencies, such as those in Guangxi Zhuang Autonomous Region, Nanning, Shenyang and Benxi, only had a list of information in the directory without information links in the list, which made the directory a mere formality. Also, even though the links released on the website of the Ministry of Justice could be opened, the information in them was just introductions to various departments. What contained in the directory on the website of the State Administration of Grain was nothing but a summary of information.

Second, the directory was unreasonably designed. Even though the directory was provided on the governmental portals of some local governments, what contained in the directory was just a list of affiliate departments. Also, in the directory on the websites of the general offices of some local governments, information disclosed by the same-level government was also found, which meant that the directory was indeed that of the local government. The problem occurred on the websites of six provincial-level governments and nine large-city governments, which illustrated that it was not a rare problem. Also, the directory and the information links of the directory on some websites were randomly arranged. For example, on the websites of Zhejiang Provincial Government and Dalian Municipal Governments, the links were directed to different content when opened in different sections.

Third, the accessibility of the directory needed to be improved. Multiple classifications of information were still not provided by many government agencies. In 2014, 22 departments under the State Council, 13 provincial-level governments and 17 large-city governments either only provided one type of classification or failed to classify the information contained in the directory at all. This brought about inconvenience for locating information.

Fourth, the search functions of the directory were not well equipped. The search functions provided on the websites of some government agencies were invalid. Some even did not provide any search function. These two problems made it inconvenient for the public to locate information. Although the combined search functions of some websites were well established and information could be searched by text number, index number, title, key words, content, time of issuance, corresponding elements such as text number and key words were not provided in the documents, which made the combined search functions a mere formality. In addition, the search functions on some websites were placed in the sub-section of the directory or the section for information disclosure and it was difficult for the public to find the functions themselves. Also, some of the combined search functions were invalid, or some information could be found by using the search functions while some others could not.

Fifth, only a few local governments provided the directory for public enterprises and institutions. The importance attached by local governments to the directory for public enterprises and institutions needed to be strengthened. Although some local governments developed the directory for public enterprises and institutions and the number of them also increased significantly compared with that of 2013, of all the links on the websites of provincial-level governments, only those of Sichuan were valid. Also, although most provincial-level governments and large-city governments developed a special section for the directory on their websites, the links in the sections were either directed to government portals or were invalid.

Sixth, the information contained in the directory was not comprehensive. In accordance with the requirements of the Regulations and previous documents issued by the General Office of the State Council, the directory for government information disclosure was an important guarantee mechanism for administrative agencies to manage government information and facilitate public access to government information. However, how to handle the relations between the directory and different sections on government portals was still unclear. The evaluation found that the directory of many government agencies failed to include the information disclosed on the portals of the same-level governments. Even when the scope of information that should be included in the directory was narrowed down to the documents that should be disclosed in accordance with the *Regulations on the Handling of Official Documents by Party and Government agencies,* the problem was still prominent. This illustrated clearly the inconsistency between the directory and the government portals. The problem led to weakened functions of the directory. Five departments under the State Council, eight provincial-level governments and eight large-city governments managed to include all the information disclosed on their government portals in the directory.

8.3 Work Information

According to the evaluation, the departments under the State Council performed well in the following aspects.

First of all, in terms of the disclosure of information about government officials, all of them provided a list of the leaders and deputy leaders of the department. Among them, 49 provided the resumes of their leaders, accounting for 89.09%; 28 provided the division of job responsibilities of their leaders, accounting for 50.91%.

Second, in terms of the disclosure of information about the functions of the departments, generally all managed to provide the information about the responsibilities of the department, the internal offices, and the affiliated departments. Among all the departments under the State Council evaluated, 53 provided their own responsibilities, 54 provided a list of their internal offices, 48 provided information about the functions of their internal offices; 35 provided a list of the divisions of their internal offices, and six provided information about the division of responsibilities of all the offices; and 24 provided contact information of all their internal offices.

Third, the performance of the departments under the State Council on disclosing information about subordinate enterprises and institutions experienced significant improvements compared with that of 2013. Except for those without subordinate enterprises and institutions, only two of all the departments under the State Council evaluated failed to provide related information.

Finally, in terms of the disclosure of annual work information, several departments disclosed their annual work plans and work summaries. The disclosure of annual work summaries, key points of work, and plans was an important means to demonstrate the achievements made by the department and to proactively receive public supervision. Also, the disclosure of such information would not only enable the public to know the work of relevant departments, but also help improve the credibility of the department. Among all the departments under the State Council, four disclosed their work summaries of previous years; nine published their key points of annual work or work plans; eight disclosed their key points of work or work plans for 2013 and before. The State Administration of Religious Affairs and the State Intellectual Property Office have been doing a fairly good job in this regard. This showed that it was not impossible to disclose such information and the main problem preventing some government agencies from doing so was that they still had some misunderstandings about the work.

Nevertheless, the evaluation also revealed the following problems in this respect, which should be taken seriously.

First, the information about government official was not fully disclosed. According to the evaluation, four departments failed to provide the resumes of their leaders, two only provided the resumes of some; 25 failed to publish the division of job responsibilities of their leaders and two only provided the division of responsibilities of some.

Second, the disclosure of information about the internal offices should be further enhanced. For example, of all the departments under the State Council evaluated, five only provided the functions of some of their internal offices; one did not provide any such information at all; the website of one could not be opened; 14 failed to provide the list of divisions of their internal offices, 43 did not provide the division of responsibilities of all the divisions and 28 failed to provide any contact information of their internal offices.

Third, not all the departments disclosed their annual work plans and work summaries. Actually, the performance of most departments on the disclosure of their annual work plans and work summaries was less than satisfactory. This was partially due to their low awareness of the work. In interviews with the Project Team, the staff at some departments claimed that such information was irrelevant with the public and could not be possessed within the department, and much of the information should not be made public.

8.4 Normative Documents

According to the evaluation, great improvements were made on the concentration and consistency of the section for normative documents, the update of normative documents, and the disclosure of the developing process of normative documents.

First, all of the government agencies evaluated developed a section for normative documents on their websites, where the normative documents developed by themselves were published and could be downloaded by the public.

Second, the consistency of normative documents disclosed in the section was enhanced. In 2014, the normative documents disclosed in the section by 19 departments under the State Council, ten provincial-level governments and 28 large-city governments were consistent with those disclosed in the directory for information disclosure. The Tibet Autonomous Regional Government did a good job in disclosing normative documents. It developed a special section for normative documents in the directory for information disclosure on its government portal.

Third, normative documents were well updated. In 2014, 48 departments under the State Council, 31 provincial-level governments and 48 large-city governments managed to provide the normative documents issued in 2014 in the section.

Fourth, many administrative agencies disclosed information about the effectiveness of normative documents. To prevent the provisions of the "Official Documents" from violating the law and thereby infringing on the legitimate rights and interests of the people, many local governments have intensified their filing and review of normative documents in recent years. They also published the directory of files that had undergone filing and review on a regular basis. Eighteen provincial-level governments disclosed the directory on their government portals or on the websites of the legislative affairs offices. Shenzhen, Dalian, Ningbo, Qingdao, Xiamen and other municipalities also disclosed the directory. Hunan Provincial Government set up a section titled "Clearance of Normative Documents" on its government portal to note in one place whether some normative documents were still effective. Also, many government agencies noted the effectiveness of normative documents in the section. Some departments under the State Council noted the effectiveness in the normative documents. For example, most of the normative documents published by the General Administration of Customs were with their own effectiveness. Some departments under the State Council published a directory of the normative documents that were still effective, for example, the State Administration of Foreign Exchange. Many government agencies also noted the effectiveness of normative documents in the list of the directory, for example, the governments of Chongqing and Hunan. Some local governments also issued a list of the normative documents that were not effective anymore, for example, Jiangxi and Sichuan. Some local governments clearly described the starting and ending time of implementation of the documents below the texts of the documents, such as Shanghai, Tianjin, Shandong, Hunan, Shaanxi, Qinghai, Shenzhen, Qingdao, Dalian, Xiamen, etc.

Fifth, great improvements were made on the disclosure of the developing process of normative documents. In 2014, 26 departments under the State Council, six provincial-level governments and 17 large-city governments developed a section for gathering public opinions on the drafts of normative documents. Twenty-one departments under the State Council, six provincial-level governments and five large-city governments published the drafts of normative documents. Thirty-five departments under the State Council, seven provincial-level governments and 21 large-city governments provided channels for submitting public opinions on the drafts of normative documents. For example, the General Office of State Food and Drug Supervision developed a special section for gathering public opinions on the drafts of normative documents, and provided detailed information about the purposes for developing the draft, the draft itself and the specific provisions contained in the draft.

Sixth, the validity of the links directed to normative documents was improved. By randomly selecting the links of ten normative documents, the Project Team the links of 51 departments under the State Council, 30 provincial-level governments and 49 large-city governments were all valid.

However, several problems were also revealed in this respect.

First, the section for normative documents was randomly developed, information was misplaced, and update delays occurred. To start with, most of the departments under the State Council and local governments developed more than one different sections for normative documents, such as polices and regulations, government gazettes, notices and announcements, and programs and plans, and the information disclosed in these sections was inconsistent with that released in the directory for government information disclosure. Only 23 departments under the State Council, 12 provincial-level governments and 25 large-city governments had only one section. Then, some departments under the State Council and local governments did not have a clear definition of normative documents, which led to the random arrangement of the normative documents. Some were placed in the section for notices and announcements while some others were in the section for news and event. For example, some non-normative documents were placed in the section titled "Policies and Regulations" section on the government portal of the Ministry of Civil Affairs. Some penalty decisions were put in the section titled "Policies" on the website of the Ministry of Housing and Urban–Rural Development. Regulations of colleges and universities were put in the section titled "Regulations" on the website of the Ministry of Education. Some documents that did not belong to normative documents were placed in the section for normative documents on the website of the Ministry of Industry and Information Technology: for example, approval results were placed in the section titled "Document Release". The random arrangement of information imposed a negative impact on public access to information and on the effectiveness of government information disclosure.

Second, the availability of the section for normative documents needed to be strengthened. To be more specific, the performance of the departments under the State Council and local governments on the classification of normative documents by items and departments needed to be improved. The 2014 evaluation found that only six departments under the State Council, one provincial-level government and three large-city government categorized normative documents by items. Only one provincial-level government managed to categorize normative documents by departments.

Third, despite the fact that improvements had been made on the disclosure of the developing process of normative documents compared with that of 2013, more efforts needed to be made. To tart with, there were still some departments under the State Council and local governments that did not develop a section for gathering public opinions on the drafts of normative documents. Also, only a few drafts were published in the section. For example, only 20 departments under the State Council, three provincial-level governments and 12 large-city governments managed to publish up to three drafts in the section with all information links valid. Then, the information disclosed was not comprehensive. Most of the information disclosed was the draft itself, and information about the purposes for developing the draft and the provisions contained in the draft was lacking. By randomly selecting one draft disclosed by each government agency, the Project Team found that only 26 departments under the State Council, six provincial-level governments and 12 large-city governments provided complete information—the purposes for developing the draft, the draft itself and the provisions contained in the draft. Some government agencies such as the State Administration of Cultural Heritage failed to provide the draft, though information for gathering public opinions was found on its website. At last, most departments under the State Council and local governments failed to provide the responses to the solicited public opinions on their websites. The 2014 evaluation found that none of the government agencies provided such responses on their websites.

Fourth, the interpretation of important normative documents needed to be strengthened. According to the evaluation, in the section for policy interpretation on the websites of some government agencies, there were not only the interpretations of local policy documents but also those of some other relevant departments. For example, on the government websites of Hunan, Hubei, Guizhou and Inner Mongolia, there were many polices interpretations issued by the departments under the State Council, while those of the government itself was less. Also, the quality of policy interpretations needed to be enhanced. Most of the interpretations issued by administrative agencies were the reports from different news media, not issued by government agencies themselves. In addition, many interpretations were just copying the description of relevant rules, regulations and normative documents, which was not only in stiff forms but also had a very limited amount of useful information disclosed.

Fifth, the number of the local governments that provided filing information needed to be increased and the update of information needed to be improved. The working mechanism for the filing of normative documents existed only in local governments, not in the departments under the State Council. In 2014, 18 provincial-level governments and 29 large-city governments managed to provide filing information. The information provided by the governments of Luoyang and Jinan was only updated to 2012.

Sixth, the disclosure of information about the elimination and modification of normative documents was less than satisfactory. According to the evaluation, only ten departments under the State Council, seven provincial-level governments and

12 large-city governments managed to publish information about the elimination of normative documents in 2014. Only four departments under the State Council, five provincial-level governments and nine large-city governments managed to provide information about the modification of normative documents. Moreover, the forms of disclosing information about the effectiveness of normative documents were different. Some (for example, the Ministry of Commerce) disclosed the effective normative documents on a regular basis. Some (for example, the General Administration of Customs) noted the effectiveness of the documents in the directory for information disclosure. Some (for example, the Ministry of Civil Affairs) developed a special section for disclosing effective normative documents. Some disclosed the results of the clearance of normative documents from time to time, examples of which included the governments of Xining and Fuzhou, and the Ministry of Agriculture.

8.5 Information About Environmental Protection

In 2014, the evaluation of information about environmental protection mainly focused on hazardous waste, radiation safety, environmental impact assessment of construction projects, completion-based environmental protection inspection and acceptance of construction projects, collection of pollution charges, response to complaint letters and visits from the public on environmental issues or environmental pollution, administrative punishment and corporate environmental credit, etc.

The 2014 evaluation found the following aspects of the work worthy of recognition.

First, the transparency of disclosing information about environmental protection of provincial environmental administrations showed positive results. Judging from the scores, provincial-level government agencies performed better on the disclosure of information about environmental protection than those of large cities, as the information disclosed by them was quite compete and standardized.

Second, great attention was paid by the environmental administrations of both provincial-level governments and large cities to the disclosure of information about environmental impact assessment of construction projects. The environmental administrations of 31 provincial-level governments and 45 large cities provided information about the acceptance of environmental impact assessment for construction projects; those of 30 provincial-level governments and 40 large cities provided the information about environmental impact assessment of projects prior to the approval of the projects; those of 31 provincial-level governments and 49 large cities provided the information about environmental impact assessment of projects after the approval of the projects. It was illustrated from the aforementioned data that all environmental administrations highly valued the disclosure of information about environmental impact assessment of construction projects.

Third, the channels for conducting interactions between governments and the public were varied and constantly innovated. Channels for the interactions between government and the public were an important platform for citizens to participate in the government affairs related to environmental protection. Most environmental administrations disclosed related information via the platforms. The environmental administrations of 26 provincial-level governments and 31 large cities provided the information about and the response to the complaint letters and visits from the public on environmental issues or environmental pollution made six months before the evaluation was conducted.

Fourth, the performance of some environmental administrations on the disclosure of corporate environmental credit showed positive results. For example, in 2013, Guangzhou and Suzhou employed the "red and yellow card system", through which enterprises were ranked by their credits to facilitate public access to the information. Meanwhile, Fujian evaluated the environmental credits of enterprises by "good" and "bad" in relevant section on its government website.

Fifth, the websites of environmental administrations were increasingly user-friendly. When searching on these websites during the evaluation, the Project Team clearly felt that increasing attention had been given by an increasingly number of environmental administrations on the accessibility of their websites. For example, the website of Ningbo Environmental Protection Bureau had different sections for individual citizens, enterprises, environmental protection information, etc., to disclose information and provide services in a targeted manner. The information was disclosed in a simple and illustrated form. Also, the websites of the environmental administrations of some government agencies, such as in Guangdong and Fujian, categorized information about administrative approval and acceptance carefully by whether it was accepted for approval, to be approved or have been approved. This enhanced public access to information.

Nevertheless, the evaluation also revealed the following problems in this respect.

First, some information about environmental protection was not made public. The environmental administrations of four provincial-level governments and 15 large cities did not provide information about the completion-based environmental protection inspection and acceptance of construction projects; those of eight provincial-level governments and 30 large cities did not provide information about the approval results of requests for the cross-provincial transfer of hazardous waste; those of two provincial-level governments and 24 large cities did not provide information about radiation safety licenses, including Beijing and Tibet. Those of three provincial-level governments and 17 large cities did not provide information about the review and approval of the environmental impact assessment of radiation projects. Those of four provincial-level governments and 16 large cities did not provide information about the completion-based environmental protection inspection and acceptance of radiation projects.

Second, information update delays occurred. This problem existed in the environmental administrations of both provincial-level governments and large cities. It was even more prominent in the protection administrations of some large cities. Among the environmental administrations of 49 large cities, 15 provided information about hazardous waste management licenses; 11 provided approval results of the application for trans-provincial transfer of hazardous waste; 15 provided information about the issuance of radiation safety licenses; 16 provided the approval results of environmental impact assessment of radiation projects; nine provided the information about completion-based environmental protection inspection and acceptance of radiation projects; and 23 provided information about the environmental protection credits of enterprises. Among the 31 provincial environmental administrations, 20 provided the approval results of the application for trans-provincial transfer of hazardous waste; and 11 provided the information about environmental protection credits of enterprises. All the aforesaid information was generated within the previous six months before the day the evaluation was conducted.

Third, the information about environmental impact assessment and completion-based environmental protection inspection and acceptance was not fully. Complete information about construction projects shall include six types of information: acceptance of environmental evaluation approval for construction projects, the information about environmental impact assessment of projects prior to the approval of the projects, the information about environmental impact assessment of projects after the approval of the projects, acceptance of application for completion-based environmental protection inspection and acceptance of construction projects, the information about environmental protection inspection and acceptance of construction projects prior to the approval, and the information about protection inspection and acceptance of construction projects after the approval. However, the performance of the environmental administrations of some local governments on fully disclosing the information was less than satisfactory. The protection administrations of four large cities did not provide information on the acceptance of environmental evaluation approval for construction projects; those of one provincial-level government and nine large cities did not provide the information about environmental impact assessment of projects prior to the approval of the projects; those of four provincial-level governments and 15 large cities did not provide information about acceptance of application for completion-based environmental protection inspection and acceptance of construction projects; those of two provincial-level governments and 13 large cities did not provide the information about environmental protection inspection and acceptance of construction projects completed prior to the approval; and those of four provincial-level governments and six large cities failed to provide the information about protection inspection and acceptance of construction projects after the approval.

Fourth, related sections were unreasonably developed on the websites of protection administrations. On some websites, information about hazardous waste licenses, approval results of radiation safety, pollution charges and administrative punishment etc. was not placed in its own sections, hindering public access to information. The sections for approval of environmental impact assessment of construction projects and acceptance of application for completion-based environmental protection inspection and acceptance of construction projects on some websites were not well constructed either. Information was mixed together. Examples included the websites of Nanning and Wuxi. Only a few websites managed to make a very detailed classification, but problems such as information to be approved was placed in the sections for the information approved still occurred.

Fifth, the disclosure of information about corporate environmental credit was not standardized. The *Interim Regulations on the Disclosure of Information about Enterprise* stated that information about administrative punishment of enterprises generated in their own government agencies shall be disclosed, and it was an important part of information about corporate credit. However, as most environmental administrations failed to develop a special section for information about corporate environmental credit, relevant information was randomly placed. This imposed a negative impact on public access to information. In addition, even some websites developed the section, no information was released in there.

8.6 Information About Administrative Approval

The 2014 evaluation found the following highlights worthy of recognition.

First, the performance on constructing online platforms for disclosing administrative approval showed positive results. Thirty-one provincial-level governments and 49 large-city governments provided the platforms in the forms of websites for government service centers, dedicated administrative approval websites, or online sections for services on their government portals. The construction of these websites made government agencies' items subject to approval and limits of authority more transparent and facilitated the access of the public and enterprises to government services.

Second, the effectiveness of information disclosure was improved by releasing the list of administrative approval authority. The evaluation found that most governments managed to proactively release a list of administrative approval authority or a list of items subject to administrative approval on the websites of their government service centers or on their government portals. The Hainan People's Government Administration Service Center developed a special section on the homepage of its website. In the section, a provincial-level list of administrative approval authority and a list of administrative approval authority applied to its provincial government service center were provided, and real-time information about the departments responsible for administrative approval, items subject to approval (including sub-items), services items (including sub-items), online application items, and full-process online approval items was also included. The websites of other administrative centers or government portals also managed to disclose the list of administrative approval authority in their own ways.

Third, the consistency of information about the items subject to administrative approval disclosed by provincial-level governments on the websites of their government service centers and government portals or department portals was enhanced. The evaluation found that 22 provincial-governments and 20 large-city governments managed to maintain the consistency.

Fourth, the elements of information about administrative approval disclosed were quite complete. By randomly selecting ten pieces of information about administrative approval on the websites of government service centers or online service websites of the government agencies, the Project Team found that the information links of the 31 provincial-level governments and those of 48 out of 49 large-city governments were al valid. With regard to the completeness of the information, the evaluation focused on whether the information included seven elements: the basis for administrative approval, approval conditions, application documents, approval procedures, approval duration, information about the office responsible for the work, and contact number of the office. Again, in terms of the selected ten information links on administrative approval provided by 31 provincial-level governments, 22 provided the basis for administrative approval in all of their ten information links; 17 provided approval conditions in all of their ten information links; 17 provided application documents in all of their ten information links; 19 provided approval procedures in all of their ten information links; 21 provided approval duration in all of their ten information links; 22 provided information about the office responsible for approval in all of their ten information links and 13 provided contact number of the office in all of their ten information links. And the number of provincial-level governments that provided the aforementioned information in only some of the ten information links was nine, 14, 14, 11, ten, seven and 16 respectively. As for the 49 large-city governments, the number of those that provided the aforementioned information in all of the ten information links was 39, 25, 41, 37, 45, 44 and 22 respectively, while the number of those that provided the aforementioned information in only some of the ten information links was eight, 18, seven, nine, three, two and 17, and the number of those that failed to provide any of the aforementioned information was two, six, one, three, one, three and ten respectively.

Fifth, more attention was paid by government agencies to the accessibility of information about administrative approval. On the websites of the government service centers or the online service section of 31 provincial-level governments and 49 large-city governments, information about administrative approvals was categorized as information for general public, information for enterprises, and information categorized by the competent departments. On some websites, the section for key information about administrative approval was developed to disclose relevant information and provide services in a targeted manner, and the information was disclosed in a clear and illustrated form.

Sixth, interpretations of the basis for administrative approval manifested that government agencies were acting in a law-biding manner and served the public. Many government agencies provided detailed information about the laws, regulations, and normative documents that were the basis for administrative approval on the websites of their service centers or in the online service section. For example, Hainan Provincial Online Approval Office provided interpretations for each basis for administrative approval it published.

Seventh, website interfaces were designed in a beautiful and user-friendly manner, and some functions provided to facilitate public access were more helpful. The construction of government service centers has also taken advantage of the continuously advanced internet technology. For example, such features such as barrier-free browsing and service obtaining, audios and animations, as well as texts and pictures were provided on the online service sections of the government portals of Beijing,

Shanghai, etc. Instructional videos were provided on the homepages of the government service centers of some government agencies (for example, Shenyang). Virtual office service halls were created by employing modern internet technology on the websites of some government agencies, such as those in Guangdong and Hefei, to offer users an immersive experience. Also, as for the questions arisen in the process of administrative approval, online assistance services were provided on some websites. Applicants could ask for help via instant chat, emails, or telephone.

Eighth, dynamic information about items subject to administrative approval was disclosed in real time. Many government agencies developed a special section on the homepage of their websites to provide scrolling dynamic information. Some developed a section for tracking the status of items, enabling the pubic to track the process and results of approvals.

Nevertheless, three major problems were revealed in this respect. First, the information about administrative approval disclosed on the dedicated website of government service centers or the administrative approval websites was inconsistent with that disclosed on the websites of same-level governments or the websites of other departments. Second, the information disclosed was incomplete. Only 11 provincial-level governments and 14 large-city governments managed to provide all the aforesaid elements of the information. Third, on the websites of some government agencies, the information disclosed by affiliated departments varied. The information disclosed by some was complete while that published by some others was not.

8.7 Request-Based Information Disclosure

Since November 20, 2014, the Project Team had successively conducted the evaluation on the disclosure of request-based information by sending requests via EMS and online platforms. In the requests filed with local governments via EMS, the Project Team mainly asked local departments of land and resources management to provide the total amount of the transfer fees of state-owned land collected from January to October 2014. Some local departments replied that the information was possessed by local financial departments, the Project Team then sent a request to the corresponding financial department. When verifying the validity of the EMS and online request channels provided by the departments under the State Council and the online request channel provided by local governments, the requested information was randomly selected. In the process, the Project Team determined the arrival time of the requests based on the time when the EMS was signed by the recipients and on the time when the emails were sent. Then a period longer than the statutory response time limit was given to the government agencies to reply to the requests.

The evaluation found that most government agencies published the qualifications and procedures of request-based disclosure. Also, some government agencies were also trying some new methods to provide the guidelines for making a request. For example, the National Health and Family Planning Commission released in the section for request-based disclosure some typical cases of requests and corresponding replies to inform applicants of the expected forms of requests and guide them to make reasonable expectations of the replies.

After sending the requests, the Project Team received replies from most government agencies. Some even made calls to confirm the details of requests.

However, several problems were also revealed in the respect.

First, the performance of some government agencies on providing descriptions of the request-based information disclosure was less than satisfactory. Providing a description of the qualifications and procedures for request-based disclosure would enable the public to submit requests in an appropriate manner. However, some failed to provide any descriptions or guidelines or the information was unreasonably placed and was difficult for the public to locate. For example, no description or guideline was provided on the websites of the State Administration of Civil Servant, Heilongjiang Provincial Department of Finance and Dalian Municipal Department of Finance. Although the guidelines on government information disclosure were provided on the website of Hainan Municipal Department of Finance, no description of request-based information disclosure was found in the guidelines. The guidelines on government information disclosure provided on the websites of the Ministry of Foreign Affairs and the China Securities Regulatory Commission could be found only through web search.

Second, request channels provided by some government agencies were limited. According to the Regulations, requests could be made through several methods such as face-to-face submission, mailing or online submission to meet the needs of different groups of people. Mailing was the most commonly used channel as almost every government agency provided this method, but many of them only provided one or a very limited number of request channels. According to the evaluation, 12 government agencies (including eight departments under the State Council and four provincial financial departments) failed to provide an online request platform or emails on their government portals. Nine government agencies (including seven departments under the State Council and two provincial financial departments) did not accept face-to-face submission. Five government agencies (including three departments under the State Council and two municipal financial departments) only provided one method, among which, the Ministry of Public Security, the State Bureau for Letters and Calls, and the State Forestry Administration only accepted mailing, while the Financial Department of Ningbo and the Financial Department of Dalian only accepted online submission.

Third, the submission channels stated on the websites of some government agencies did not match with reality. The evaluation found that the submission channels stated in the guidelines on government information disclosure on the websites of 30 government agencies (including 17 departments under the State Council, 11 provincial finance departments, and two municipal finance departments) were not consistent with the reality. According to the guidelines on government information disclosure on the websites of seven government agencies (including four departments under the State Council and three provincial finance departments), online requests platforms were provided, but in reality, no online platform was found on their websites. These seven government agencies were: the State Administration of Industry and Commerce, the State Administration of Surveying, Mapping and Geographic Information, the State Administration of Foreign Exchange, the State Administration of Traditional Chinese Medicine, the Finance Department of Inner Mongolia Autonomous Region, the Finance Department of Ningxia Hui Autonomous Region and the Finance Department of Hebei. Although the Finance Department of Guangdong provided an online request platform on its website, the platform was only open to local residents of Guangdong. The inconsistent requests provided in the different sections of government agencies would be misleading. It would also cause the delay of the applicant's request, and damage public rights and interests in requesting for government information disclosure.

Fourth, information about the department responsible for handing requests was not fully disclosed. Getting to know the competent department was a precondition for applicants to appropriately submit requests. However, some government agencies did not provide necessary information about the department and applicants were unable to fill in the information of the recipients of the requests, thereby failing to submit requests. For example, in the guidelines on government information disclosure of the State Bureau for Letters and Calls and the Finance Department of Xinjiang Uygur Autonomous Region, no address of the competent department was provided, In the guidelines of the Finance Department of Shanxi, the Finance Department of Hainan and the Finance Department of Xinjiang Uygur Autonomous Region, no postcode of the competent department was provided. The seven government agencies ((including six ministries and commissions and one provincial finance department) that did not provide the contact number of the competent departments in their guidelines were: the Ministry of Housing and Urban–Rural Development, the National Health and Family Planning Commission, the General Administration of Quality Supervision, Inspection and Quarantine, China Insurance Regulatory Commission, China Securities Regulatory Commission, National Energy Administration, and the Finance Department of Xinjiang Uygur Autonomous Region. The 24 government agencies (including 15 ministries and commissions, seven provincial finance departments, and two municipal finance bureaus) that did not provide the email address of the competent department were: The Ministry of Foreign Affairs, the Ministry of Finance, the Ministry of Housing and Urban–Rural Development, the Ministry of Public Security. the Ministry of Justice, the Ministry of Human Resources and Social Security, the Ministry of Agriculture, the Ministry of Culture, the State Forestry Administration, the State Letters and Visits Bureau, the Civil Aviation Administration of China, the State Administration of Foreign Exchange, the State Grain Administration, the State Oceanic Administration, the State Post Bureau, the Finance Department of Shanxi, the Finance Department of Gansu, the Finance Department of Sichuan, the Finance Department of Zhejiang, the Finance Department of Hainan, the Finance Department of Hubei, the Finance Department of Xinjiang Uygur Autonomous Region, the Finance Department of Qingdao, and the Finance Department of Shenzhen.

Fifth, the replies to requests given by some government agencies were not standardized. Instead of replying in written forms, some government agencies just informed applicants of the replies by telephone. Some replies given via emails were also not in a formal format. For example, the Department of Land and Resources of

Jiangxi gave two replies to the Project Team by emails, however, both the content and the email address used were different. In one of the two emails, there was only one sentence: "Please search for the information on the website of the State Land and Resource Trading Center of Jiangxi Province" and no letterhead or signature was in it. The eight government agencies that did not provide any legal basis of their replies were: the Department of Land and Resources of Shanghai, the Department of Land and Resources of Shandong, the Department of Land and Resources of Guangxi Zhuang Autonomous Region, the Department of Land and Resources of Inner Mongolia Autonomous Region, the Department of Land and Resources of Liaoning, the Department of Land and Resources of Zhejiang, the Department of Land and Resources of Heilongjiang and the Department of Land and Resources of Hubei. Also, no further assistance methods were provided by many governments agencies for the applicants whose requests had been rejected.

8.8 The Annual Report on Government Information Disclosure

As of 24:00 on March 31, 2014, 51 departments under the State Council, all the provincial-level governments and large-city governments had released their annual reports for the previous year.

Most annual reports disclosed were comprehensive and detailed. Many reports provided detailed information about voluntary disclosure, request-based disclosure and related administrative reviews, proceedings, and complaints, with the major problems of same-level government's work on information disclosure summarized and corresponding measures and potential improvements proposed.

More attention was paid by some government agencies to the accessibility of the annual reports. Some government agencies emphasized the diversity and vividness of the form of annual reports. Some also focused on the readability of the content. For example, the annual reports of Beijing, Shanghai, and Sichuan were in the form of Flash brochures with exquisite styles and complete content, being both creative and practical. Many government agencies provided charts in their annual reports, which enhanced the accessibility of annual reports. In some annual reports, comparison was made between the performance of the year and that of previous years, providing richer content in a simple manner. Some listed in their annual reports the names of the regulations, rules and normative documents that had been disclosed voluntarily, with information links to their content also provided. Some provincial-level governments also included the annual reports of municipal governments in their own sections for the annual reports. The Shanghai Municipal Government developed a search drop-down box in its section to facilitate public search. The aforesaid designs and measures all brought convenience for the public to understand and locate information.

What was worth mentioning was that some departments under the State Council, such as the Ministry of Commerce and the State Administration of Cultural Heritage, also disclosed their monthly reports on government information disclosure. The practice was to inform the public their work of government information in real time. The State Administration of Cultural Heritage also released the monthly reports on government information submitted by local cultural heritage management agencies.

However, the evaluation also revealed some problems in this respect, the most prominent one of which was that some important data was not included in the annual reports. The evaluation found that 26 departments under the State Council listed the items with top requests in their annual reports; 19 provided the number of requests categorized by different submission methods; 21 provided data categorized by the content of replies (such as to be disclosed, not to be disclosed or to be partially disclosed); nine provided data categorized by the reasons why the request had been refused (such as involving state secrets or personal privacy); and only six managed to provide data on the number of administrative proceedings, reviews and complaints involving government information disclosure. Eight provincial-level governments provided the number of requests received in the previous year categorized by same-level government, lower-level and affiliated departments in their annual reports; 14 provided the number of requests received in the previous year categorized by only same-level government and lower-level government or same-level government and affiliated departments; seven listed the departments that received top requests; 21 listed the items with top requests; 20 provided the number of requests categorized by different submission methods; 24 provided data categorized by the content of replies (such as to be disclosed, not to be disclosed or to be partially disclosed); nine provided data categorized by the reasons why the request had been refused (such as involving state secrets or personal privacy); and only 11 managed to provide data on the number of administrative proceedings, considerations and complaints involving government information disclosure.

In addition, information on request-based disclosure provided in the annual report of some government agencies was oversimplified. Some was only summarized in one sentence. For example, in the 2013 annual report of one provincial-level government, it was stated that government officials highly valued request-based disclosure, but only a few sentences in the annual report were about request-based disclosure, and neither whether some types of information would be disclosed nor the reason why the information would not be made public was provided.

8.9 Recommendations

First, Strengthen the establishment and integration of departments responsible for government information disclosure. Government agencies shall establish a special department in charge of information disclosure, and professional staff shall be assigned to conduct the work. Also, the competent department shall lead the work of disclosing information, constructing websites, external publicity, operating and maintaining Weibo and WeChat, and the observation and response of public opinions, so as to integrate and systematize the work.

Second, standards for voluntarily disclosing information in key fields shall be gradually developed. It is suggested that the standards be developed with the cooperation of relevant departments in the key fields stated in the annually issued key tasks in disclosing government information. It is also recommended to develop a list of top- down power list for certain industries, clarifying the division of responsibilities and powers between different levels of government agencies and establishing clear standards and paradigms for the disclosure of information about administrative approval, punishment and coercion. In addition, it is advised that the departments under the State Council refer to the practice of the Ministry of Education's release of the list of the disclosure of information about colleges and universities; sort out the government information in the industries that should be voluntarily disclosed; compile the information in one list and then make it public as a minimum requirement for relevant government agencies to disclose relevant government information; and update the list according to the changes and improvements of relevant laws and regulations as well as social development. Strict standards shall also be developed for the release of the annual reports, so as to prevent the high similarities in the structure and content of annual reports of different years.

Third, the work of request-based disclosure shall be further strengthened. Judging from the current situation facing government agencies, it is likely that both the quality and complexity of requests will continue to rise in the future and the cases that requests are made to be the alternatives of complaint letters and visits will also increase in the short term. Given this, government agencies at all levels shall standardize the processing procedures of request-based disclosure, provide accurate guidelines on request-based information disclosure, and offer diversified and effective channels for the public to submit requests. Enough professional and full-time staff members shall be assigned to handle the work. The consultation mechanism for handling difficult, major and complicated requests shall be established, so that when the competent departments are faced with difficult requests, officials from relevant departments and experts can have a discussion. Regular and targeted trainings shall also be conducted to tackle problems encountered in practice. Government offices at all levels shall play a leading and guiding role, have a unified control over the work on handling requests at the same-level government, and promptly intervene when difficult, major, and complicated requests appear, so as to guide and help relevant departments to make appropriate responses and replies.

Fourth, the work of government information disclosure and the construction of a law-based government shall be promoted simultaneously. Instead of being isolated, government information disclosure is closely related to the construction of a law-based government. The problem that the work of some government agencies on government information disclosure was stressful and some requests were difficult to handle not only resulted from the lack of clarity and practicability of related standards, but also more from the inappropriate and unregulated management due to underperformed administration. Some government agencies did not have the capacity and courage to tackle problems occurred in request-based disclosure. Therefore, the work of government information disclosure and the construction of a law-based government shall be promoted simultaneously, and efforts need to be made not only in tackling the problems occurred in government information disclosure, but also in strengthening law-based administration to further regulate the operation of power. The disclosure of government information is conducive to regulate power, and only when power is operated in a regulated manner, can full government information disclosure be truly achieved.

Chapter 9
The 2015 Evaluation of China's Government Transparency

9.1 Overview of the Work of Government Information Disclosure in 2015

In 2015, China high valued the work of government information disclosure and incorporated it in all areas of government administration, and made remarkable progress in this aspect.

First, government information disclosure was considered as an essential approach to government administration. To start with, the role of government information disclosure in building a rule-based government has been further clarified. As per the *Implementation Outline on Building a Rule-Based Government (2015–2020)* issued by the Central Committee of the Communist Party of China (CPC) and the State Council, states clearly that information disclosure shall become a regular government practice and non-disclosure only happens in exceptional cases. The central government shall continue to promote the openness of the decision-making, execution and administration process, facilitate public access to administrative services and results, improve the government information disclosure systems, broaden the channels for government information disclosure, and further clarify the scope and content of government information disclosure. Also, government information was viewed as an important means of encouraging innovation. The *Opinions on Strengthening Efforts to Build New Types of Think Tanks with Chinese Characteristics* issued by the General Office of the CCCPC and the General Office of the State Council, sets forth the requirements to enhance information disclosure and enable the think tanks to have timely access to government information. A number of policies issued by the State Council also mention driving innovation through openness, including the *Action Outline for Promoting the Development of Big Data*, the *Guiding Opinions of the State Council on Vigorously Advancing the "Internet Plus" Action*, the *Notice of the State Council on Standardizing Administrative approval*s by *Departments under the State Council to Improve Work Related to Administrative approvals*, and the *Notice of the General Office of the State Council on Simplifying and Optimizing*

Y. Lv and H. Tian, *Evaluation on Government Transparency Index in China (2009–2016)*, Understanding China, https://doi.org/10.1007/978-981-16-5032-1_9

the Public Application procedures to Facilitate the Public to Get Access to Government Services and Start Their Own Business. Then, the state regarded government information disclosure as a significant approach to strengthening supervision. The *Guiding Opinions on Promoting the System of Listing the Power of Local Governmental Departments at all Levels*, the *Circular of the General Office of the State Council on Promoting Random Inspection to Regulate the In-process and Ex Post Supervision*, and the *Circular of the General Office of the State Council on Enhancing Supervision and Law Enforcement in Work Safety*, issued by the General Office of the CPC Central Committee and the General Office of the State Council, require to strengthen the supervision over administrative agencies through openness. The *Implementation Opinions of the General Office of the State Council on Comprehensively Promoting the Comprehensive Reform of All Public Hospitals at the County Level, the Opinions of the General Office of the State Council on Enhancing and Improving the State-Owned Assets Supervision to Prevent the Loss of State-Owned Assets of Enterprises* and other policies to exercise the social supervision through openness. Last, the country treated government information disclosure as an all-new supervisory approach. Policies including the *Several Opinions of the General Office of the State Council on Strengthening the Services and Supervision over Market Entities by Means of Big Data Analysis*, the *Opinions of the General Office of the State Council on Strengthening the Governance of Infringement and Counterfeiting Behaviors in the Field of Internet*, and the *2015 Major Tasks for the Nationwide Crackdown on IPR Infringements and on the Production and Sale of Counterfeit and Shoddy Commodities* also talk about making enhanced efforts to promote the information publicity of market entities and foster a market environment of integrity.

Second, the top-down instructions urged and promoted government information disclosure. In 2015, the General Office of the State Council further issued the *Key Points in the Work of Government Information Disclosure in 2015*, which has set forth requirements and arrangements for government agencies at all levels to perform well in government information disclosure. On November 18, 2015, the Office of Government Information Disclosure and Openness of Government Affairs of the General Office of the State Council responded to questions—how to determine the time point at which a request for information disclosure is received and whether to stop calculating time during the rectification period—raised by the Information Disclosure Office of the State-owned Assets Supervision and Administration Commission of the State Council (SASAC) in the *Letter for Requesting the Clarification of Issues Regarding the Processing Procedures for Information Disclosure upon Request*.

Third, the requirements for government information disclosure were becoming increasingly high and detailed. For example, the *Key Points in the Work of Government Information Disclosure in 2015* requests the government agencies at all levels to provide a detailed description of their budget and final accounts. The governments and government agencies at all levels are requested to prepare and disclose the budget and final accounts by expenditure functions. The public budget expenditure shall be made publicly available for economic purposes. The budget and final accounts for special transfer payment shall be disclosed by detailed items. The *Circular of the Ministry of Finance on Making Efforts to Accomplish the Work of Government Procurement Information Disclosure* also specifies the requirements for the disclosure of government procurement information in great details.

Fourth, third-party evaluations have become another tool with which government agencies can promote information disclosure. In 2014, the Office of Government Information Disclosure and Openness of Government Affairs of the General Office of the State Council entrusted the Institute of Law of the Chinese Academy of Social Sciences with the task of conducting a third-party evaluation on the work of government information disclosure nationwide for the first time[1]. The evaluation was published in 2015. In 2015, third-party evaluations continued to be conducted. The provincial-level governments of Shandong, Heilongjiang and others also adopted the same approach in their own work in this area. Third-party evaluation would help rectify the malpractices that may occur when government agencies conduct self-evaluation, thereby effectively pushing forward the work of government information disclosure nationwide.

9.2 Information Disclosure Sections on Official Government Websites

The Project Team chose not to focus too much on analyzing the directory for information disclosure itself as it had found one common issue among government agencies in recent years—the information made publicly available by these agencies on their official websites was inconsistent with that disclosed under the directory. This discrepancy could be attributed to the fact that different information management systems were often used for maintaining the website and the directory. This inconsistency could easily cause repetitive disclosure and affect the overall results of disclosure. As internet search technologies became increasingly sophisticated, the public can obtain what information they were looking for by employing the search functions on related websites. From a long-term perspective, the official websites of government agencies shall be integrated with websites and sections set up specifically for purpose of information disclosure. These sections colud also support most of the directory's functions. The Project Team decided, for these reasons, not to take the directory development as a key indicator since 2015.

The evaluation found that the official websites of evaluation objects were generally developed with a special section for the disclosure of government information, though the key elements in some sections were missing, including the basis for information disclosure, the directory for information disclosure, the guidelines on information disclosure, the sub-section for publishing the annual report on government information disclosure. Most of the evaluation objects set up a special section on their official websites and also had the above four key elements included. Among the

[1] Third-Party Assessment Report on the Disclosure of Government Information in China (2015), China Social Science Press.

organizations being evaluated, 35 departments under the State Council, 23 provincial-level governments and 31 large-city governments had the four key elements in the section, accounting for 63.64%, 74.19% and 63.27% respectively. Nevertheless, still a moderate proportion of the evaluation objects failed to provide the four elements.

The performance on providing the basis for the disclosure of government information was less than satisfactory. In the evaluation, the organizations being evaluated were asked to publish not only the Regulations and relevant rules issued by the superior agencies in the special section, but also relevant regulations concerning the disclosure of government information formulated by the government agencies thereof. However, the evaluation found that 13 departments under the State Council, eight provincial-level governments and 13 large-city governments failed to provide the basis for government information disclosure in their special section. One common issue was that what some evaluation objects published as the basis were the Regulations or rules issued by their superior agencies rather than the regulations formulated by themselves.

9.3 Normative Documents

The evaluation found that all the evaluation objects developed a special section for the disclosure of normative documents in an organized manner. However, some issues have been identified.

First, the section was developed in unstandardized manner. The normative documents of some evaluation objects were published concurrently in several sections and the problem was the most prominent among the departments under the State Council. Fourteen departments under the State Council disclosed the normative documents in several sections, accounting for 25.93%. Similar problem was found among three provincial-level governments and three large-city governments, accounting for 9.68% and 6.12% respectively. What's worse, some normative documents were mixed up with other documents such as policies, laws, regulations and rules, bringing extra difficulties for the public to find the information they need.

Also, many evaluation objects did neither disclose the collected opinions on the proposed drafts of normative documents nor feedback from government agencies. The evaluation set a rather low standard—the evaluation objects would be deemed to meet the requirements as long as they had made publicly available the drafts and the feedback for at least once. However, 30 departments under the State Council (55.56%), 20 provincial-level governments (64.52%) and 28 large-city governments (57.14%) failed to disclose the proposed drafts on their websites. Even if the drafts were published, the organizations generally failed to disclose the information about collected opinions and whether the opinions were adopted. Only one department under the State Council, three provincial-level governments and four large-city governments made publicly available the collected opinions, among which only the National Development and Reform Commission (NDRC) disclosed the information about whether the collected opinions were adopted. If government agencies only collected opinions but did not provide explanations on what opinions were collected, what collected opinions were adopted and why they adopted some opinions instead of others, it would be less helpful for exercising the public oversight over the government decision-making process and winning the trust of the people.

Last, most of the evaluation objects failed to mark the validity of normative documents. Normative documents without validity marked might mislead the public. Only a very few of them marked the validity of the normative documents on their websites, including the General Administration of Customs (GAC) and the governments of Chongqing, Hunan, Shanghai, Shandong, Guangdong, Jilin, Xi'an, Guangzhou, Xiamen and others.

9.4 Financial Information

The evaluation of the disclosure of financial information mainly focused on the information about budget, final accounts and "three types of public expenditures". The evaluation found that the departments under the State Council provided more detailed information in the disclosure of the budget and final accounts. Fifty-three departments under the State Council made publicly available a description of the 2015 budget statement and that of the 2014 final accounts. The statements were also very detailed and developed by functions or economic purposes.

Nevertheless, some problems were also identified.

First, the information about budget and final accounts was disclosed in an unstandardized manner. The information was either misplaced or disclosed in different forms. Only a few departments under the State Council and local governments failed to develop a special section for disclosure of the financial budget and final accounts. In some cases, the budget and final accounts were made publicly available in other sections, such as "government announcement", "announcement information" or "news release". Also, although some departments under the State Council and local governments developed a special section for disclosure, they placed the information for disclosure in the notice and announcement section or the news release section instead of in that for disclosure.

Second, the performance of both the provincial-level governments and large-city governments on the disclosure of the budget statements and final accounts descriptions shall be improved. Twenty-five provincial-level governments and 27 large-city governments disclosed a description of the 2015 budget statements on their government websites and the websites of the financial departments, accounting for 80.65% and 55.10% respectively. Eighteen provincial-level governments and 21 large-city governments published a description of the 2014 final accounts on the government websites and the websites of the financial departments, only accounting for 58.06% and 42.86% respectively.

Third, the statements disclosed by provincial-level governments and large-city governments were not detailed. Very few governments disclosed them by functions or economic purposes. The Project Team evaluated six statements in total, including the public budget expenditure, the public final expenditure accounts, the consolidated budget expenditure, the consolidated final expenditure accounts, the basic expenditure in general public budget and the basic expenditure in general public final accounts, and the following issues was identified: to begin with, most of the local governments failed to provide comprehensive statements. Nine provincial-level governments and 13 large-city governments did not disclose the public final expenditure accounts. Three provincial-level governments and 11 large-city governments failed to disclose the public budget expenditure. Also, some local governments disclosed the statements in a less standardized manner. For instance, only 11 provincial-level governments and two large-city governments published the basic expenditure in general public budget by economic purposes, and only one large city disclosed the basic expenditure in general public final accounts by economic purposes.

Last, some evaluation objects failed to provide details about the "three types of public expenditures". Only 35 departments under the State Council and two provincial-level governments disclosed a complete description of the "three types of public expenditures" on their websites and the websites of their financial departments. Some local governments only published a brief description of their "three types of public expenditures". The information provided by some departments under the State Council and local governments was incomplete, as some key information was missing. One department under the State Council, 26 provincial-level governments and 45 large-city governments failed to disclose the number of overseas trips and people travelling abroad for business. Ten departments under the State Council, 26 provincial-level governments and 44 large-city governments did not disclose the number of official vehicles purchased in 2014. Six departments under the State Council, 25 provincial-level governments and 45 large-city governments failed to disclose the number of official vehicles owned as of the end of 2014. Ten departments under the State Council, 27 provincial-level governments and 47 large-city governments did not disclose the number of domestic official receptions and people involved. In addition, these government agencies often neglected to provide an explanation why the budget for the three types of public expenditures was increased or cut. Three departments under the State Council, 18 provincial-level governments and 40 large-city governments did not disclose the reasons for budget increase or cut.

9.5 Information About Environmental Protection

The following highlights on the disclosure of information about environmental protection have been noticed.

First, the performance of provincial-level governments on the disclosure of information about environmental protection was generally at a high level. The performance of environmental protection departments at the provincial level in terms of the disclosure of the information about the environmental impact assessment of construction projects, environmental protection inspection and acceptance upon the completion of construction projects, review and approval of radiation safety, issuance of radiation safety permits, key pollutant-discharging enterprises or key environmentally regulatory objects held a significant lead over that of the large-city governments. For instance, all of the provincial-level environmental protection departments evaluated promptly disclosed the information about the environmental impact assessment of construction projects and the information about environmental protection inspection and acceptance upon the completion of construction projects.

Second, the overall performance on the disclosure of information about the environmental impact assessment of construction projects showed positive results. The environmental protection departments of 30 provinces and 44 large cities disclosed their information about acceptance of application for environmental impact assessment of projects constructed in 2015, accounting for 96.77% and 89.80% respectively. Those of 30 provinces and 47 large cities published the information about environmental impact assessment of projects constructed in 2015 prior to the approval of the projects, accounting for 96.77% and 95.92% respectively. Those of 31 provinces and 42 large cities disclosed the information about environmental impact assessment of projects constructed in 2015 after the approval of the projects, accounting for 100% and 85.71% respectively. Those of 29 provinces and 38 large cities disclosed the information about the acceptance of application for environmental protection inspection and acceptance upon the completion of construction projects in 2015, accounting for 93.55% and 77.55% respectively. Those of 30 provinces and 37 large cities disclosed the information about environmental protection inspection and acceptance of construction projects completed in 2015 prior to the approval, accounting for 96.77% and 75.51% respectively. Those of 31 provinces and 42 large cities provided the information about protection inspection and acceptance of construction projects completed in 2015 after the approval, accounting for 100% and 85.71% respectively.

Third, the overall performance on the disclosure of information about key pollutant-discharging enterprises was satisfactory. The environmental protection departments of 31 provinces and 40 large cities disclosed the information about key pollutant-discharging enterprises or key environmentally regulatory objects within the provinces in 2015, accounting for 100% and 81.63% respectively.

Fourth, the overall performance on the disclosure of information about review and approval of radiation safety and issuance of permits showed positive results. Among provincial-level environmental protection departments, 25 disclosed the results of review and approval of environmental impact assessment of radiation projects constructed in 2015, accounting for 80.65%; 23 provided the results of environmental protection inspection and acceptance for radiation projects constructed in 2015, accounting for 74.19%; 25 disclosed the information about issuance of radiation safety permits in 2015, accounting for 80.65%. Among the large-city governments, those of Chengdu, Hefei, Shantou, Suzhou and Luoyang disclosed all of the aforesaid three types of information in 2015.

Nevertheless, the following two issues were also identified.

First, the performance of large cities on the disclosure of information about radiation safety was less than satisfactory. Information about radiation safety consisted of the results of review and approval of environmental impact assessment of radiation projects, the results of environmental protection inspection and acceptance for radiation projects, and the information about issuance of radiation safety. The evaluation found that the performance of the environmental protection departments of large cities on the disclosure of information about radiation safety was poor. Among environmental protection departments of large cities, 34 did not disclose the results of review and approval of environmental impact assessment of radiation projects, accounting for 69.39% and only 12 disclosed the results for radiation projects constructed in 2015, accounting for 24.49%; 36 failed to disclose the results of environmental protection inspection and acceptance for radiation projects, accounting for 73.47% and only nine provided the results for radiation projects constructed in 2015, accounting for 18.37%; 25 failed to disclose the information about issuance of radiation safety permits, accounting for 51.02% and only 18 provided the information about permits issued in 2015, accounting for 36.73%.

Second, the channels used for the disclosure of information about environmental protection shall be further integrated. An increasing number of governments developed a special section on their websites besides the existing information disclosure section to disclose the information in key fields, of which the information about environmental protection was considered as an important component. However, instead of being categorized, the information about environmental protection in some sections was simply listed there, bringing extra difficulty for the public to locate the information they need. Also, the information provided by some local environmental protection departments was inconsistent with what was disclosed in the information disclosure section on government websites, which would confuse the public.

9.6 Information About Administrative Approval

The following highlights have been noticed in the disclosure of information about administrative approval.

First, the overall performance on the disclosure of directory for items under administrative approval showed positive results.

Thirty-one provincial-level governments and 47 large-city governments disclosed the list of items under administrative approval on their websites, accounting for 100% and 95.92% respectively.

Second, the sections developed by some evaluation objects were very clear and information was easily accessible.

On the homepage of some official government websites, the lists of powers and responsibilities were published at a prominent position. The section for information about administrative approval was user-friendly with the lists there sorted according to corresponding government agencies and the procedures for administrative approval clearly explained. The complete and standardized guidelines on public services were also provided and easy to find. Taking the government websites of Hebei, Henan, Zhuhai and Jinan as an example, the layout of the homepages was reasonably designed, which not only further highlighted the section of administrative approval, but also optimized the presentation of items by types of administrative approval to enhance user experience. Heilongjiang designed its government website with elegant simplicity. The lists of powers and responsibilities on the website can be easily located by searching the types of powers on the upper side of the homepage or selecting the name of the department on the left side, both of which provided convenience for the public.

Third, most of the evaluation objects disclosed the basis for administrative approval, application qualifications, application documents, and approval procedures.

Among provincial-level governments, 24 directly disclosed the basis for administrative approval in the approval lists, accounting for 77.42%, four disclosed the basis in the public service section instead, and other three disclosed the basis in some of the items under administrative approval. Among the government of large cities, 47 disclosed the basis on their websites, accounting for 95.92%, of which 39 directly disclosed the basis in the approval lists while eight in the public service section instead.

Twenty-two provincial-level governments disclosed information about application qualifications, accounting for 70.97%, among which two disclosed the information in the list of items subject to approval and 20 in the public service section instead. Meanwhile, 39 large-city governments disclosed information about application qualifications, accounting for 79.59%, among which eight provided the information in the list of items subject to approval and 31 in the public service section instead.

Twenty-four provincial-level governments disclosed information about application documents, accounting for 77.42%, among which three disclosed the information in the list of items subject to approval and 21 in the public service section. Meanwhile, 44 large cities disclosed information about application documents, accounting for 89.80%, among which 12 have disclosed the information in the list of items subject to approval and 32 in the public service section.

Twenty-four provincial-level governments disclosed information about approval procedures, accounting for 77.42%, among which five disclosed the information in the list of items subject to approval and 19 in the public service section. Meanwhile, 44 large cities disclosed information about approval procedures, accounting for 89.80%, among which13 disclosed the information in the list of items subject to approval and 31 in the public service section.

Fourth, the vast majority of the evaluation objects that were selected for random inspection disclosed the approval results.

In terms of provincial-level governments, the departments responsible for the supervision and administration of production safety were selected. The evaluation found that among the departments selected, 28 disclosed the results of administrative approvals, accounting for 90.32%. In terms of the large-city governments, the departments responsible for the supervision and administration of food and drugs were selected. The evaluation found that among the departments selected, 47 disclosed the approval results, accounting for 95.92%.

Nevertheless, the following problems were identified.

First, the guidelines on public services disclosed were less than accurate. The guidelines disclosed in the list of items subject to approval shall be consistent with the ones that disclosed in the public service section on the website. However, what the evaluation found was quite opposite. Among provincial-level governments, only eight disclosed the guidelines with consistency between the approval list and the public service section, accounting for 25.81%; and eight provided the guidelines with consistency between the approval list and the government affairs service center, accounting for 25.81%. Among the large-city governments, 17 disclosed the guidelines with consistency between the approval list and the public service section, accounting for 34.69%; while 16 disclosed the guidelines with consistency between the approval list and the government affairs service center, accounting for 32.65%.

Second, most of the government websites did not have a special section for disclosing the results of permit application. Only 17 provincial-level governments developed a special section on their websites, accounting for 54.84% of total provincial-level governments, among which 15 developed on the government websites and two on the website of administrative service centers. Twenty-three large-city governments developed a special section on their websites, accounting for 46.94% of the total, among which 19 developed a section on the official website and four on the website of administrative service centers.

9.7 Request-Based Information Disclosure

In the name of an ordinary citizen, the Project Team submitted requests for information disclosure via registered mail to 54 departments under the State Council, 31 provincial-level pricing regulatory departments and 49 civil affairs departments of large cities on November 10, 2015. The information requested varied among different departments under the State Council. The information requested from 31 provincial-level pricing regulatory departments was "the current admission fees of 5A-level tourist sites in the province and the ticket prices of specific spots within the tourist sites (including but not limited to the list of tourist sites, the ticket price of each tourist site at high season and low season, ticket prices of spots within the tourist sites, and the basis for pricing)". The information requested from the civil affairs departments was "the list of the names of existing public welfare and charity organizations registered at the municipal government." Then, the Project Team started to review whether these departments provided a reply within 15 working days, calculated from the second working day from the date when the requests were delivered to these departments.

According to the evaluation, the evaluation objects performed well in the following aspects.

First, the channels for submitting requests by mail were generally accessible.

Among the evaluation objects, 53 departments under the State Council, 30 provincial-level pricing regulatory departments and 48 municipal-level civil affairs departments of large cities provided accessible channels for submitting requests by mail. All registered mails sent by the Project Team to these organizations were signed upon receipt, accounting for 98.15%, 96.77% and 97.96% respectively. The channels provided by three organizations were inaccessible, they were: State Administration of Cultural Heritage—the mail was returned due to "change of address"; Hainan Pricing Administration—the mail was returned due to "rejection by security" and later "overdue for pickup"; and Guangzhou Civil Affairs Administration——the mail was returned also due to "rejection by security" and later "overdue for pickup".

Second, the majority of administrative agencies replied in a timely manner.

Most of them provided an official replay via mail or email within the statutory period. Forty-one departments under the State Council, 23 provincial-level pricing regulatory departments and 37 civil affairs departments of large cities provided either an written or electronic reply within 15 working days after the date when they received the request, accounting for 75.93%, 74.19% and 75.51% respectively.

Third, most of the administrative agencies replied in a standard format.

The replies provided by mail were all in a standard format with all stamped with the official seal of the agency. Most of the replies provided via email were in a standard format, either attached with an electronic copy of the reply stamped with the official seal of the agency, or clearly specifying the letterhead or signature of the agency. Statistically speaking, 23 out of the 26 departments under the State Council, nine out of 18 provincial-level pricing regulatory departments, and 13 out of 34 civil affairs departments of large cities replied via mail in a standard format. In addition, it can be seen from the above data that, compared with provincial-level pricing regulatory departments and civil affairs departments of the large cities, departments under the State Council performed better in this respect.

Fourth, most of provincial-level pricing regulatory departments and the civil affairs departments of large cities disclosed the information requested.

The aforesaid information requested by the Project Team to provincial-level pricing regulatory departments and civil affairs departments of large cities was information that can be disclosed, either by voluntary disclosure or request-based disclosure. Twenty-three out of 27 provincial-level pricing regulatory departments and 35 out of 37 municipal-level civil affairs departments of large cities fully or partially disclosed the requested information in their replies. Among the remaining four provincial-level pricing regulatory departments, one replied that the information did not exist, and the other three replied that the agency was not in the position of disclose the information requested. Meanwhile, one of the remaining two civil affairs departments of large cities partially disclosed the information in its reply while the other replied that the information did not exist.

Nevertheless, the following problems were identified in request-based disclosure.

First, a few administrative agencies failed to provide effective channels for submitting requests by registered mail.

The channels for submitting requests by registered mail provided by a few government agencies either failed to work or might cause delay of submissions. One cause of this problem was the failure of the agencies responsible for processing the requests to timely update its address in the guidelines on government information disclosure. For example, the request submitted to the State Administration of Cultural Heritage was returned due to "change of address", which illustrated that the address was not updated promptly. Another example was that the request filed with the National Bureau of Surveying, Mapping and Geographical Information was submitted by the Project Team on November 10, 2015 and signed off upon delivery on December 18, 2015. However, when receiving the call from the Project Team on December 21, 2015, a staff member said that they had just received the request due to wrong address, which also illustrated that the address was not updated. Another cause was that the address provided in the guidelines on government information disclosure was inaccurate. For example, the Project Team submitted the request to the State Intellectual Property Bureau on November 10, 2015 based on the address provided in its guidelines. However, while receiving the call from the Project Team on December 1, 2015, a staff member said that due to the wrong address, which was actually the address of its office of letters and visits, the request was delayed as it had taken a quite long time to redeliver it.

Second, a few administrative agencies failed to reply within the statutory period.

Four provincial-level pricing regulatory departments replied to the requests after the required deadline. Twenty-one government agencies—8 departments under the State Council, two provincial-level pricing regulatory departments and 11 civil affairs departments of large cities—did not replied at all. One department under the State Council and one provincial-level pricing regulatory department asked the Project Team to supplement request materials, and three other departments under the State Council requested the Project Team to provide materials explaining the use of information. In addition, a few government agencies refused to provide written replies. For instance, A staff member of Kunming Municipal Bureau of Civil Affairs told the Project Team over phone that they could only reply by phone and refused to reply by other methods without giving any reason. In the end, Kunming Municipal Bureau of Civil Affairs did not provide any formal response.

Third, the format of replies provided by a few government agencies via email was still not standardized.

Three out of 26 departments under the State Council, nine out of 18 provincial-level pricing regulatory departments and 21 out of 34 civil affairs departments of large cities replied via email in a less standardized format. This was reflected in the way that the attached reply was not stamped with the official seal of the agency, or the email itself did not include the letterhead or the signature of the agency. For instance, the reply of Harbin Bureau of Civil Affairs was sent via QQ mailbox, and there was nothing but one link included. The recipient did not know who the sender was until the link was clicked.

Fourth, the content of reply provided by some administrative agencies was not standardized.

Among the 41 departments under the State Council that replied, 18 disclosed all the information requested, two disclosed part of that, one refused to disclose any of that, three replied that the information was out the scope of disclosure, four replied that they the information did not exist, seven replied that the agency was not responsible for disclosing the information requested, one replied that the agency was responsible for processing and compiling the information, one replied that some part of the information did not exist and they agency was not in the position to disclose the other part. three replied that the request shall be deemed as policy consultation instead, and one replied that the information was out of the scope of disclosure. Among the 27 provincial-level pricing regulatory departments replied, 23 disclosed the information, one replied that the information did not exist, and three replied that the agency was not in the position to disclose the information. Among the 37 civil affairs departments of large cities replied, 35 disclosed the information, one provided part of that, and one replied that the information did not exist.

Some government agencies did not provide clearly the links of or the searching channels for information that had been voluntarily disclosed, neither did they inform the Project Team of the legal basis for reply and the relief channels. Also, in the relief channels provided by a few government agencies, the prescribed period for administrative proceedings was inaccurate. In the *Administrative Litigation Law of the People's Republic of China*, the period has been revised to six months, but some administrative agencies—for example, China Earthquake Administration—failed to update the information in the reply. Then, some administrative agencies experienced decreased experience in this respect. For instance, during the evaluation of government information dis closure in 2014, the Ministry of Finance provided a contact number for the General Office of Financial Information Disclosure to the Project Team in the Notification to Make Rectification. The Project Team made several calls but nobody answered. In 2015, the Ministry of Finance did not even leave a contact number in the Notification they sent to the Project Team.

Fifth, the scope of policy consultation defined by a few administrative agencies was too broad.

In the evaluation, the Project Team requested the State Administration of Taxation for policy information. Instead of communicating with the Project Team over phone, the agency replied via email that the request was a policy consultation, and suggested that the Project Team shall either make a supplementary request or search the information online. A policy itself is the basis for the administrative actions of the government agencies and belongs to government information. When the content of the relevant policy were requested, government agencies shall treat it as a request for government information disclosure; when applicants have trouble in understanding the content of the policy, it is a policy consultation then.

9.8 Annual Report on Government Information Disclosure

The Project Team completed the evaluation of the disclosure of annual reports by April 1, 2015. The evaluation found that the majority of administrative agencies managed to disclose the annual report within the statutory period. After searching on the website of the government agencies, the Project Team found that, as of 24:00 on March 31, 2014, the only one department under the State Council that failed to issue the annual report was the Ministry of Justice, and all of the provincial-level governments and large cities have issued theirs in a timely manner. The Ministry issued its annual report later, with the release dated marked as March 31, 2015.

Most of the evaluation objects summarized and analyzed their work on voluntary disclosure in 2014. A description of the collected data for voluntary disclosure was provided by 53 departments under the State Council, 31 provincial-level governments and 47 large-city governments.

Most of the evaluation objects disclosed the general results of accepting and replying to requests. The number of the departments under the State Council, provincial-level governments and large cities that provided the number of requests received was 54, 31 and 48 respectively; while the corresponding number of those that made public their replies in general was 54, 28 and 45 respectively.

The following problems were also identified in this respect.

First, the development of the section for and the release of the annual report of some government agencies were not standardized. For example, Yinchuan Municipal Government developed a special section for information disclosure on its homepage but failed to develop a section for publishing the annual report. Its 2014 annual report was placed in the public announcement section instead and it took quite a long time to locate it. Hohhot Municipal Government was another example, it developed a section for government affairs disclosure but fail to develop a section for publishing the annual report either. The government did not provide its 2014 annual report on its website. Its annual reports of 2009–2014 were ere found under the annual report directory on the website of the Inner Mongolia autonomous region. Some of the annual reports developed by the government departments, district-level or county-level governments of Hohhot was disclosed in such sections as "official documents and announcements", "news of banners, counties and districts", "department news" on the website of the municipal government. Also, Hubei only disclosed the 2014 annual report under the directory for annual report on information disclosure. The annual reports of other years were not provided there but could be found on Baidu. Hunan published not only the annual report developed by the provincial-level government but also those by various departments and district-level governments under the directory. As these annual reports were not categorized, searching for the documents was quite difficult.

Second, the content of the 2014 annual report disclosed by some governments and that of previous reports were highly repetitive. By comparing the annual reports of different years, the Project Team found that the 2014 annual report disclosed by China Earthquake Administration, the State Administration of Foreign Exchange, the State Administration of Traditional Chinese Medicine, and the Government of Xinjiang Uygur Autonomous Region and their 2013 report were highly repetitive.

Third, details about relevant items were not provided in the annual report. For example, in the 2014 annual report of 35 departments under the State Council, eight provincial-level governments and 21 large cities, the items with top requests were not provided. Another example was that in the 2014 annual report of 25 departments under the State Council, five provincial-level governments and ten large cities categorized statistics on the replies to the requests were not provided.

9.9 Suggestions Based on the 2015 Evaluation

In 2016, the General Office of the CCCPC and the General Office of the State Council issued the *Opinions on Comprehensively Promoting the Openness of Government Affairs,* which stipulated clear requirements on the work of comprehensively promoting the disclosure of government affairs. How to implement the requirements to improve the effectiveness of the openness is a topic currently facing government agencies at all levels. It is recommended that government agencies strengthen government information disclosure from the following aspects.

First, promote the information disclosure work with rule-based mindset and practices. Government at all levels are advised to conduct a comprehensive review of the existing relevant laws and regulations base on the current social situation and administration needs while taking the amendments to the Regulations into account. The review shall focus on the regulations concerning disclosure and confidentiality and the public authority and responsibilities of various government agencies, so as to promptly fill the system gap, modify outdated regulations and strengthen coordination between relevant laws and regulations.

Second, focus on boosting standardized and regulated disclosure. The departments under the State Council and provincial-level governments shall focus on top-level system design, strengthen the instruction of wok on government information disclosure in related industries and regions, and issue detailed requirements for the work. Meanwhile, based on the functions and responsibilities of government agencies at different levels, their respective disclosure obligations and responsibilities shall be clarified, so as to prevent the requirements made for them are too general. In addition, it is recommended that the lists of items for voluntary disclosure be developed in different industries, to develop specific requirements for the subjects, objects, scope, approaches and timeline of disclosure, and ensure that information of the same kind can be disclosed in accordance with the same standards.

Third, promote the disclosure of government affairs and the establishment of a law-based government simultaneously, and consider the entire decision-making and execution process with the mindset that information disclosure shall be the norm. The final decisions of all administration segments of government agencies, including some internal affairs, cannot be made without undergoing a legality review, social risk evaluation, and a disclosure attributes review. It is necessary to review whether the information generated in each administration stage can withstand future public tests in the light of the fact that all information may be requested by the public in the future or be voluntarily disclosed.

Fourth, consider public demands as both the initial intention and the ultimate goal of government information disclosure. The self-centered disclosure mindset and practices shall be completely changed. Government agencies shall figure out what items about government administrations citizens want to know, study and make judgment on the situations facing government information disclosure through public participation, survey on public needs, analysis of the current situation and the future trend of government information disclosure. The work or government information disclosure shall be changed from a "set menu" developed by governments to having the public do "a la carte"—instead of disclosing what the government agencies want to made public, government affairs and information can be disclosed according to the needs of the public, in the ways they want, in an accurate, comprehensive, effective, and timely manner. Also, the different information needs and information acquisition capabilities of different groups of people shall be considered and information shall be proactively sent to targeted audience. For people living in developed regions and those who are capable of using information technology or willing to do so to obtain information, information shall be disclosed on government portals and other online platforms, while for people living in backward areas and those who are unable to use information technology, more conventional ways such as bulletin boards or brochures should be employed.

Chapter 10
The 2016 Evaluation of China's Government Transparency

10.1 Overview of the Work of Government Information Disclosure in 2016

In 2016, the General Office of the CCCPC and the General Office of the State Council issued the *Opinions on Comprehensively Promoting the Openness of Government Affairs*, and the General Office of the State Council issued the *Detailed Implementation Rules of the 'Opinions on Comprehensively Promoting the Openness of Government Affairs'*" and the *Key Tasks in Promoting the Transparency of Government Affairs in 2016*, etc. All of these illustrated that the comprehensive promotion of the disclosure of government affairs was highly valued by governments at all levels and they proactively worked on the disclosure of decision-making, implementation, administrative procedures, government services and implementation results. In other words, the release of the *Opinions on Comprehensively Promoting the Openness of Government Affairs* signified a new chapter for the construction of a transparent government since the release of the Regulations.

The evaluation found that, large cities performed better than county-level governments in terms of government affairs disclosure. Statistically speaking, in terms of the construction of government information disclosure platforms, 83.67% of large-city governments and 73% of county-level governments developed a special section for government information disclosure on their portal websites and provided complete information in the sections; in terms of the disclosure of normative documents, 75.51 percent of large-city governments and 45 percent of county-level governments developed a section for disclosure of normative documents and also categorized the documents; in terms of the disclosure of information about administrative approval, 100% of large-city governments and 98% of county-level governments published the list of items subject to administrative approval; and in terms of the disclosure of the annual report on government information disclosure, all large-city governments and 92% of county-level governments disclosed their 2015 annual report.

Y. Lv and H. Tian, *Evaluation on Government Transparency Index in China (2009–2016)*, Understanding China, https://doi.org/10.1007/978-981-16-5032-1_10

Also, after analyzing the performance of county-level governments and large cities in 2016, the Project Team found that, the level of voluntary disclosure was gradually increasing and request-based information was becoming more standardized.

First, the disclosure of information in some key areas was increasingly detailed and standardized. The performance of government agencies in various regions on the disclosure of information in some key areas such as the power list, information about environmental protection, information about shanty town redevelopment, information about social assistance, and information about education showed positive results in general as they were stepping up their efforts in this respect. For example, Beijing Municipal Government re-examined and released a three-level list of items for disclosure including the power list. The lists consist of 4909 standards, and they were categorized under 959 directories and applied to governments at the municipal, district and county level respectively. The standards required the governments at the three levels to disclose information for public inquiry. The municipal and county-level governments nationwide also disclosed the power list. In terms of the disclosure of information about administrative approval, governments in various regions examined and published the guidelines on public services and the implementation results in according to the requirements for boosting the "Internet + Government Services" model.

Second, evaluation objects generally valued highly the construction of government portal. Government portal shall serve as the primary platform for government affairs disclosure. Having a well-constructed government portal and releasing reliable information is the fundamental assurance for government agencies to succeed in disclosing government affairs in an information era. The evaluation found that the government portals of the evaluation objects were generally well constructed. The elements of the sections were relatively completed. The searching functions on most websites were effective. Quite a few websites also developed the barrier-free browsing function for the visually disabled.

Third, the evaluation objects disclosed the local information in one place on their government portals, which was easily accessible. To start with, many governments developed a sub-section for information in key fields under the special section for government information disclosure of their government portal. In the sub-section, key departments' information in critical fields that were related to the people's livelihood or of huge public concern was disclosed in one place. Also, in terms of the disclosure of government services, governments in many regions, such as Guiyang and Lanzhou, set up a dedicated platform to release guidelines developed by the departments or counties and county-level cities under jurisdiction. A few governments also disclosed at one place the information in the same fields but from different departments. One example is the disclosure of the information about the water quality monitoring of drinking water from centralized supply sources. Suqian Municipal Environmental Protection Bureau in Jiangsu province disclosed in one place on its website the information about the water quality of drinking water from supply sources, the information about the water quality of outlet water from the water plants, and the information about the water quality of the user-end tap water, which the Municipal Environmental Protection Bureau, the Municipal Water Resources Bureau and the

Municipal Health and Family Planning Commission were responsible for publishing respectively. Provided in one place, information was more easily accessible to the public, thus improving the disclosure result.

Fourth, the channels for submitting requests for information disclosure were generally accessible and replies were provided in a standard format. The verification result showed that almost all the channels provided by the evaluation objects were accessible, except one channel of submission via mail, which did not work. The majority of administrative agencies were managed to reply within the statutory period, with both the format and content of the replies being standardized.

Nevertheless, some common issues in the work of government affairs disclosure were revealed, which shall be taken seriously by governments when promoting the work.

First, some details of the work shall be further clarified. To start with, there is no clear boundary line among the "Five Types of Disclosure"—the disclosure of decision-making, administrative procedures, government services, execution and implementation results. The five types are sometimes overlapped and unclear, making it difficult for local governments to implement the work. Also, the standards for disclosure are not clear enough. Despite the fact that many local governments have develop a special section for the "Five Types of Disclosure" and relevant information has been disclosed in different categories, the information disclosed was mainly news rather than the information about government affairs. Then, the government agencies responsible for the disclosure of information in key fields are unclear. In the *Key Tasks in Promoting the Transparency of Government Affairs in 2016* issued by the General Office of the State Council, the key information that shall be disclosed in 2016 was provided, but it did not specify which government agencies were responsible for disclosing such information. For example, the 2016 *Key Tasks* only required to disclose housing security information. However, in the *Guiding Opinions of the General Office of the State Council on Construction and Management of Affordable Housing Projects(No. 45 [2011] of the General Office of the State Council)*, it was stipulated that the organizations responsible for disclosing housing security information shall be county-level and municipal governments.

Second, county-level governments and their departments need to upgrade their capacity for government portal development, which directly impacts disclosure results. The evaluation found that many local governments, especially county-level governments and their departments, were affected due to a lack of the capacity and disclosure results. To start with, most county-level government websites had floating windows, and those on some websites could not be closely, which seemed like a means to force people to read. Also, a few websites were poorly built. For example, the website of the Ongniud Banner Education Bureau in Inner Mongolia autonomous region consisted of only one picture, and all links were invalid except one at the bottom of the website that directed to the list of schools. Then, the sections on some websites were in a chaos and confusing. Examples include the section on the websites of Yima Municipal Government in Henan province, Zhuanghe Municipal Government in Liaoning province, Lixia District Government of Jinan City in Shandong province and Rongchang District Government of Chongqing, the functions of all of which were unclear and none of which was reasonably designed. Lastly, the information about some pages of a few websites was not normally displayed. For example, on the website of Hunan Changsha County Government and under the guidelines on the application for the support for extremely poor people and temporary assistance, error messages were showed.

Third, the same information has been disclosed on too many platforms. Many local governments set up several platforms to disclose information of the same type, which made people confused about the information disclosure channels and brought about extra difficulties for public inquiry. Taking the release of the annual report as an example, many local governments released their annual reports both on their government portals and on that of their superior governments. However, the information disclosed on the two platforms by some evaluation objects was either overlapped or both incomplete. The release of information was in a chaotic and random manner.

Fourth, information of the same type disclosed on different platforms was inconsistent. Many local governments disclosed information of the same kind on several platforms. However, the information was inconsistent and could easily mislead the public. Taking the release of guidelines on public access to the items subject to administrative approval as example, the guidelines on same type of items subject to administrative approval were disclosed on the websites of local governments, government service centers and relevant departments. However, the information about the basis for government services, application procedures, documents to be submitted and the office locations was often inconsistent. What's worse, the problem of inconsistency between the information disclosed online and that published offline existed.

10.2 Platforms for Government Information Disclosure

The following two highlights were found in this respect.

First, the special section for government information disclosure was generally developed in a standardized manner.

To start with, the special section developed by most evaluation objects was equipped with complete elements. Statistically speaking, 41 large-city governments and 73 county-level governments developed a special section which contained the sub-sections for publishing the basis for information disclosure, the guidelines on information disclosure, the annual report on information disclosure and the information about request-based disclosure, accounting for 83.6% and 73% respectively.

Also, some evaluation objects disclosed information of the same type from their subordinated departments, districts and counties in the special section to facilitate public inquiry. For example, the governments of Guangzhou, Qingdao, Jingjiang in Jiangsu province, Duolun County in Inner Mongolia autonomous region disclosed the information from their departments and subordinates in such way. Some evaluation objects also published the information about request-based disclosure in corresponding sub-section in a centralized way. For instance, the municipal governments of Ningbo and Hefei developed some level-three sections—including sections for information about disclosure procedures, approaches, inquires, form downloads and fee standards—under the sub-section for requested-based disclosure.

A few evaluation objects disclosed their replies to requests for information disclosure or the statistics about request-based disclosure. One example is the government of Nanchang County in Jiangxi province, which developed a request-based disclosure sub-section under the special section for information disclosure. The items of request received and their replies were disclosed in the sub-section. Another example is Hefei Municipal Government, which created a level-three section for statistics about request-based disclosure under the sub-section for request-based disclosure. In the level-three section, the statistics about requests received by the government and its departments and their replies were published.

Second, most evaluation objects equipped their websites with the barrier-free browsing function.

The evaluation found that the governments of 28 large cities developed the function on their government portal, among which, 27 provided a reading aid function—users could enlarge the texts or the pages, accounting for 55.10%; 26 provided another reading aid function—users could change the background of the page or the color of the texts, accounting for 53.06%; and 22 provided a speech aid function, accounting for 44.90%.

Nevertheless, the following problems were also identified.

First, the performance of a few evaluation objects on the development of the special section for information disclosure was less satisfactory.

The elements of a few governments' special section were incomplete. Among all the evaluation objects, eight large-city governments and 19 county-level governments failed to equip their special section with a sub-section for publishing the basis for information disclosure; six county-level governments did not have a sub-section for publishing the guidelines on information disclosure; four county-level governments failed to provide a sub-section for publishing the annual report on information disclosure; and one government of large cities and 11 county-level governments did not have a sub-section for request-based disclosure.

The special section of a few evaluation objects was developed in a less standardized manner, making it inconvenient for the public to search information. For example, Hubei developed a uniform government information disclosure platform across the province, with which a special section for information disclosure for Jinzhou City was equipped. In the special section, the guidelines and annual reports on information disclosure and other information were published. However, there was no access to the special section or the platform on the official website of Jinzhou Municipal Government.

A few evaluation objects failed to have a clear understanding of what should be published in the special section. One example was that what was placed in the subsection for the basis for information disclosure on the government website of Golmud in Qinghai province was not the basis. Also, in the sub-section for the guidelines on information disclosure on the government websites of Xiaoyi City in Shanxi province,

Yima City in Henan province, Shenqiu county in Henan province, and Golmud City in Qinghai province, information unrelated to guidelines also existed.

Second, information was not fully or accurately disclosed in the special section.

A few evaluation objects did not provide the information developed itself. In the sub-section for the basis for information disclosure of three large-city governments, 18 county-level, no document about government information disclosure was found. In the sub-section for guidelines on information disclosure of five county-level governments, no guidelines developed by themselves were found. In the sub-section for the annual reports of one county-level government, no annual report developed by the government was found.

Some content of the guidelines on government information disclosure provided by a few evaluation objects was inaccurate. Information about the ways to request for information disclosure provided by five county-level governments—the governments of Pingfang District of Harbin City in Heilongjiang province, Wuchang District of Wuhan City in Hubei province, Huichuan District of Zunyi City in Guizhou province, Tengchong City in Yunnan province and Pingluo County in Ningxia Hui autonomous region—in the sub-section for guidelines on information disclosure was inconsistent with that provided in the sub-section for information about request-based disclosure. For example, in the guidelines provided by the government of Pingfang District, it said that information could be requested via emails, however, no email address of the responsible agency was provided in the guidelines. At the same time, the guidelines did not describe online request as a method, though an online request platform was already provided on the website.

Third, the performance of some evaluation objects on the searching function was less satisfactory.

The evaluation found that some governments either failed to provide any searching function or the function provided was invalid. The government of one large city and 12 county-level governments failed to provide the function; four large-city governments and 26 county-level governments provided invalid function.

Fourth, some evaluation objects failed to provide the barrier-free browsing function on their websites.

In accordance with the *Guiding Opinions on Improving the Barrier-free Service Capabilities of Websites,* jointly issued by China Disabled Persons' Federation and the Office of the Central Leading Group for Cyberspace Affairs, the barrier-free service capabilities of websites shall be enhanced according to relevant national standards and a barrier-free service environment for the public access to network information shall be comprehensively fostered. Among all large-city governments evaluated, 21 failed to equip their official website with the barrier-free browsing function, accounting for 42.86%. one example was that though Harbin Municipal Government provided the access to barrier-free browsing function, the link was invalid. Among the 28 large-city governments that provided the barrier-free browsing function, six only provided a reading aid function but not a speech aid function; while one was quite the opposite.

10.3 Normative Documents

The following seven highlights were found in this respect.

First, some evaluation objects disclosed information about the solicitation of public opinions on normative documents in a relatively standardized manner.

Information elements about the solicitation published by some governments were complete. The elements included drafts of normative documents, channels for opinion collection and time period of the solicitation. The evaluation found that 32 large-city governments and 16 county-level governments provided the aforesaid elements, accounting for 65.31% and 16% respectively.

A few evaluation objects innovated their approaches to publish information about the solicitation of public opinions on normative documents. For example, Guangzhou Municipal Government developed a sub-section for diagrams of opinion solicitation. In the sub-section, charts were provided to illustrate the solicitation process of some normative documents. It improved the readability of the drafts and was an effort to proactively interpret policies earlier.

Second, some evaluation objects valued highly the disclosure of feedbacks.

Some published the feedbacks on opinion solicitation. The governments of 11 large cities and two county-level governments disclosed general information about the solicitation of public opinions on normative documents. Among them, Shenzhen Municipal Government provided a summary of the opinions and suggestions solicited, and described the number of the opinions, the categorized statistics about the opinions collected in different ways, and the main points of the opinions. The governments of five large cities provided information about whether the opinions were adopted or not. Among them, Suzhou Municipal Government also provided detailed reasons why some opinions were rejected.

Some published the feedbacks on the solicitation of opinions on the drafts of rules and regulations. The governments of 11 large cities provided general information about the solicitation. Among them, one stated that it did not receive any opinion; six provided the information about which opinions were adopted; and five gave reasons why some opinions were rejected. For instance, Xiamen Municipal Government detailed in its feedbacks the background of developing rules and regulations, the process of opinion solicitation, the summary of opinions solicited, and information about which opinions were adopted and why.

Third, the information about opinion solicitation and feedbacks provided by some evaluation objects was easy for the public to search.

Some published the information about the solicitation of opinions on normative documents together with the feedbacks to make it easier to search. For example, the municipal governments of Guangzhou, Shenzhen and Suzhou developed two sub-sections—one for public opinions solicited and one for feedbacks—under the section for opinion solicitation, to make it easier to search related information. For another example, the municipal governments of Fuzhou, Xiamen, Wuxi and the government of Hepu County in Guangxi Zhuang autonomous region developed a sub-section for feedbacks beside the information about opinion solicitation that had been published, directing to the corresponding feedback.

Fourth, some evaluation objects categorized normative documents in multiple ways.

The categorization of normative documents by year, type of document, issuing department, related item or validity would make it more convenient to search. Among the 49 large-city governments and 98 county-level governments that developed a section for publishing normative documents, eight large-city governments and ten county-level governments classified their normative documents in more than two ways.

Fifth, some evaluation objects marked the validity of their normative documents.

Marking the validity of normative documents helped clarify whether the document was still effective. Two ways of marking the validity were found in the evaluation. One was to mark in the list of the documents or on the top of a specific page, evaluation objects using this method including the governments of Yinchuan City, Jinan City and Changsha City. The other one was to stipulate the validity at the time when the document was developed and published, evaluation objects using this method including the governments of Shantou City and Xinjin County in Chongqing. The evaluation found the 13 governments or large cities and 12 county-level governments marked the validity of all of their normative documents, accounting for 26.53% and 12% respectively; 21 large-city governments and 23 county-level governments marked that of some, accounting for 42.86% and 23% respectively.

Sixth, some evaluation objects performed well on the disclosure of information about the removal of invalid normative documents from websites.

In accordance with the *Opinions of the State Council on Strengthening the Building of a Government Ruled by Law*, administrative agencies shall publish the deletion result of normative documents. Invalid normative documents could be deleted on a regular basis or in a timely manner. The evaluation found that 38 large-city governments and 33 county-level governments published the result in recent two years. Among them, 12 employed the latter method, e.g. deleting in a timely manner, while 59 used the former approach. Changsha Municipal Government published on its website the report on the validity of normative documents every month.

Seventh, some evaluation objects performed relatively well on the disclosure of information about the filing review of normative documents.

The *Opinions of the State Council on Strengthening the Building of a Government Ruled by Law* clearly stipulated that the directory of regulations and normative documents that passed the filing review shall be released to the public on a regular basis. The evaluation found that 24 large-city governments and one county-level governments published the information about the filing review of normative documents. Among them, some evaluation objects, such as the municipal governments of Harbin, Luoyang, Nanchang, Qingdao, Jinan, Zibo, and Ningguo in Anhui province, published the information about a quarterly basis; a few large-city governments, such as those of Nanning, Xiamen and Guangzhou, disclosed the information about a monthly basis.

Nevertheless, the following five problems were also identified.

First, the majority of evaluation objects failed to properly publish the information about the solicitation of opinions on normative documents and feedbacks.

Most evaluation objects failed to disclose information about the solicitation of opinions on the drafts of normative documents. The governments of 15 large cities and 80 county-level governments failed to do so, accounting for 30.61% and 80% respectively. Also, among the 34 large-city governments and 20 county-level governments that disclosed the drafts, the governments of Benxi City, Xining City, Xintai City in Shandong province, Changsha County in Hunan province, Beibei District of Chongqing, and Mian County in Shaanxi province did not provide the channels for opinion solicitation; and the governments of Benxi City, Xining City, Xintai City in Shandong province, Beibei District of Chongqing and Mian County in Shaanxi province failed to provide the duration of the solicitation.

A few evaluation objects failed to disclose information about the solicitation of opinions on the drafts of normative documents in a timely manner. For example, it showed on the website of Harbin Municipal Government that the deadline for collecting opinions on the draft of a normative document was April 3, 2016. However, the message appeared online on April 5, 2016.

The duration of the solicitation provided by a few evaluation objects was too short. For example, Wuhan Municipal Government published a message on the website of the Legislative Affairs Office on October 14, 2016 to collect opinions on the draft of a normative document. The deadline for the collection was October 20, 2016—only six days were given. Similar circumstances were also found on the websites of the municipal governments of Hefei, Ningbo and Jinan.

Most evaluation objects failed to publish the feedbacks on the solicitation of opinions on normative documents or on regulations and rules. The governments of 37 large cities and 98 county-level governments did not publish any feedbacks on the solicitation of opinions on the normative documents, either a summary of the collected opinions or which opinions were adopted, accounting for 77.51% and 98% respectively. Among the remaining 12 government of large cities and two county-level governments, one large-city government only published the opinions adopted and did not provide the summary; seven large-city governments and two county-level governments only published the summary and did not disclose information about which opinions were adopted; one large-city governments stated that all opinions were adopted, and two large-city governments only provided a summary of the opinions collected and information about which opinions were adopted, but did not give any reasons to explain whether some opinions were rejected.

Most evaluation objects also failed to provide feedbacks on the solicited opinions on rules and regulations. The governments of 38 large cities did not provide any feedbacks, either a summary of the collected opinions or which opinions were adopted. Among the remaining 11 large-city governments, four only published the summary but did not explain which opinions were adopted.

Second, a few evaluation objects needed to develop the section for normative documents in a more standardized manner.

A few evaluation objects failed to develop any special section for publishing normative documents—2 county-level governments, to be exact.

A small number of evaluation objects failed to categorize their normative documents. Among the 49 large-city governments and 98 county-level governments that developed the section for normative documents, 12 large-city governments and 55 county-level governments did not categorize their normative documents.

The section for normative documents developed by a few evaluation objects was disorganized. The governments of 11 large cities and 15 county-level governments misplaced information unrelated to normative documents in the section. For example, Handan Municipal Government placed the rules and local laws and regulations in the section for normative documents, and normative documents were found in the section for publishing the government rules and regulations instead. Local laws and regulations were also found in the section for normative documents of Kunming Municipal Government.

Third, the performance of most evaluation objects on marking the validity of normative documents needed to be improved.

The governments of 15 large cities and 65 county-level governments failed to mark the validity or duration of validity of their normative documents that had been disclosed.

Fourth, most evaluation objects performed poorly on disclosing information about the removal of invalid normative documents.

The governments of 11 large cities and 67 county-level governments failed to do so in the recent two years.

Fifth, the performance of most evaluation objects on the disclosure of information about the filing review of normative documents needed to be enhanced.

The governments of 25 large cities and 99 county-level governments failed to provide any related information.

10.4 Information About Administrative Approval

The following three highlights were found in this respect.

First, evaluation objects were generally published the list of items subject to approval.

The list of items subject to approval was a major component of the list of powers. The disclosure of the list of items subject to approval on government portals could facilitate the public to the public to access government services and exercise oversight over the government. The evaluation found that 49 large-city governments and 98 county-level governments disclosed the list on their government portals, accounting for 100% and 98% respectively.

Second, the vast majority of evaluation objects released the guidelines on administrative approval.

The governments of 49 large cities and 95 county-level governments published the guidelines. Among them, 19 large-city governments and 38 county-level governments provided complete information in the guidelines, including the basis for administrative approval, application qualifications, application documents, approval procedures, approval timeline and fee standards. Also, Jinan Municipal Government provided a link of the sample of the document beside each application document required and users could download the sample document.

Third, some evaluation objects developed the section for publishing the results of administrative approval.

The governments of 38 large cities and 33 county-level governments developed the section to publish in one place the results of approval, accounting for 77.55% and 33% respectively. Some developed a "Dual disclosure" special section for publishing the results of approval, and the results were categorized by issuing department, district and county, such as Tangshan City and Dongcheng District of Beijing. In addition, the results disclosed by the issuing departments of a few evaluation objects the type of business. For example, Shenyang Municipal Food and Drug Administration categorized the results of approval by food, drug, medical equipment, and GSP.

Nevertheless, the following five problems were also identified.

First, a few evaluation objects failed to properly disclose the list of items subject to approval.

There were still two county-level governments failed to publish the list. Also, the content in the section for the lists of powers and responsibilities was not standardized. For example, other information was misplaced in the section for the lists of powers and responsibilities of Tongcheng in Anhui province, and the webpage for the disclosure of the lists of some departments was blank.

Second, the list of items subject to approval disclosed by some evaluation objects was not updated in a timely manner. In accordance with the *Circular of the Ministry of Civil Affairs on Accomplishing the Work of Cancellation of Qualification Accreditation Items for Welfare Enterprises*, the items subject to qualification accreditation for welfare enterprises have been canceled. Therefore, the evaluation objects should update their list of items subject to approval accordingly. However, 11 large-city governments and 33 county-level governments still had the item in their list, accounting for 22.45% and 33% respectively.

Third, the performance of most evaluation objects on the disclosure of guidelines on public access to the items subject to administrative approval needed to be strengthened.

A few evaluation objects failed to release the guidelines, including the governments of Lang County in Tibet autonomous region, Jiangyuan District of Baishan City in Jilin province, Gongzhuling City in Jilin province, Yima City in Henan province and Jingjiang City in Jiangsu province.

The elements of guidelines provided by most evaluation objects were incomplete. The complete elements shall consist of the basis for administrative approval, application qualifications, application documents, approval procedures, approval timeline and fee standards. However, the basis was not provided in part of the guidelines issued by five large-city governments and nine county-level governments; application qualifications was not specified in part of the guidelines issued by 17 large-city governments and 29 county-level governments; application documents was not specified in part of the guidelines issued by four large-city governments and 18 county-level governments; approval procedures was not included in part of the guidelines published by 11 large-city governments and 21 county-level governments; approval timeline was not provided in part of the guidelines published by three large-city governments and seven county-level governments; and fee standards was not specified in part of the guidelines published by 12 large-city governments and 28 county-level governments.

The application qualifications specified in the guidelines on public access to the items subject to administrative approval issued by some evaluation objects were unclear. In accordance with the *Guiding Opinions of the State Council on Accelerating the Advancement of "Internet plus Government Services"* (No. 55 [2016] of the State Council), no extra requirements shall be added upon those prescribed in the guidelines. However, the evaluation found that the application qualifications provided by 25 large-city governments and 45 county-level governments were unclear. Some used ambiguous words like "others", "relevant" or "etc." when referring to the application qualifications, such as the municipal governments of Taiyuan, Datong and Ningbo. Some provided the qualifications by saying only "in accordance with a relevant document" or "see the document for details". Examples including the municipal governments of Jilin, Chengdu and Renqiu in Heibei province, and the governments of Tiedong District of Anshan City in Liaoning province and Dunhua City in Jilin province. The application documents provided by some were unclear. A clear list of application documents would help the public not spend too much time on getting the public service. However, 19 large-city governments and 50 county-level governments still used ambiguous words like "others" or "etc." when referring to the application documents. the fee standards provided by some were not clear. For example, Tianchang Municipal Government in Anhui province only provided the document numbers of the basis for fee collection for some items subject to administrative approval and did not provide specific fee standards.

Fourth, the content of the guidelines on public access to the items subject to administrative approval published by some evaluation objects was not accurate enough.

A few evaluation objects failed to update the items subject to administrative approval under the section for the guidelines. For example, in the lists of powers and responsibilities of Pingjiang County in Hunan province, the qualification accreditation for welfare enterprises was no longer an item subjected to approval. However, it was still found in the section for publishing guidelines. The items provided on two platforms were inconsistent.

The guidelines on public access to the items subject to administrative approval released by a few governments on different platforms contradicted with each other. Some evaluation objects released the guidelines both in the list of items subject to approval and in the section or hall for online application or the online government services center. However, the guidelines released by 29 large-city governments and 25 county-level governments on multiple platforms were found inconsistent.

The content of some guidelines published by a few evaluation objects was inconsistent with the existing regulations. For example, in accordance with the *Measures for the Administration of Concession for Infrastructure and Public Utilities, the* concession period for infrastructure and public utilities shall not exceed 30 years.

However, the valid time limit of a license for a municipal public utility concession project in Change of Henan Province was 30 days. It could be a clerical error.

Fifth, the performance of some evaluation on the disclosure of the approval results was less than satisfactory.

The disclosure of approval results is a major component of online government services. The evaluation mainly reviewed the disclosure of the results on government portals, administrative service center websites and the websites of selected departments. Among them, six large-city governments failed to disclose the results in the field of food and drug administration, and 62 county-level governments did not publish the results in the field of health and family planning.

The approval results of a few evaluation objects were not disclosed in a standardized manner. For instance, Changge Municipal Government in Henan province used the same title for all results of administrative approval in the section for the disclosure of information about administrative approval, making it difficult to distinguish the specific approval results.

10.5 Information About Administrative Punishment

This section evaluated the disclosure of the list of items subject to administrative punishment and that of results of administrative punishment on enterprises involved.

The following two highlights were found in this respect.

First, evaluation objects generally published the list of items subject to administrative punishment.

Statistically speaking, 47 large-city governments and 95 county-level governments disclosed the list provided by the government departments at the corresponding level. Among them, the municipal governments of Dalian, Taiyuan, Urumqi, and Benxi classified the list of items by department, making it easier to search.

Second, the performance of evaluation objects on the disclosure of administrative punishment results relating to environmental protection showed positive results.

Most evaluation objects published the administrative punishment results relating to environmental protection. Statistically speaking, 46 large-city governments and 73 county-level governments disclosed the results. Among them, the elements of the results—including the name of the entity subject to punishment, description of illegal acts, basis for enforcing punishment and results of punishment—were complete.

However, the following three problems were also identified.

First, the performance of a few evaluation objects on the disclosure of the list of items subject to administrative punishment was less satisfactory.

In the evaluation, two large-city governments and five county-level governments failed to release the list. Among of the 47 large-city governments and 95 county-level governments that released the list, two large-city governments and one county-level government did not provide the legal basis; and one county-level government did not provide the legal basis for part of the items subject to administrative punishment.

The legal basis provided by a few evaluation objects was unclear. The legal basis provided by seven large-city governments and eight county-level governments did not include the complete titles of laws and regulations, clause number and content of clauses. For instance, the legal basis provided by the governments of Changsha City, Fuzhou City, Fengrun District of Tangshan City in Hebei province, Renqiu City in Hebei province, Lingqiu County in Shanxi province and Taijiang District of Fuzhou City in Fujian province did not include any content of clauses.

Second, performance on the disclosure of the results of administrative punishment needed to be enhanced.

A few evaluation objects failed to provide the results of administrative punishment relating to environmental protection—3 large-city governments and 27 county-level governments, to be specific. The elements of the results provided by a few evaluation objects were incomplete. Among those published the results, two county-level governments did not provide any description of the illegal acts at all; one county-level government did not provide a description of the illegal acts for part of the punishment results; one large-city government and seven county-level governments failed to provide the basis for enforcing punishment.

Most evaluation objects did not provide the administrative punishment results relating to safety production. The evaluation found that 25 large-city governments and 77 county-level governments failed to do so. The elements of the results provided by a few evaluation objects were incomplete. Among those published the results, three large-city governments and one county-level government did not provide a description of the illegal acts; two large-city governments and one county-level government failed to provide the basis for enforcing punishment; one large-city government and one county-level government did not provide the results of punishment.

Third, multiple platforms were used to disclose the results of administrative punishment.

Some evaluation objects published the results on different platforms. The websites used by governments in various regions included departmental website, government portal, and enterprise credit information website. Among the 46 large-city governments that published the administrative punishment results relating to environmental protection, 24 disclosed the results on the website of municipal-level environmental protection department; six on both the website of municipal-level environmental protection department and the enterprise credit information website; seven on both the website of municipal-level environmental protection department and the government portal; and nine on all the three websites. Disclosing information about multiple platforms tended to incur chaotic information disclosure and further lead to the inconvenience for information search.

10.6 Information About Environmental Protection

The following three highlights were found in this respect.

First, information about the water quality monitoring of drinking water from supply sources and that of outlet water from water supply plants was generally disclosed in a standardized manner.

Compared with the disclosure of the information about the quality of user-end tap water, most evaluation objects provided the information about the water quality monitoring of drinking water from supply sources and that of outlet water from water supply plants in a timely manner. Among the large-city governments evaluated, 46 published the information about the water quality monitoring of drinking water from supply sources on a monthly basis; 40 provided the information about drinking water safety of outlet water from water supply plants on a quarterly basis; and only 24 disclosed the information about the quality of user-end tap water.

Compared with what was required in related documents, most evaluation objects disclosed the information about the water quality monitoring of drinking water from centralized supply sources more frequently. Among all the large-city governments evaluated, one published the information about the water quality monitoring of drinking water from supply sources on a weekly basis; 25 provided the information about drinking water safety of outlet water from water supply plants on a monthly basis, one at the beginning, middle and end of each month, four on a weekly basis and five on a daily basis; 17 published the information about the quality of user-end tap water on a monthly basis, one on a weekly basis and one on a daily basis.

Second, evaluation objects generally performed well on the disclosure of information about pollution charges.

Most evaluation objects disclosed information charging standards and fee collection for pollution discharge. Statistically speaking, 42 large-city governments published charging standards and 40 large-city governments disclosed the information about fee collection.

Third, the performance on the disclosure of the information about environmental impact assessment of construction projects showed positive results.

Most evaluation objects published the public notice for acceptance of applications for environmental impact assessment of construction projects, public notice for applications subject to approval and decision on application of 2016. Among all the large-city governments evaluated, 47 provided the public notice for acceptance of applications; 47 disclosed the public notice for applications subject to approval, and 46 provided the decision on application for environmental impact assessment of construction projects.

However, the following three problems were also identified.

First, a small number of evaluation objects failed to properly disclose the information about the water quality monitoring of drinking water from centralized supply sources.

A few failed to disclose the information about the water quality monitoring of drinking water from supply sources on a monthly basis. To be specific, one large-city government disclosed the information on a quarterly basis and two even did not publish the information.

A few failed to disclose the information about drinking water safety of outlet water from water supply plants on a quarterly basis. To be specific, two large-city governments failed to disclose the information regularly, and seven even did not provide the information.

Most evaluation objects failed to provide the information about the quality of user-end tap water on a quarterly basis. To be specific, four large-city governments failed to disclose the information on a regular basis, and 21 even did not provide the information at all.

Second, a few evaluation objects did not provide the information about pollution charges.

To be specific, seven large-city governments did not publish charging standards, and nine failed to provide the fee collection of pollution discharge.

Third, the performance on disclosing the information about environmental impact assessment of construction projects needed to be strengthened.

A few evaluation objects did not disclose the public notice for acceptance of applications for environmental impact assessment of construction projects, public notice for applications subject to approval and decision on application. Statistically speaking, two large-city governments failed to provide the public notice for acceptance of applications for environmental impact assessment of construction projects; two did not provide the public notice for applications subject to approval and three did not provide the decision on application.

The elements of the public notice for acceptance of applications provided by a few evaluation objects were incomplete. In accordance with the *Notice on Printing and Distributing the guidelines for Disclosing Government Information about the Environmental Impact Assessment of Construction Projects (Trial)*, the public notice for acceptance of applications shall consist of project name, construction location, construction unit, environmental impact assessment agency, date of acceptance, environmental impact report, all application forms, and contact information for collecting public feedback. Seven large-city governments failed to disclose environmental impact report and all application forms.

The elements of the public notice for applications subject to approval provided by a few evaluation objects were incomplete. In accordance with the *Notice on Printing and Distributing the guidelines for Disclosing Government Information about the Environmental Impact Assessment of Construction Projects (Trial), the* public notice for applications subject to approval shall consist of project name, construction location, construction unit, environmental impact assessment agency, project overview, main environmental impacts, approaches and measures to prevent or mitigate the negative environmental impacts, public participation, commitment documents provided by construction unit or local government relating to the environmental protection measures, notification of the right of hearing, contact information for collecting public feedback. Among all the large-city governments evaluated, three failed to provide approaches and measures to prevent or mitigate the negative environmental impacts; 26 did not provide information on public participation; and 41 failed to publish commitment documents provided by construction unit or local government relating to the environmental protection measures.

10.7 Disclosure of Information About Shanty Town Redevelopment

This section evaluated the disclosure of information about land-use planning on shanty town redevelopment and related projects.

The following three highlights were discovered in this respect.

First, most evaluation objects had a high awareness of disclosing information about shanty town redevelopment.

Among all the large-city governments evaluated, 31 disclosed the land-use planning on shanty town redevelopment in 2016 or the land-use planning on security housing/state-owned construction that includes shanty town redevelopment, accounting for 63.27%; 43 provided basic information about fundamental redevelopment projects in 2016, accounting for 95.92%; and 44 published the information about the implementation of fundamental redevelopment projects in 2016, accounting for 89.80%.

Second, some also disclosed the information about shanty town redevelopment in districts and counties within their jurisdiction.

Among all the large-city governments evaluated, 11 disclosed in their land-use plans on shanty town redevelopment the land-use planning on shanty town redevelopment in 2016 developed by the governments at the municipal, district and county level, accounting for 22.45%; 22 published the information about the fundamental redevelopment projects in 2016 at the municipal, district and county level, accounting for 44.90%; and ten provided the information about the implementation progress of the fundamental redevelopment projects in 2016 at the municipal, district and county level, accounting for 20.41%.

Third, the information about shanty town redevelopment disclosed by a few evaluation objects was quite detailed.

The land-use planning on shanty town redevelopment in 2016 published by Changchun Municipal Government was quite detailed, with information such as location, name of land, coverage area in four directions and overall land area included. The municipal governments of Kunming, Zhengzhou, Luoyang and Jinan provided basic information about the shanty town redevelopment projects in 2016, including project name, project location, publishing agency, publishing date, number of apartments provided through replacement, number of apartments provided through cash settlement, and planned groundbreaking date. The municipal governments of Suzhou, Zhuhai and Huainan provided information about the implementation of shanty town redevelopment projects, including project name, project location, implementation progress, construction unit, source of funds and fund payment, number of apartments planned for construction, number of apartments being constructed, and number of apartments completed.

Nevertheless, the following three problems were identified.

First, the formats in which evaluation objects disclosed the information about land use for shanty town redevelopment were inconsistent with each other.

Among the large-city governments evaluated, 21 provided the information in table format, accounting for 42.86%; only ten published the information in both text and table formats, accounting for 20.41%.

Second, the information about shanty town redevelopment projects disclosed by some evaluation objects was not detailed.

The basic information about the shanty town redevelopment projects in 2016 of the municipal governments of Datong, Qiqihar, Zibo, Harbin and Haikou was released in news and the information was quite simple and general. The information of Shenyang Municipal Government was published in the *Letter on Record of the Shanty Town redevelopmentProjectsin2016*, which could confuse the public. The implementation progress of redevelopment projects of the municipal governments of Shenyang, Harbin, Nanjing, Kunming and Hangzhou was also disclosed in news.

Third, the information disclosed by a few evaluation objects was incorrect.

For example, the 2016 land-use planning on shanty town redevelopment of Hohhot Municipal Government disclosed on the website of the Municipal Land Resources Bureau was empty, which was inconsistent with the information disclosed on the website of the Municipal Housing Administration Bureau.

10.8 Information About Social Assistance

This section evaluated the disclosure of information about the standard for urban and rural minimum living security and the application guidelines, the standard for the support of the extremely poor and the application guidelines, the standard for medical assistance and application guidelines, the standard for temporary assistance and the application guidelines.

The following two highlights were discovered in this respect.

First, some evaluation objects published comprehensive application guidelines on social assistance.

The application guideline is an important document to guide the public to apply for social assistance. In the evaluation, 43 county-level governments disclosed complete application guidelines on urban and rural minimum living security; 32 county-level governments published complete application guidelines on the support of the extremely poor; 36 provided complete application guidelines on medical assistance; and 37 disclosed complete application guidelines on temporary assistance.

Second, a few evaluation objects established a uniform online service platform to facilitate the public to obtain social assistance services.

The disclosure platform built and uniformly maintained by provincial-level governments was conducive for the public to search information. On the platform built by Zhejiang Provincial Government, the information about public access to government services and the items subject to administrative approval at the municipal and county level was disclosed, including the application guidelines on urban and rural minimum living security, support for the extremely poor, medical assistance and temporary assistance with complete elements of the guidelines and detailed application procedures provided.

Nevertheless, the following two problems were also identified.

First, most evaluation objects failed to properly disclose the information on social assistance standards.

Some did not disclose any social assistance standard. In the evaluation, 26 county-level governments did not release the standard for urban and rural minimum living security; 44 county-level governments did not provide the standard for the support of the extremely poor; 23 county-level governments failed to provide the standard for medical assistance, and 34 county-level governments failed to provide the standard for temporary assistance.

Second, the performance of most evaluation objects on the disclosure of application guidelines on social assistance needed to be enhanced.

The elements of the application guidelines on social assistance published by some evaluation objects were incomplete. The elements consisted of the basis for administrative approval, application qualifications, application documents, application procedures, application timeline and fee standards. The elements of the application guidelines on urban and rural minimum living security provided by 47 county-level governments, on the support of the extremely poor provided by 42 county-level governments, on medical assistance provided by 49 county-level governments, and on temporary assistance were incomplete.

Also, the content of the application guidelines on social assistance provided by some evaluation objects was inaccurate. For example, the elements of guidelines published on the government website were inconsistent with those disclosed on the website of the civil affairs bureau at the corresponding level. The problem occurred on the websites of Dongcheng District of Beijing, Laixi City in Shandong province, Boxing County in Shandong province, Longhui County in Hunan province, Lingui District of Guilin City in Guangxi Zhuang autonomous region, Longzhou County in Guangxi Zhuang autonomous region, Rongchang District of Chongqing City, Xinjin County in Sichuan province, Wudang District of Guiyang City in Guizhou province, Huichuan District of Zunyi City in Guizhou province and Mian County in Shaanxi province.

A few evaluation objects failed to release the application guidelines on social assistance.

Among all the county-level governments evaluated, ten did not provide the application guidelines on urban and rural minimum living security, 26 failed to provide the application guidelines on the support of the extremely poor, 15 did not provide the application guidelines on medical assistance, and 19 did not provide the application guidelines on temporary assistance.

10.9 Information About Education

This section evaluated the disclosure of information about the division of compulsory education enrollment areas and the enrollment of children living with migrated parents, both of which are of high public concern.

The following two highlights were discovered in this respect.

First, over half of the evaluation objects disclosed the information about the division of compulsory education enrollment areas.

In the evaluation, 55 county-level governments disclosed the information about the division of primary school enrollment areas in the region in 2016. Among them, 54 disclosed the information on the portal of the county-level government or the website of the education department at the corresponding level; one on the portal of the superior government. Forty-eight county-level governments disclosed the information about the division of high school enrollment areas in the region in 2016. Among them, 47 disclosed the information on the portal of the county-level government or the website of the education department at the corresponding level; one on the portal of the superior government or the website of the education department.

Second, a small number of evaluation objects disclosed the information about the enrollment of children living with migrated parents.

In the evaluation, 35 county-level governments disclosed the information about the enrollment of children living with migrated parents, including enrollment qualifications, application documents and application procedures. Among them, 32 disclosed the information on the portal of the county-level government or the website of the education department at the corresponding level; three on the portal of the superior government.

Nevertheless, the following three problems were also identified.

First, approximately half of the evaluation objects still did not disclose the information about the division of compulsory education enrollment areas.

In the evaluation, 45 county-level governments failed to disclose the information about the division of primary school enrollment areas for the current year, while 52 failed to disclosed the information about the division of high school enrollment areas for the current year. For example, the government of Mian County in Shaanxi province disclosed the information about the division of primary school and junior high school enrollment areas for 2014 on the website of the education department, but did not disclose the information for the current year. The government of Yanchi County in Ningxia Hui autonomous region only provided the information about the division of compulsory education enrollment areas up to 2015.

Second, most evaluation objects failed to properly disclose the information about the enrollment of children living with migrated parents.

Some did not disclose enrollment qualifications, application documents and procedures. In the evaluation, 47 county-level governments did not provide any enrollment qualifications of children living with migrated parents, 33 county-level governments failed to release application documents, and 60 county-level governments did not provide any application procedures.

The information about the enrollment of children living with migrated parents disclosed by a few evaluation objects was unclear. Enrollment qualifications and application documents were core component of the enrollment policy of the children living with migrated parents. Proving them in a clear and specific manner helped improve application efficiency. Although two county-level governments provided enrollment qualifications, the qualifications were unclear. Similarly, although 16 county-level governments disclosed application documents, they were unclear too.

Third, most evaluation objects failed to disclose the information about education on uniformed platforms.

Most evaluation objects disclosed the information about education in random locations. There was neither uniformed disclosure platform nor navigation functions provided, which made it difficult for the public to locate quickly the information they need. Some disclosed the information in the section for notice and announcement; some in the section for government services, some in the section for government documents, and some in the section for planning. Chengdong District Government of Xining City in Qinghai province disclosed the information about the division of compulsory education enrollment areas in the section for notice and announcement of education departments; Yidu Municipal Government in Hubei province in the section for publicity and announcement of education departments; and West District Government of Panzhihua City in Sichuan province in the section for documents and notices of education departments. Although a special section for publishing the education information of districts and counties in a centralized manner was developed on the website of Beijing Municipal Government, the special section was placed in a hidden location—"more—education and employment—ongoing special topic on compulsory education enrollment in Beijing" at the second part of the front page. Moreover, thee section was not included in the "Convenient Public Services" section, making it difficult for the public to find.

10.10 Annual Report on Government Information Disclosure

The following two highlights were found in this respect.

First, evaluation objects generally disclosed the annual report on government information disclosure.

In the evaluation, 49 large-city governments and 92 county-level governments published the 2015 annual report.

Second, the content of the annual report disclosed was detailed and comprehensive.

The content of the 2015 annual report published by most evaluation objects was detailed and comprehensive. This was illustrated in the following five aspects: (1) A description of voluntary information disclosure was provided in all the 2015 annual reports released. (2) Forty-nine large-city governments and 89 county-level governments provided the total number of requests for information disclosure they received. Among them, except 15 county-level governments that did not receive any request in 2015, 48 large-city governments and 71 county-level governments also provided the number of requests they have replied. (3) A description of fee collection for government information disclosure was provide in the annual report of 42 large-city governments and 75 county-level governments. (4) Forty-eight large-city governments and 85 county-level governments provided the total number of the administrative reviews due to the request for government information disclosure. (5) a description of the major problems faced by evaluation objects in government information disclosure during the previous year was provided in all reports. Requirements for future work were also proposed in the annual report of most evaluation objects.

Nevertheless, the following six problems were also identified.

First, some evaluation objects failed to disclose all annual reports as required.

The 2015 annual report or those of previous years of some evaluation objects was not found. In accordance with the Regulations, government agencies at all levels shall release their annual report since 2008. However, however, 16 large-city governments and 60 county-level governments failed to do so. Among them, the 2015 annual report of eight county-level governments was not found on their website.

Second, a few evaluation objects misplaced the annual reports, making it difficult to locate.

Publishing the annual reports on a uniform platform or in a specific section and categorizing them by year, issuing department or hierarchy would make it more convenient to search information. However, a few evaluation objects did not publish the annual report on a uniform platform. For example, Lhasa Municipal Government published the 2008–2014 annual reports on its government portal but the 2015 annual report was published on the government portal of Tibet autonomous region. A few evaluation objects published the annual reports developed by all administrative agencies in one section but did not classify them. Example included the governments of Xinxing County in Guangdong province and Lixia District of Jinan City in Shandong province.

Third, the naming of the annual reports released by a few evaluation objects was not standardized.

The annual reports published by different subordinate departments of a few evaluation objects had the same title, making it difficult to differentiate them. For example, some administrative agencies of Meilan District of Haikou City in Hainan province published the annual report with the same title the *2015 Annual report on government information disclosure* on the website of the district-level government in a centralized manner, making it difficult to search and identify.

Fourth, the originality of the annual report issued by some evaluation objects shall be enhanced.

When comparing only the sections of overview, existing problems and measures for improvement in the annual reports of the recent three years published by 49 large-city governments and 100 county-level governments, the Project Team found that the annual reports published by four large-city governments and 24 county-level governments had a repetition rate of over 90%. Among the large-city governments, the 2015 annual report and the 2013 one published by Jinan Municipal Government had the highest repletion rate—96.05%. Among the county-level governments, the 2014 annual reports and the 2013 one published by the government of Lingui District of Guilin City in Guangxi Zhuang autonomous region and the government of Tengchong City in Yunnan province had the highest repletion rate—100%.

Fifth, most evaluation objects failed to provide detailed information on request-based disclosure.

Three county-level governments did not provide any information on request-based disclosure in the 2015 annual report, either the requests they received or the replies they provided.

Some evaluation objects failed to provide categorized descriptions of request methods. Seven large-city governments and 31 county-level governments did not provide a description of request methods—e.g. by mail, email or in person—in their annual report.

Eight large-city governments and 36 county-level governments failed to provide categorized descriptions of the replies they provided. Instead of disclosing the information by types of reply, they only described the results as "all completed" or "all promptly replied". In addition, 22 large-city governments and 24 county-level governments did not provide categorized explanations of the reasons why they rejected the disclosure of some information. For example, the government of Wuchang District of Wuhan City in Hubei province did not explain why six items of information was refused to disclose. For example, the item may involve state secret, commercial secret, personal privacy or others.

Sixth, some date in the annual report of a few evaluation objects was inaccurate.

The annual report shall present the work results of evaluation objects through comprehensive and accurate data. However, the data provided in a few annual reports were less than accurate. For example, the government of Yanchi County in Ningxia Hui autonomous region stated in its 2015 annual report that there was no administrative review case during the year, but the attachment to the annual report showed that there were three cases. The government of Xinjin County in Sichuan province stated the section for "fee collection" in its 2015 annual report that "the county's expenses on the disclosure of government affairs for 2014 were RMB 453,600, of which RMB 108,200 was spent on procurement of facilities and equipment, RMB 253,600 on document printing, RMB 42,800 on business training and RMB 49,000 on others". The time was incorrect and the sum of all items did not equal the total cost. For another example, Datong Municipal Government stated in the annual report that "In 2015, the governments and departments at all levels in Datong received a total of 146 requests for government information disclosure and all have been replied. Among the 146 replies, 27 were "agree to disclose", zero was "refuse to disclose" and 51 were "the information requested is not a part of government information", "the government information does not exist" or "the government agency is not responsible for disclosing the information requested". The sum of the numbers in total obviously did not equal 146.

Also, the accuracy of the information provided in the annual report of a few evaluation objects was questionable. For example, the accuracy of the numbers of requests for information disclosure, applications for administrative reviews and administrative litigations stated in the 2015 annual report of the government of Jinzhou City in Hebei province was questionable. The annual report showed that the government did not receive any application. However, it was found that five cases pending for administrative review actually happened in 2015. Even if the cases were occurred due to applications received in 2014, a detailed explanation should be given to avoid misunderstanding.

10.11 Request-Based Information Disclosure

The following two highlights were discovered in this respect.

First, channels for submitting requests by mail were generally accessible.

Among the 149 evaluation objects, 148 managed to receive the requests sent by mail, accounting for 99.33%. Only the letter sent to the local taxation bureau of Wuchang District of Wuhan City in Hubei province was returned.

Second, the procedures, formats and content of the replies provided by some administrative agencies were clear and standardized.

Some administrative agencies managed to provide clear and standardized procedures, formats and content of the replies strictly in accordance with the relevant laws and regulations. For example, the Project Team sent a request by mail to Shenyang Municipal Justice Bureau on November12, 2016. On November 21, the bureau sent to the applicant's email address a message for confirmation of delivery, the *Receipt for Accepting the Requests for Government Information Disclosure* and the *Notification on Government Information Disclosure*, and told the applicant that a reply would be provided by via email. On November 23, the bureau provided the official reply by sending the *Reply to Applications for Government Information Disclosure* and a message for confirmation of delivery. The procedures were complete and each document provided was attached with the official stamp. For another example, the Project Team requested to Lanzhou Municipal Justice Bureau for government information disclosure on November 9. The bureau officially replied via email on November 21 and the information provided was quite clear. In the forms provided in the reply, the bureau described the work of community correction carried out at the municipal, district and county level as well as the village, town and street level in great detail, and explained the number of community correction officers categorized by the staffing of the central government, local administrative departments and the institutional organizations.

Also, the format of replies provided by some administrative agencies was standardized. For example, the municipal justice bureaus of Guangzhou, Jinan, Fuzhou, Ningbo, Zhuhai and Chengdu and the local taxation bureaus of Wuqing District and Hexi District of Tianjin provided a document number in their reply and attached the document with the official stamp of the bureau. The municipal justice bureaus of Jinan and Ningbo also provided the channels to apply for relief in the reply beside the information requested.

Some administrative agencies also made it easier for the applicants to obtain more related information descriptions of their work, contact number and fax number, etc. For example, when disclosing the information requested, Dalian Municipal Justice Bureau provided the *Introduction to the Work of Community Correction in Dalian*, which briefly introduced the general work of community correction and the progress in team building, and the contact number was also provided. The justice bureaus of Ningbo, Hefei, Xiamen and Nanning also provided contact details in their reply to make it convenient for the applicants to make inquiries.

Nevertheless, the following four problems were also identified.

First, some evaluation objects failed to reply or to reply in within the statutory period.

As of March 1, 2017, among the 148 evaluation objects with accessible request channels, 84 did not provide any reply. Among them, 19 were the administrative agencies of large cities, accounting for 38.78%; 65 were administrative agencies of county-level governments, accounting for 65.66%. In addition, nine administrative agencies of large cities replied over phone rather than providing an official reply, accounting for 18.37%. Among the 64 administrative agencies that provided an official reply, six replied after the deadline. Among 30 administrative agencies of large cities that provided an official reply, two replied after the deadline, accounting for 6.67%. Among the 34 administrative agencies of county-level governments that provided an official reply, four replied after the deadline, accounting for 11.76%.

Second, the procedures of the reply provided by some evaluation objects were inconsistent and not standardized.

Administrative agencies shall maintain consistency and use the same standards when providing a reply. However, the replies provided by some administrative agencies were contradicted and not standardized, resulting in a lower credibility of the replies. For example, after receiving the request for information disclosure, Qingdao Municipal Justice Bureau first informed the applicant that the staffing information requested was confidential and could not be disclosed. However, the information was disclosed orally later. Inconsistency occurred in such practice. Also, in accordance with the Article 21 of the Regulations, administrative agencies shall notify the applicant to make changes to an application or provide supplemental information if the request is unclear. However, instead of informing the Project Team to make changes or provide supplemental information before it made an reply, Zhuhai Municipal Justice Bureau simply replied in the official letter that "the request is unclear and therefore no specific reply can be provided."

Third, the formats of the reply provided by some evaluation objects were confusing.

Standardized formats of replies could not only clearly inform applicants of the information requested, but also reflect the level of standardization of replies. However, the formats of the replies provided by some government agencies, such as the municipal justice bureaus of Shijiazhuang and Nanjing, and the local taxation bureaus of Ningguo City in Anhui province and Pizhou City in Jiangsu province, were confusing. They replied by using personal emails of their staff. The names of the senders were various and the name of the replying agency was not specified in the email subject. Also, for some administrative agencies that replied later than required, the name of the replying agency cannot be found in either the subject or main body of the email, or the letter of notification. Therefore, it was difficult to figure out who the sender was.

Fourth, some content of replies provided was either incorrect or missing.

Incorrect information was provided in the reply of some administrative agencies. For example, a type error was found in the subject of the email sent by the local taxation bureau of Huaiyuan County in Anhui province, in which "残保金" (employment security funds for the disabled) was written as "残暴金" (deposit for atrocity). For another example, in the official reply letter provided by the local taxation bureau of Xinjin County in Sichuan Province, "印发" (printing and issuing) was written as " 印花"(stamping).

The basis or reasons for refusing disclosure provided by some administrative agencies were either missing or unreasonable. Among the 64 administrative agencies that provided official replies, 25 of large cities and nine of county-level governments disclosed the information requested. Among the remaining five of large cities and 25 of county-level governments that refused to disclose the requested information, four of large cities and six of county-level governments did not provide the legal basis for refusal; and 11 of county-level governments did not provide the reasons for refusal. Also, the reason for refusal provided by the local taxation bureau of Xinjin County in Sichuan province was unreasonable. The reason provided by the bureau was "taxation agencies are required to disclose the information about the employment security funds paid by the employers in the region for the previous year by the end of March each year. It is still in the reporting period of the security funds for the disabled now, so the information about the security funds paid by the employers cannot be disclosed at this moment." However, the reality was that the information requested by the Project Team was that for the year 2015. In accordance with the legal provision cited by the local taxation bureau of Xinjin County, it should have disclosed the information by the end of March, 2016.

10.12 Recommendations

First, clearly define the content, subjects and standards of information disclosure. We recommend that administrative agencies gradually review from top to down the relevant guiding documents on the work of disclosing government affairs developed and issued to ensure that the content, subjects and standards, especially the responsibility of the agency itself, have been clearly identified in related documents. Adjustments shall be made to the documents that contain contradictory content. The content, subjects and standards for the disclosure shall be further clarified if requirements in certain areas provided in certain documents were ambiguous. When preparing documents concerning the work of government affairs disclosure, administrative agencies shall define the key information to be disclosed, and also develop the detailed rules to clearly specify the work requirements, including the content, subjects and standards for disclosure. In addition, dynamic adjustment of the list of government affairs to be voluntarily disclosed shall be made.

Second, strengthen the people-oriented concept of government information disclosure. By processing and analyzing the statistics about the number of page views and clicks of the information that has been voluntarily disclosed, and that of request-based disclosure on government websites, a situation analysis of government information disclosure shall be made to figure out the main public demands and to strengthen the work of voluntary disclosure effectively.

Third, strengthen legislation for government information disclosure. At present, the implementation of work of government information disclosure is mainly driven by policies. Except the Regulations and the *Interim Regulations on the Disclosure of Enterprise Information*, there are no other higher-level laws and regulations on disclosure. The requirements and boundaries for information disclosure, especially the definition of items undisclosable, are not clear enough. Therefore, Legislation in this area shall be further enhanced.

Fourth, optimize the way that the information is presented, integrate disclosure platforms and strengthen the inter-linkage of various types of information. The highly repetitive disclosure platforms developed by governments of higher and lower levels, administrative departments and their subordinates shall be closed. By using links, the uniformity of disclosure platforms can be guaranteed, and accuracy of information can also be improved. Similar information, such as policy documents and their drafts, policy interpretations, policy documents and their implementation information, shall be well linked to realize the correlated reading.

Chapter 11
Conclusion

A decade has passed from the release of the *Regulations on the Disclosure of Government Information* by the State Council in 2007 to the completion of the *2016 Evaluation of China's Government Transparency* by the Project Team now in 2017. The implementation of the government information disclosure system has been conducted for over nine years, and the time from which the policy of openness of government affairs was adopted was even earlier. With the top-down strong efforts made by Chinese government and the increased public demands, openness and transparency has been deeply rooted in the hearts of the people and become a required work in government administration. The evaluations of China's government transparency conducted by the Project Team of the Institute of Law of the Chinese Academy of Social Sciences for nearly nine years successively have witnessed the whole development process.

On one hand, the following three highlights have been identified in the process.

First, the attention paid by government agencies at all levels to the disclosure of government information and affairs has been continuously increased. A substantial number of regulations and policies on government information disclosure have been developed since the implementation of the Regulations. This has greatly facilitated to delineate information disclosure in various fields. In 2016, the *Opinions on Comprehensively Promoting Open Government Work* was approved on the 20th meeting of the Central Leading Team of Comprehensively Deepening the Reforms. This was a concrete step taken to fully implement the principle proposed by the *Decisions of the CPC Central Committee on Major Issues Pertaining to Comprehensively Promoting the Rule of Law* that information disclosure shall become a regular government practice and non-disclosure only happens in exceptional cases, and to enhance the disclosure of decision-making, implementation, administrative procedures, government services and implementation results, collectively known as "five disclosures". It was also a necessary requirement to build an open government and to accelerate the construction of a government ruled by law. The Opinions will be a guiding document to promote the openness of government affairs for some time to come and

Y. Lv and H. Tian, *Evaluation on Government Transparency Index in China (2009–2016)*, Understanding China, https://doi.org/10.1007/978-981-16-5032-1_11

it has made overall arrangements and macro requirements for promoting the openness of government affairs and improving government transparency in many respects. Many government agencies would contact the Project Team after the Institute of Law released our evaluation reports every year. They would like to figure out the problems in their work, to learn from the highlights of others, and to seek recommendations for improving their work. Many public service-oriented suggestions provided by the Project Team during the interactions were adopted by corresponding government agencies and were integrated into their work on government information disclosure.

Second, the awareness of government information disclosure has been continuously raised. To start with, the ongoing work on promoting the openness of government affairs fully reflects the concept of deepening reform in public services. The key to deepening reforms, streamlining administration and delegating power, and transforming government functions is to delegate power to market and society, and to enable various types of entities to make their own decisions in carrying out activities. However, this by no means suggests that government administration should be totally abandoned. Only by fully understanding the policy trends, regulatory dynamics, social developments and market changes, can entities clearly anticipate the risks of their own activities and make rational choices, and can power be successfully delegated. To this end, as per *the Key Points of Promoting the Openness of Government Affairs in 2017* issued by the General Office of the State Council in March 2017, government agencies shall promote the disclosure of financial policies and their implementations, so as to provide market entities with such market supervision elements as policy trends, implementation results and market conditions. This can help entities develop clear and accurate anticipations and judgments about economic operations and social development. Hence they can make reasonable decisions on their activities and reduce government direct intervention in markets. Also, the ongoing work on promoting the openness of government affairs fully reflects the major changes occurred in government administration means and concepts. Historically, government administration was conducted by various means of direct interventions in markets and society such as administrative approval, penalties and coercion, all of which directly affected the administrative counterpart or the market. However, this method has three main weaknesses: high administrative cost; heavy and direct interventions in markets and society; and conflicts between the government and administrative counterparts could be easily triggered. By comparison, the ongoing work on promoting the openness of government affairs focuses on the disclosure of information about policies, projects and data in key areas. By promoting information disclosure across the board, the government means to enable entities in markets and society to fully understand the policy trends and actual situations in related areas, to develop adequate anticipations of their future development and possible risks, and to make reasonable choices that are beneficial to them. In other words, by promoting the openness of government affairs, the government aims to change the previous direct government control to indirect takeover, direct intervention to indirect regulation, and to give more freedom to entities in markets and society to make their own judgments and choices. This is a major shift of the methods and concepts of government regulation, and it illustrates that promoting the openness of government affairs has become an important means of government regulation. In addition, the ongoing work on promoting the openness of government affairs also fully reflects a triple disclosure-interpretation-reply concept. The work of promoting the openness of government affairs used to mainly focus on the disclosure of government information itself, without paying enough attention to disclosure results. However, at present, it is required in almost all aspects of the work that information shall not only be disclosed but also be interpreted to make it accessible to the public, and that major policies, data and results shall not only be disclosed but also be interpreted in a means of expression that is popular among the public, bringing them a sense of gain. What's more, the government should also respond to social concerns promptly. As for the major public concerns reflected in public opinions, consultations and complaints, the government should also avoid the "Ostrich Effect", and proactively provide them with accurate and timely responses to avoid public misunderstandings. In particular, when disclosing government information, the government should try hard to identify the focuses of social concerns through the public opinions collected, analyze and judge the public opinion risks of the disclosure, and then disclose and interpret information in a targeted manner. Instead of being a passive process as it used to be, promoting the openness of government affairs should be an integrated process of disclosure, interpretation and response, with key public demands identified and disclosure results improved.

Third, significant improvements have been made on government information disclosure. Since 2009, the indicators of the evaluations have been becoming increasingly complex, and the focus of the evaluations has shifted from the work of government information disclosure itself to the quality of information disclosed. As the disclosure in many aspects improved year by year, some indicators were more strictly evaluated while some others were no longer used. The evaluation objects used to fail in most indicators, but now they could get quite desirable results. Earlier in the evaluations, some evaluation could only score a dozen points[1] even after the Project Team gave them ten free points, and they could just score zero in many respects[2]. But now, most of them could get a pass, and the highest score continues to rise. Although the main purpose of the Project Team is to identify problems and weaknesses of government information disclosure exposed in the evaluations, obvious progress can be seen in the disclosure of government information by government agencies at all levels. One example is the release of the annual report on government information disclosure. The 2011 evaluation found that all of the 59 departments under the State Council managed to publish their 2010 annual reports without delay. However, as of the end of 2016, four departments under the State Council had not published their 2009 annual reports. Among the 43 large cities evaluated, 34 published their annual reports of the previous year in 2009, 37 in 2010, and 43 in 2012. Another

[1] In the 2009 Evaluation Report, government agencies with a government portal were all given ten points.

[2] See "Many Government Agencies Scored Zero on the Work of Government Information Disclosure", *Legal Daily*, February 25, 2011, 2nd edition.

example is the disclosure of financial budgets and final accounts. The 2010 evaluation revealed that the departments under the State Council performed poorly on the disclosure of budgets and final accounts. This was mainly manifested by the fact that little information was disclosed and the information disclosed was not detailed enough. Among the 59 departments under the State Council evaluated, only 27 had a special section for financial budgets in the directory or on the homepages of their websites, accounting for 45.8%; 43 managed to disclose their own financial budgets in different ways, accounting for 72.9%; none provided detailed descriptions of their budget standards for revenues and expenditures; only three provided descriptions of the items whose budget changed significantly compared with the previous year in their overall budgets, one of which briefly explained the reasons; two provided the items whose budget changed significantly compared with the previous year in their financial appropriation budget, one of which briefly explained the reasons. By contrast, the disclosure of budgets and final accounts, and expenditures to buy and use cars, travel overseas and host meetings - collectively known as "three types of public expenditures" has become quite standardized and is becoming increasingly detailed.

One the other hand, many problems facing the construction of a transparent government have been exposed. The performance of information disclosure varies largely among different regions, levels of governments and aspects. The contradiction between the slow openness of government affairs and the ever-increasing public demands on government information is always there. Hence, it is recommended that government agencies at all levels take the following measures to effectively implement the work of promoting the openness of government affairs.

First, promote the openness of government affairs by employing rule-based frameworks and means. Promoting the openness of government affairs is an inevitable requirement for the comprehensive construction of both a government and a state ruled by law. To ensure its implementation, it must be promoted according to law. As promoting the openness of government affairs means properly dealing the relations between information publicity and information security, and that between guaranteeing the public's freedom of information and the normal administration of government agencies, implementation of the work requires corresponding institutional arrangements and legal authorization. Hence, it shall be completed within the rule-based framework, with clear boundaries between openness and confidentiality set, and the practice of "captain's calls" or "feeling-based decision making" in government information disclosure avoided. Government agencies shall, in accordance with the requirements proposed on the 18th CPC National Congress and the 3rd, 4th, and 5th Plenary Sessions of the 18th CPC Central Committee on constructing a government ruled by law, with the arrangements of the work on promoting the openness of government affairs made by the General Office of the CPC Central Committee and the General Office of the State Council, and with the *Decisions of the CPC Central Committee on Major Issues Pertaining to Comprehensively Promoting the Rule of Law,* comprehensively review existing laws and regulations. Government agencies shall also, based on the current social situation and administration requirements as well as the revisions of the Regulations, conduct a comprehensive review of the provisions concerning information disclosure and confidentiality, and the powers and responsibilities of various government agencies, to fill the gaps in the system promptly, revise obsolete regulations, strengthen the coordination among relevant laws and regulations. In doing so, the work of promoting the openness of government affairs will be supported by legal basis, disclosure requirements be fixated by institutional arrangements, and the work itself be unaffected by changes in government officials' priorities.

Second, further standardize the work of promoting the openness of government affairs. The biggest problem facing the work in recent years is that disclosure standards are not clearly developed, contributing to too much liberty of government agencies in conducting their work. The problem is reflected in the following aspects: different sections of the same type of information are published by different government agencies, causing decreased information usability; information is disclosed through different platforms such as special sections, LCD screens, press conferences, government portals, or the official websites of other agencies, bringing inconvenience for the public to access the information they need. Given this, the standardization of government information disclosure shall be improved by tackling the existing problems and meeting the demands on government information collecting, mining, and utilization in the big data era. To start with, departments under the State Council and provincial-level governments shall strengthen the guidance of the work in this field and in the regions within their jurisdiction, and identify clearly the disclosure authority, methods, and time limit of lower-level agencies by issuing detailed requirements. Also, corresponding responsibilities and obligations of different departments on the work shall be clearly defined based on their functions, so as to prevent the requirements from being too general. In addition, the lists of voluntary disclosure shall be gradually developed by industry, and specific requirements such as the subject, object, scope, method, and time limit of government information disclosure shall be clarified therein, so as to ensure that information in the same category is disclosed in accordance with the same standard.

Third, simultaneously advance the work of promoting the openness of government affairs and the construction of a government ruled by law, and decisions in the work and the whole implementation process shall both be based on the concept of "disclosure as a regular practice". Instead of being isolated, the work shall be closely connected to the construction of the law-based governments at all levels. Some government agencies face huge pressure in conducting the work. This is because their administration is not fully exercised in accordance with the law and is not well regulated to some extent. This discourages them from disclosing government information. The openness of government affairs is not isolated, and necessary reviews shall be conducted at an earlier stage to support the work. The principal that information disclosure shall become a regular government practice and non-disclosure only happens in exceptional cases is not just a slogan. Instead, it is a basic principle and requirement in constructing a government ruled by law. Technically, information about government activities in various respects can all be requested by the public. Hence, all administrative activities conducted by government agencies, including internal affairs, shall not only experience legality review and social risk evaluation, but also the determination and review of disclosure attributes before final decisions can be made. All information related to administrative activities shall be reviewed on the assumption that all information may be requested by the public or may be voluntarily disclosed in the future.

Fourth, make public demands both the motive and the goal of the work, so as to offer the public a sense of gain. A large amount of information has been disclosed and much efforts have been made by government agencies in promoting the openness of government affairs in recent years. However, there is still a gap between the disclosure and pubic demand for information. This is mainly manifested by the fact that some information needed by the public to gain government services, relate to national interests and the people's livelihood has not been disclosed in a detailed and comprehensive manner. The root cause of this problem is that government agencies only conduct their work based on their own points of view, and there is a serious supply–demand mismatch between the government agencies and the public. Given this, the self-centered concept of government agencies' philosophy and patterns of information disclosure shall be completely abandoned. By taking steps such as involving public participation, conducting public demands surveys, and analyzing government information disclosure requests trend, government agencies shall figure out what the public wants to know about government administration, grasp and judge the situation facing government information disclosure, and therefore instead of disclosing what the government agencies want to make public, government affairs and information shall be disclosed according to public demands, in the ways they want, in an accurate, comprehensive, effective, and timely manner. Also, different information demands and information acquisition capabilities of different groups of people shall be taken into consideration when disclosing information proactively. For example, for people in developed regions and those who are good at using information technology to obtain information, information can be disclosed on government portals and other online platforms, while for people living in backward areas and those who do not have access to information technology, more conventional ways such as bulletin boards and brochures should be employed.

Fifth, strengthen the construction of government information disclosure platforms. Constructing disclosure platforms is a crucial element in performing well on government information disclosure. Therefore, government agencies shall leverage both conventional platforms and the emerging digital ones to promote the all-round government information disclosure. Governments at all levels shall strengthen the use of websites to publish information. To start with, government portals shall be clearly identified as the chief platform and as the most authoritative channel of disclosure. This means that all government information that should be disclosed, regardless of whether it has been released on any other platforms, shall be disclosed on government portals to facilitate public access to the information. Second, government portals shall be constantly revised and optimized to offer better accessibility. Sections on government websites shall be well designed and arranged instead of relying on arbitrary decisions, so as to ensure the unified release of information, thus facilitating public access to information. Third, online disclosure platforms shall be further integrated. If the lower-level departments are incapable of building and maintain their own websites, sections for them to publish information shall be set up on the government portals of the same-level governments. Government portals and dedicated websites for government information disclosure shall be managed in a systematical way, so as to ensure the consistency and comprehensiveness of information disclosed on different platforms. In addition, the relations between government portals and dedicated websites shall be carefully managed. As disclosing government information is one of the major functions of government portals, there is no need to establish dedicated websites or platforms. In the future, these dedicated websites and platforms shall be gradually integrated into government portals to weaken the function of the directory and to completely resolve the problem of information inconsistency among different platforms. The sections on government portals shall be optimized and government portals should be more user-friendly to facilitate public access to information. however, the main function of the directory shall be managing internal information to strengthen government agencies' ability to manage their own information. Finally, government information disclosure and public access to information should become more intelligent with the help of internet technologies. The function of intelligent information push should be gradually developed to provide information in a targeted manner, realizing the transition from "people searching information" to "information being tailored to specific people".

Sixth, explore to implement the triple disclosure-interpretation-reply model. At the stage of developing policies that are not confidential or the disclosure of which will not cause public or market fluctuations, interpretation of the policies shall be provided when gathering public opinions on the drafts, so as to show the government's sincerity and determination to seek public advice. As for the opinions and suggestions proposed by the public, relevant departments shall provide feedbacks on whether the opinions and suggestions will be adopted and why not as long as confidentiality is not broken. Interpretation of some information that is not policy, such as data, financial budgets and final accounts, audit reports, shall be highly valued, and the interpretations shall be developed in a way that the public can understand and that they would love to read. Government agencies should gradually explore the mechanism for understanding public concerns through public opinions, website interactions, and channels for consulting and complaints. By doing so, government agencies can understand and judge the public opinions risks of government administration and information release accurately and promptly, so as to develop response plans. Meanwhile, the relations between government information disclosure and news release shall also be appropriately managed. A basic requirement for promoting the openness of government affairs, especially that of the performance of duties, is to release reliable information in a standardized way. Information shall be released comprehensively with all elements included, so as to enhance the authority of the openness of government affairs, and unstandardized information disclosure through news release shall be avoided. However, this does not necessarily mean that the role of news media should be ignored in the process. The advantages of news media, such as its accessibility, large audience and strong dissemination power, should be utilized to widely disseminate information about government activities and their outcomes, so as to increase its permeability. When conducting their own work on promoting the openness of government affairs, government agencies at all levels should also actively employ new media platforms, such as Wechat, Weibo and other news apps to disseminate information about government activities in a manner and language that is popular among the public.

Seventh, strengthen public supervision and review to establish a strong accountability mechanism. In addition to guaranteeing public access to information through administrative reconsideration and lawsuits in accordance with the law, it is necessary to further expand channels for the public to report and make complaints, and innovate the methods of higher-level government agencies' inspections and spot checks, so as to enhance internal supervision and accountability. Furthermore, the role of third-party evaluation shall be better exerted, and an independent, objective, and scientific third-party evaluation mechanism shall be employed to carry out "physical examinations" on the effectiveness of the openness of government affairs aperiodicity, so as to identify the lists of issues facing the openness of government affairs. A third-party evaluation can avoid biased self-evaluation, in which government agencies may turn a blind eye to problems as they have been accustomed to them. By resolving the issues identified in third-party evaluations, government agencies can constantly improve their work of promoting the openness of government affairs.

The manufacturer's authorised representative in the EU is Springer Nature Customer Service Centre GmbH, Europaplatz 3, 69115 Heidelberg, Germany. If you have any concerns regarding our products, please contact ProductSafety@springernature.com

Printed and bound by CPI Group (UK) Ltd, Croydon, CR0 4YY
30/09/2026
02225290-0006